INTEGRAL HUMANISM

INTEGRAL HUMANISM

A Distinct Paradigm of Development

Ashok Gajanan Modak

Indian Council of Social Science Research

₹1250; US$ 41.70
ISBN: 978-93-88691-94-9

First Published in India in 2023

Integral Humanism: A Distinct Paradigm of Development

Published by:
SHIPRA PUBLICATIONS
LG 18-19, Pankaj Central Market
I.P. Ext., Patparganj, Delhi 110092, India
Tel.: +91 11 2223 5152/6152; 96500 28065
E-mail: info@shiprapublication.com
www.shiprapublication.com

Indian Council of Social Science Research
(Ministry of Education, Government of India)
Aruna Asaf Ali Marg, New Delhi 110 067

Acknowledgement

The writer of the collection of research papers titled "Integral Humanism: A Distinct Paradigm of Development" would like to acknowledge sincere gratitude to Prof. Dhananjay Singh, the present Member Secretary of the ICSSR for his immediate consent to publish this collection!

That the prestigious institution like Indian Council of Social Science Research is publishing a compilation of my research papers is the most memorable event! This is why, let me articulate how sincerely I feel grateful towards Prof. Dhananjay Singh. Let me also inform readers that two worthy gentlemen - Shri Ashwani Kumar and Shri Abhinav Paliwal, who shoulder due responsibilities in the ICSSR office rendered full help to me in the task of proof correction, as a result of which the present collection of my research papers is being released.

Heart felt Thanks!

Ashok Modak

Contents

Part - III

Part - IV

1

Introduction

It was in January 2015, that Human Resource Development Ministry of the Government of India offered National Research Professorship to the author. And it was, incidentally in 2015 only that all of us remembered quite gratefully the life and mission of Pandit Deendayal Upadhyay because first, the year 2015 marked the culmination of a half centenary of Pandit Deendayalji's lecture series on Integral Humanism in Mumbai, and secondly, 2015 also inaugurated the beginning of the year preceding to the birth-centenary of Pandit Deendayal Upadhyay. Several universities and institutes in India then thought it wise to organise symposia, seminars and workshops to commemorate inspiring legacy of Deendayal. Quite a few of them invited the author to participate in such programmes. Compliance with these invitations through paper presentations followed by interactions with scholars assembled there enabled me to know different aspects of Pandit Deendayal's line of thinking. It was noted that Pandit Deendayal Upadhyay who started his political career in 1951 in the capacity of the first General Secretary of Bharatiya Jana Sangh, a new political formation fully succeeded in building this party from the scratch. The most successful growth of Jana Sangh by 1967 under Pandit Deendayal's leadership impressed all political analysts. Workers of Jana Sangh unanimously elected Pandit Deendayal as the All India President in 1967 in acknowledgement of his contribution in making Jana Sangh a formidable formation. It was in the midnight of 10th February 1968 that unfortunately Pandit Deendayal passed away. He was thus alive hardly for 43 days after getting elected as All India President of Bharatiya Jana Sangh!

People found in him a totally different type of political leader, who called himself as an ambassador of Indian culture and civilization in the political field of India. Pandit Deendayal, indeed, articulated India-centric views and thoughts throughout his life. Least wonder, his writings and speeches were imbued quite deeply with unique qualities, such as his confidence in India-centric approach, his faith in Indian unity, his belief in symbiotic relationship between an individual and society as well as his viewpoint that social activists must always give precedence to divine tendencies over satanic instincts. According to Pandit Deendayal, Lokmanya Tilak and Mahatma Gandhi were the two most towering and ideal leaders of India's freedom-struggle; because according to him these two visionaries, being genuinely affirmative showed the path conducive to Indian ethos to be followed by India in the post freedom years.

Pandit Deendayal's India-centric Approach vs Mainstream Mania for Euro-centric Thinking

It was during the two decades of 1950s and 1960s when Pandit Deendayal was busy in organisational activities (pertaining to progressive unfoldment of Jana Sangh) and articulating his India-centric opinions, mainstream Indian leaders and thinkers of that period were tepid enthusiastic towards India-centric approach. They had developed fascination for Euro-American model of development. They did not accordingly show any interest even in Gandhi's views and thoughts as well. Prof. Amiya Kumar Dasgupta, who presided over All India Economic Conference held in Chandigarh in 1960 subsequently delivered two lectures in 1969 in honour of Gandhi-birth centenary year for expressing his despondency over the mainstream economist's apathy in this regard. Pulin Nayak's write-up informs us that the dominant Indian citizenry - in the media, in academics and elsewhere (during 1950s and 1960s) did not want to share Gandhian mode of thinking, that the opinion makers of that era were uninterested in implementing Gandhian precepts. "And that was why", the write-up adds, "Prof. A. K. Dasgupta was quite upset over the thinking process of the then prevailing opinion makers".[1] It was the fascination for the European paradigm of development that must have persuaded Indian leaders in general and intellectuals in particular to be apathetic about

1. Pulin B. Nayak, "A. K. Dasgupta on Gandhi and the Economics of Austerity", in *Economic and Political Weekly* (Mumbai), 16 December, 2017, p. 45.

Indian ethos. The very fascination dissuaded them from pondering over Gandhian precepts and practices. Dr. Ram Manohar Lohia also vented his agony over the thinking process of the then existing academic circles.

The extract given below from Lohia's writings evidences this agony quite vividly: "Like the team of blinkered oxen in an oil press, they go on and on, researching into sectional conditions with Europe's tools and without a thought, that these tools are inadequate and require to be refashioned".[2]

The above lines have been drawn as a rough sketch of the mindset of opinion makers of the post freedom years of India. This mindset mirrored attraction for a curious crossbreed of Marxism, and capitalism, in the sense that it wanted to implement modified Marxism in the field of economy and similarly it wished to pursue democracy; of course, duly amended democracy prevalent in the capitalist world. This mindset remained predominant till the emergence of 1991-LPG-trends (Liberalization, Privatization and Globalization trends). Certain events such as the collapse of the Berlin-wall, demise of the USSR and withering away of Soviet empire in East Europe caused severe shocks to the devotees of Marxism. Subsequent happenings like terrorist death blows on twin-towers of World Trade Centre in New York and Lehman crisis of 2007-2008 as well as lingering and deepening challenges confronting capitalist countries issued shockwaves for the followers of capitalism.

It was thus the indifference of mainstream Indian leaders and academicians regarding Indian ethos during post freedom years of India that had prompted them to be apathetic and tepid toward Gandhism. In contrast, Pandit Deendayal's conviction in Indian ethos had triggered a unique bond between the advocate of Integral Humanism and the writer of Hind Swaraj. The Present compilation of papers therefore contains an essay underscoring commonalities between these two stalwarts of modern India. Pandit Deendayal, following the footsteps of Gandhi, vented his foreboding about the future of Euro-American world. Thus his apprehension that the artificial creation of Soviet Union would dig its graveyard through heavy, rather exclusive reliance on the institution of state proved true in 1991 and his analysis that the excessive pursuit of satanic instincts like desire, greed and temptation would cause existential threat to the capitalist world proved its mettle at the time of

---

2. Rammanohar Lohia, "Interval During Politics", quoted by Yogendra Yadav, "What is Living and What is Dead in Rammanohar Lohia? In *Economic and Political Weekly* (Mumbai), 02 October, 2010, p. 95.

the Lehman crisis in 2008. Indian philosophy was the common fountainhead for Gandhi as well as Deendayal. Several thinkers in the West as well as in the East and their counterparts in India have astonishingly come ahead during post 1991 years to pay obeisance to Indian philosophy. Succinct review of their writings attempted in the next section is thus logical in the discourse of the preface.

Global Obeisance to Indian Philosophy

It is immensely revealing to note that during post-cold war years (post 1991) several Euro American and Eastern scholars and leaders as well as Indian academicians have realized the worth and relevance of Indian philosophy in the present era. A perusal of their views is a 'must' because it will inform us of the significance – of Gandhism and Integral Humanism in the 21st century. This section intends to peruse these views by referring to Gorbachevian elaboration of 'Perestroika' or 'restructuring' as it initiated the termination-process of the cold-war. Mikhail Gorbachev thus rationalized 'restructuring-process' by underscoring "the great thirst for mutual understanding and mutual communication in the world".[3] According to Raghavan Iyar, "the rationale provided by Gorbachev for 'Perestroika' was an echo of the ancient Indian thought that entire cosmos and all human souls are continually sustained by the principles such as harmony, universal interdependence, solidarity and concord".[4]

Secondly, views of Vaclav Havel, the first president of the Czech Republic also deserve our attention, because they inform us of the withering away of the fake influence of Marxism and materialism in east Europe in the aftermath of the demolition of Soviet Empire. These views given below evidence realization that Descartes-sponsored mind body dichotomy is no longer acceptable: "Without a global revolution in the sphere of human consciousness, nothing will change for the better and the catastrophe towards which the world is headed will be unavoidable".[5]

Vaclav Havel has thus acknowledged the Indian line of thinking that when an individual acts with social interest in mind and the society acts unitedly as one mind, it generates the most effective power on earth. He has moreover endorsed that consciousness – transformation is basic, if compared to institutional change! According to David

3. Mikhail Gorbachev, *Perestroika* (New York, 1987), pp. 53-54.
4. Raghavan Iyer, 'Introduction', Introduction to the Essential Writings of Mahatma Gandhi, p. 2.
5. Quoted in Barney Wee & Agnes Lau, *Choices of Now* (San Diego, CA, USA, 2014), p. 244.

Hawkins, Gandhi epitomized the revolutionary shift in human consciousness, as the latter demonstrated the superiority of the power of selflessness over the force of self-interest.[6]

Thomas Friedman has explicitly appreciated the role played by Indian culture in making a due transformation in Indians' collective consciousness. He has admired 'adaptability' as well as 'adoptability' of Indian culture and substantiated his viewpoint by informing us of a laudatory extract from a June 21, 2004 essay in Forbes, penned by the British historian Paul Johnson. The extract runs as follows: "Hindu religion is tolerant and permissive and Hindus residing in India or in foreign lands are known for hard work, strong family bonds and devotion to education".[7]

As per Jeremy Rifkin's book *The Zero Marginal Cost Society*, present times require partnership culture, in the sense that we should opt for partnership and cooperation in the place of domination and competition. Riffin's suggestion is worth reproduction here: "Business corporations should adopt an intra-corporate partnership approach and the partnerships so created should endeavour to lever not only the conjoint financial resources of the partners but also their non-financial assets".[8]

Rifkin's recommendation in favour of partnership culture reminds us of the fact that India has been pursuing such culture in its nation building process from centuries together. One may thus say that Rifkin has complimented India's second nature.

Rajan Gurukul, the present Vice-chairman of the Kerala State Higher Education Council of India has expressed his anxiety over state sponsored development – decentralization in India, as it mirrors 'merely a localization of class governance based on the status quo'.[9] His prescription "that local, voluntary institutions and organisations 'emana -ting from grass roots' must be developed for concreting genuine decentralization invites our attention to the analysis of participatory democracy made by Gandhi and Pandit Deendayal. It may be reminded to Gurukul that his apprehension regarding the fate of democracy in the capitalist paradigm of development has been ventilated quite vividly by Vivekananda, Gandhi and Pandit Deendayal".

6. David Hawkins, *Power vs. Force* (London, 2012), p. 156.
7. Thomas Friedman, *The World is Flat* (London, 2006), p. 422.
8. Quoted in Vikram S. Mehta, "CSR: Corporations should Reach out", in *The Indian Express* (Mumbai), 04, August 2015, p. 13.
9. Rajan Gurukul, "Death of Democracy: An Inevitable Possibility under Capitalism", in *Economic and Political Weekly* (Mumbai), 25 August, 2018, p. 107.

Likewise, Vikram Mehta, Chairman of Brookings India has appealed to business corporations in India, through his newspaper-write -up that they should implement Corporate Social Responsibility Act 2013. Their allocation of two percent from their average net profits for social projects would enhance social capital; that it would cement harmonious relations in society at large. He informs that the CSR Act 2013 is not mandatory; it merely requires corporations to "comply or explain" and the latter unfortunately opt for drafting explanations.[10] Vikram Mehta thus expects business companies to keep in mind their commitment towards social welfare and do justice to the concept of trusteeship. For several years, Milton Friedman's comment: 'the business of business is business' dictated business corporations. At present, however, every corporation is supposed to bring in practice typical Hindu term of 'trusteeship'.

For several years, thinkers condoned three inhibitions coming in the way of the evolution of the world into more harmonious global civilization. Barney Wee and Agnes Lau, two scholars from Singapore have called Scienceism, Survivalism and Humanism as three inhibitions or blocks to 'our advancement'. Both of them have however brought to notice that these barriers are no longer condonable, that the present world is eager to find out ways and means for removing these blocks.[11] A separate segment deserves to be spared in this essay for elaborating these major blocks to world evolution.

Major Blocks to Our Healthy March

a) *Scienceism*: As for the block or barrier of Scienceism, Barney Wee and Agnes Lau invite our attention to the role played by Rene Descartes in offering a unique status to science. They thus point out that Descartes, a 17th century French philosopher noted how two scientists, Copernicus and Galileo had successfully challenged biblical scripture and how the split between religion and science became unbridgeable. The solution found out by Descartes, according to Wee & Lau was unique; as it made the split between religion and science or that between mind and body permanent forever. Rene Descartes thus handed over 'mind' to the jurisdiction of religion and 'body' to that of science. He thus prohibited religion from interfering in the material domain and similarly

10. *See* the Note no. 8.

11. Barney Wee & Agnes Lau, *See* the Note no. 5, pp. 253-260.

proscribed science in intervening in the domain of 'mind' and 'soul'. Descartes-sponsored mind-body dichotomy thus freed material world of any domination from God; it also liberated physical world from the influence of consciousness and spirit. Descartes, in short, questions: "Why to allow consciousness to dominate physical world, which is comprehensible through physical senses?" Such sort of naked materialism remained quite predominant throughout the world for two centuries. Materialism, in alliance with reductionism and determinism ruled our world view almost for two hundred years. This world view is called Scienceism. If reductionism informs us of the possibility of reducing any system into different parts or components, it also underscores the necessity to reduce God to nonentity. Determinism means certainty to determine and manipulate results of nature on the basis of prior events. Scienceism, in short considers matter as basic and spirit, consciousness, etc. as irrelevant.

At the outset of the 20th century the world, however, realized that human consciousness is more significant than human body, that holistic outlook is superior to fragmentary approach, that faith in divinity of a human being ennobles human transactions. World accordingly became skeptical regarding determinism. Vaclav Havel's advice to revolutionise our consciousness has indeed acquired a significant status in the present era. Present world has indeed noted the urgency of implementing Lord Krishna's appeal to restrain physical senses and to emancipate minds from the clutches of the body.

b) *Survivalism*: The book: 'Choices of Now', penned by Barney Wee & Agnes Lau gives a very interesting piece of information that the December 2008 – issue of National Geographic Magazine contained a write-up titled "The Other Darwin". Readers must have realized through that write-up that Alfred Russell Wallace a contemporary of Charles Darwin gave a message, diametrically opposite to that of Darwin and this very message is quite apt for today's world. As per Wallacean message, our survival depends not on Competition but on completion. Charles Darwin has asked us, to pursue Killer's instinct because 'Survival of the fittest' is the worthy maxim. Wallace has however asked us to adjust to our environment with a view to remaining 'fit' in the world. If

Darwin expects us to opt for competition, Wallace wants us to prefer completion to competition. And present world has acknowledged the relevance of Wallacean advice to get tuned to surrounding circumstances. 'Choices of Now' very rightly concludes that the spirit of cooperation and coordination has enabled us to survive, that the message of Wallace to the people at large to develop harmonious relations with each other and with the nature has won the race. Do we not remember here the golden counsel articulated in 'Hind-Swaraj' and repeated later in 'Integral Humanism' to care for dumb and deaf? We are not, in other words expected to be harsh about the pains and strains of vulnerable and marginalized sections of our society. The World-acclaimed imperative is to complete and not to compete! Let me now elucidate third block or barrier to our advancement and that block is called 'Humanism'.

c) *Humanism*: The world view of Humanism presently seems to be a block or inhibition in our march toward noble civilization, because 'scienceism' and 'survivalism' have projected ideal man as a homocentric or anthropocentric being. If scienceism has uprooted God from the world, survivalism has justified the operation of the law of the jungle. Resultant exile of divine tendencies like renunciation, compassion, empathy, sacrifice, etc. has created a horrible vacuum, in the human life. History of the genesis and growth of 'Humanism' in Europe informs us that during 15th and 16th century Protestants fought against Catholics with a view to enabling a human being to have a personal contact with God. Protestants thus fought for making a human being free from the Catholic priesthood and Roman domination. They did not, however fight against history-centrism of Catholics. "They actually continued to endorse the 'otherness' of God. Logically they did not find it essential to cultivate inner consciousness as a gateway to the divine".[12] Subsequently Descartes underscored mind-body dichotomy. As this dichotomy remained influential upto the beginning of the 20th century, Europe sponsored 'Humanism' did not recognise any role of consciousness in the human life at least for two hundred years. Still later, in the aftermath of the emergence and consolidation of nation-states in Europe, initially autocracy and later plutocracy caused incalculable torture to a common man. That

12. *See* Rajiv Malhotra, *Being Different* (Noida, U.P. India, 2013), p. 158.

was why, Europe observed a new incarnation of 'Humanism' in the form of the campaign for human rights.

Marxism came ahead in reaction to capitalism to rid common man of alienation and fetishism. The remedial measure of statism prescribed by Marxism, however proved catastrophic, because statist grabbing of society converted ordinary man into a nut-bolt and screw. Least wonder, the continuation of the campaign for human rights for shaping 'Humanism' has become an uninterrupted journey towards unreachable 'El-Dorado'.

Barney Wee and Agnes Lau have called present campaign for 'Humanism' as a block or a barrier in the path towards advancement, because the human beings nurtured through this campaign are homocentric, interested in the exclusive pursuit of naked selfishness. 'The Humanism' of the present era, with its encouragement to desire, greed and temptation and through its endorsement of the Darwinian principle of "the survival of the fittest", has posed serious challenges, threatening the rise of noble healthy civilization.

The above mentioned two Singapore-scholars have however failed to notice that the roots of the present-day Humanism are traceable in the history. As has been mentioned above that during 15th and 16th centuries Protestants had sowed the seeds of current 'Humanism', as they thought it essential to free the common man from the clutches of the Holy Roman Empire of Catholics. Thus, the roots of Europe sponsored 'Humanism' were located in reaction against Catholic priests. Protestants, however, continued to believe in history centrism; in the 'otherness' of God, etc. They did not believe in the intrinsic divinity of each human being. We can thus legitimately comment that the Protestant-sponsored 'Humanism' originated in reaction and not out of conviction in the significance of human consciousness. Secondly, Protestants like Luther and Calvin, did fight, no doubt for offering each human being a right to get direct access to God; but they never fought for offering every human being a right to free himself from the grip of satanic instincts. Protestants, in other words fought for human freedom to gain access to God; but they failed to fight for human freedom from greed, jealousy, etc.

It may be remembered here quite spontaneously that the 'Humanism' preached in India and advocated by Gandhi and Pandit Deendayal Upadhyay is definitely superior to its West-Sponsored counterpart. It is important, in other words, to imbibe in ourselves the imprints of inherent human divinity with a view to expediting our march towards noble civilization. We must advocate Cosmo-centric and not homo-centric Humanism! It seems that Gandhi carried ahead Vivekananda's legacy of spiritual Humanism and Pandit Deendayal Upadhyay further enriched the same legacy. Cosmo-centric Humanism and spiritual Humanism are the two sides of the same coin. Naturally, social dimension of India-sponsored Humanism was underscored by Swami Vivekananda and Gandhi as well as Pandit Deendayal Upadhyay who all implemented this dimension. One can, incidentally refer here to some quotations from Vivekananda's speeches and writings, as they evidence social dimension quite vividly.

a) "We want a religion.... Which will give us faith in ourselves, a national self-respect and the power to feed and educate the poor and relieve the misery around-us. If you want to find God, serve him".
b) "Do you love your fellow-man? Where else should you go to seek for God? Are not all the poor, the miserable, the week-Gods? Why not worship them first?"
c) "Service to man should be the further religion of the world!"

It has been elucidated in this segment how scienceism, survivalism and Humanism have emerged at present as major blocks in the path of our advancement. It has also explained how the present global think tank has noted the relevance of Indian philosophy in this connection. Prof. Vamsee Julury, who has been quoted in the body of the present book in certain places has rightly informed us that "Gandhi and Pandit Deendayal Upadhyay responded in strongly similar idioms, with non-violence as a central concept, in trying to chart an ethical course for a newly decolonized India".[13] The following extract from Julury's write up aptly sums up the crux of India's civilization:

13. Vamsee Julury, "Ahimsa has no political hue", in *The Hindu* (Chennai), 02 October, 2015, p. 15.

> "the real genius of India's civilizational legacy perhaps is its ability to engage with diversity deeply and meaningfully enough to restore the primacy of what is important, and dismiss the distractions of the superficial, the deleterious".[14]

It has been stated in the beginning of this 'Preface' that Prof. A. K. Dasgupta a well-known Indian economist vented his despondency through his lecture in 1971 over the then prevailing mainstream-sidetracking Gandhian thoughts. He was, however, optimistic. He was confident that "in future Indian thinking in general and Gandhian thinking in particular would definitely receive due obeisance". His optimism or confidence well-articulated in the extract given below has proved true. The narration of several specimens attempted in the preceding lines endorses Prof. Dasgupta's optimism. One can quote a lucid articulation of this optimism, "Marxian revolution was originally meant for the industrialised West, but was actually adopted, against Marx's own prediction, by the undeveloped East. Can it not be that this reversal of venue will be repeated in the case of Gandhian revolution too? It may well happen that it will catch the affluent West sooner than one would imagine. May be that the suitable soil for a peaceful revolution such as Gandhi envisaged is for an affluent society and not an immature one. It makes smooth going to settle on a plateau once you have climbed the hill; the journey uphill is arduous".[15]

The fact that Gandhian line of thinking and in actuality entire Indian philosophy has presently attracted the affluent West, rather whole world is undeniable. This very fact places heavy responsibility on our shoulders. Indians should now delve deep into the treasury of our ethos with a view to finding genuine solutions and relief to the globe. Present compilation of such essays is merely a small step in that direction. Readers will, hopefully appreciate this initiative.

Succinct Introduction

Thirteen research papers or essays compiled here need to be introduced succinctly in the preface. First paper highlights the life and mission of Pandit Deendayal Upadhyay. Pandit Deendayal Upadhyay's life was really a miracle. It was he who accomplished the mission of his life within around one and half decades. He built a formidable political party which subsequently revolutionized the polity of India. Pandit

14. *Ibid.*
15. *See* the Note no. 1.

Deendayal Upadhyay epitomized Sage Vashishtha's golden counsel given to Lord Ramachandra. The counsel runs as follows: "Remain fully unattached in all your public dealings". Deendayal's writings and speeches dive deep into the happenings and bring out permanent out of evanescent dimensions. They thus remain evergreen!

Barring the first essay of the present compilation, all other papers, twelve in number deal with different facets of Deendayal sponsored Integral Humanism thus doing justice to the title: 'Integral Humanism: A Distinct Paradigm of Development'. Remaining papers can be classified into four groups. First group thus comprises three write-ups. If one of them focuses on the fact that Gandhi's 'Hind-Swaraj' and Pandit Deendayal Upadhyay's 'Integral Humanism' offer impressively similar interpretations of Indian ethos, the other essay brings to our notice, interesting and revealing commonalities between Lohia's socialism and Pandit Deendayal Upadhyay's Integral Humanism. Second group, accommodates three papers. First one of this group elaborates how Integral Humanism can be presented as the apt unfoldment of Swami Vivekananda's Spiritual Humanism. This group has two more papers one on 'Swaraj in Ideas' and second one 'Gita Rahasya' the magnum-opus of Lokamanya Tilak appears to be the fountain head of Integral Humanism.

Third group, shelters two essays. 'Integral Humanism and Marxism' is the title of the first paper of this group, which highlights commonalities and contrasts between these two 'isms'. Finally, the last paper of this group conveys to readers that 'Integral Humanism' assures sustainable development for India. The philosophy of Integral Humanism has accordingly become a precursor to the present UNDP-pleaded mission of Sustainable Development Goals.

Final group, hosts four papers. First essay, quite lengthy, puts forth detailed elucidation of seven unique features of Integral Humanism. The second one, delineates how the concept of Indian Nationalism presented in Integral Humanism is far superior to the recently rooted Euro-American Nativism. Third write up, in this section, convincingly proves that Integral Humanism is quite capable of providing antidotes apt for countering contemporary world challenges. The last paper of the book demonstrates how Integral Humanism is immensely relevant at present, and that's why this chapter is aptly titled as 'Integral Humanism: A Timely Treatise'. Readers will hopefully share the viewpoint that Integral Humanism really happens to be, a distinct paradigm of development.

My sincere heartfelt thanks to Professor V. K. Malhotra, the Member Secretary of the Indian Council of Social Science Research, for his offer to publish the present compilation of thirteen research papers on Integral Humanism. This inspired me to expedite the collection of relevant material with a view to giving final shape to each paper. And, this is the ultimate outcome in humble homage to Pandit Deendayal Upadhyay, the modern Indian sage in whose sacred memory this volume has been devoted.

2

Life and Mission of Pandit Deendayal Upadhyay

As the study of Pandit Deendayal Upadhyay's writings and speeches triggered passion for grasping Lokamanya's matchless attributes, it is quite relevant and befitting to describe Pandit Deendayal's life and mission in the light of the latter's life history.

Thus, just as Lokamanya Tilak practised Karma-Yoga principles before articulating Karma Yoga 'Mantras' in *Gita-Rahasya* during his stay in Mandalay-Jail, Pandit Deendayal first mirrored the unique attributes of Ekatma Manava in his transactions before articulating the fundamentals of Ekatma Manava Darshan.

It was in the year 1871 that Bal Gangadhar Tilak had decided to write his commentary on Bhagvad Gita. In actuality, the year 1911 witnessed the completion of the writing of this commentary in the jail at Mandalay, Burma. Lokamanya Tilak elaborated through this commentary that esoteric import of Gita lies in the preaching of Karma-Yoga (Desireless or Unattached Actions). World of course noticed during forty years between 1871 and 1911 that the life led by Tilak during this period was full of anecdotes and happenings mirroring Karma-Yoga only. One can in fact aver that Tilak never abandoned the path of Karma-Yoga. What impressed Pandit Deendayal most was the very indivisibility in Lokamanya's life between precept and practice.

We observe similar type of integrity in Pandit Deendayal's life as well between contemplation and action. We all know that Pandit Deendayal expounded the philosophy of Integral Humanism in the evening of his life. He however showed the signs of Integral Man since the early years of his life. Thus, it was during the early years of his life that Pandit Deendayal faced through remarkably restrained emotions the ordeal of the deaths of seven close relatives including parents, grandparents, brother, sister, etc. During these very years, moreover, he was constrained to move from one place to another, from one educational institute to another. He nonetheless shouldered several family responsibilities and passed every test or examination (whether in a school or in a college) with flying colours. Such signs of well-balanced mental condition of Pandit Deendayal prompted the editor of Political Diary (compilation of Pandit Deendayal's essays) to remind us of his feat in the following words:

"Deendayal was an outstanding child. He was all brains and nerves. He did his matric from Kalyan High School, Sikar, standing first class first in the Ajmer Board examinations. He was awarded a gold medal each by the Board and the school. Two years later, he stood first class in the Intermediate examination from Birla College, Pilani. Again, he got two gold medals one from the Board and the other from the college. He did his B.A. in Mathematics from S.D. College, Kanpur with first division. Panditji joined St. John College in Agra to do his M.A. in English but left it midway and went to Allahabad where he did B.T. During his college career he was the recipient of a monthly scholarship".[1]

Here one recollects the following stanza of the Bhagavad Gita: (Stanza 13 Chapter 2)

> "देहिनोऽस्मिन् यथा देहे कौमारं यौवनं जरा। तथा देहान्तरप्राप्तिर्धीरस्तत्र न मुह्यति।।" (When the embodied soul passes in this body from boyhood to youth and from youth to old age and later passes into another body at death, a sober person is least bewildered by such a change.)

What is remarkable is the fact that despite various adversities including deaths of seven close relatives faced by Pandit Deendayal during his student-years, he took initiative in forming 'Zero Clubs' with a view to rendering essential educational assistance to his dull colleagues. One can indeed state that Pandit Deendayal demonstrated during very adverse formative years of his life a bunch of unique qualities like rare calmness of mind, proneness to shoulder family responsibilities and deep compassion for vulnerable colleagues.

---

1. Deendayal Upadhyay, *Political Diary* (Bombay, 1968), p. XI

Kandarpa Ramachandra Rao, whose book titled 'Integral Humanism'has been acclaimed as the most authentic treatise on Deendayal's mission offers us in the following paragraph very lucid narration of 'Integral Man'.

'The Integral Man is one whose consciousness filled with love and compassion embraces the whole mankind. He is the one who has freed himself from the magnetic pulls and attachments of the physical world and thereby established himself in the peace of the soul within and in the harmony of nature around. His ego is completely effaced and he is one with all life and consciousness. In his experience, he is face to face with the Creator who has manifested Himself in all beings and objects around. He lives in the peace and bliss of his oneness with the Creator".[2]

Juxtaposition of this narration side by side with the sketch drawn in the preceding lines of the happenings during early years of Pandit Deendayal's life prompts one to notice marks of Integral Man in Pandit Deendayal's during those years.

Pandit Deendayal Upadhyay as the R.S.S. Pracharak

It was in 1941 that Pandit Deendayal became a fulltime worker of R.S.S. (Rashtriya Swayamsevak Sangh), but his association with R.S.S. as a Swayam sevak or a worker began in 1937 only. He was lucky to hear about R.S.S. mission from Dr. Hedgewar and Veer Savarkar the two key stalwarts of Hindutva ideology. As has been explained above, he had shown the marks of Integral Man in the early years of his life. He could naturally grasp the mission of R.S.S. within no time. One can in fact point out that Pandit Deendayal and R.S.S. were made for each other. It seems that three dimensions of R.S.S. mission deeply impressed Pandit Deendayal Upadhyay.

Rashtriya Swayamsevak Sangh thus aims at advocating the cause of geo-cultural nationalism in the place of territorial nationalism. It is moreover interested in pursuing development trajectory based on Indian ethos. Thirdly, it wants to invest in human capital as it has faith in the transformation of individual consciousness. It is essential now to elaborate these dimensions in detail.

Geo-Cultural Nationalism

As for geo-cultural nationalism, one can observe that a nation connotes confluence of land, people and culture. It is the culture which

2. Kandarpa Ramachandra Rao, Integral Humanism (Hyderabad, 1995), p. 123.

unites people and links them with land. In India since the years of Vedas and Upanishads one single culture based on 'Chiti' has kept Indians together. We thus find common faith among Indians in certain principles such as 'unity in diversity', 'symbiotic relations between individual and society', 'superiority of divine tendencies over satanic instincts', etc. This faith, (termed as 'Chiti') in our ethos has kept us united. The R.S.S. therefore avers that as the faith in cultural and civilizational bonds in India is strong, neither foreign invaders, nor adverse rulers has ever succeeded in crushing our national spirit. The very silken bonds keep us linked with the hoary past through the memories of our rich heritage. It was on the basis of these links, which are most cultural and least biological that Pandit Deendayal used to assert our ancient roots.

Pandit Deendayal must have noticed that whereas all political parties then existing in pre independence India, (barring of course Hindu Maha Sabha) were pleading in favour of territorial or geographical nationalism, R.S.S. was an energetic votary of geo-cultural nationalism. He must have observed that whereas most of the activists were interested in forming political receptacles due to conviction that, it was only a political receptacle that could transform India. Hedgewar was totally unwilling to convert R.S.S. into a political party. Pandit Deendayal shared this line of thinking because of his conviction that it was the role played by Rishis, Munis and Yogis and not that by Kings and Queens which sowed the seeds of our nation. His liking for affirmative thinking was also in tune with that of Hedgewar, Savarkar and Golwalkar. The R.S.S. leadership was, no doubt quite uneasy with the Indian followers of obdurate Islam and Christianity, as both of these sects refused to get assimilated into Indian ethos. The leaders of R.S.S. nonetheless opted for affirmative stance, they always stated that the R.S.S. had come into existence not in opposition / reaction to non-Hindus but out of confidence that the gravity or dignity and spirituality of the organised Hindu society is bound to move all non-Hindus within its field. Pandit Deendayal must have felt that if pseudo secularist forces were bent on bargaining with non-Hindus and on compromising with solid truth, R.S.S. was marching in the right direction of apt assimilation between Hindus and non-Hindus.

Our Development Trajectory

The second dimension of the R.S.S. mission is to generate faith among Indians that "We, the natives of India can shape our destiny, that our development trajectory can be chalked out on the basis of our ethos". It was well known that Hedgewar, the founder of R.S.S. was an active worker of Indian National Congress in the years preceding to the formation of R.S.S. and in 1920, during the All India conference of Congress Party held at Nagpur, Hedgewar moved a resolution expressing resolve to put an end to imperialism throughout the world.

Much later in 1929 when the Indian National Congress decided at Lahore to march towards 'Poorna Swaraj', Hedgewar appealed to R.S.S. *shakhas* to welcome this decision through organising public functions. R.S.S. mission to strengthen Swadeshi spirit in India with a view to chalking out indigenous strategy of development was thus in full consonance with its past. That Pandit Deendayal was also fond of, rather insistent on indigenous development trajectory can be corroborated by referring to reminiscences of Dr. Murali Manohar Joshi, a former Central Minister and a previous president of B.J.P.

It was in 1949 that Pandit Deendayal was Saha-pranta Pracharak of U.P. and Joshi was a post graduate student in Allahabad University. The student's hostel there used to be visited quite often by all India leaders of all parties and organisations. The jargon used by such stalwarts, according to Joshi, "was steeped in Western standards in the sense that they used to evaluate Indian events by Western yardsticks or parameters". Joshi states that "Pandit Deendayalji however, used to state very strongly that we must create our own standards, why should we be judged by a literary history of 300 or 400 years old or even in philosophy why should we be compared with a philosophy which started only with Socrates or Plato. Why not with Indian philosophers? Pandit Deendayal, indeed introduced Indian jargon within an Indian system of analysis".[3]

Dr. Mahesh Chandra Sharma's very valuable Ph.D thesis entitled – "Pandit Deendayal Upadhyay: Kartritva evam Vichar" has rightly demonstrated through the following content how Pandit Deendayal's thinking was in total agreement with R.S.S. mission to make Indians self-confident of their ability to chalk out India's development trajectory. He wanted to preserve India's Indianness but not through delinking it from the world. He expected India to pursue modernisation. He however refused to treat modernisation as equivalent to Westernisation. He wanted India to contribute to the world treasury of knowledge, undoubtedly, on the basis of its spiritual inheritance".[4]

3. Murali Manohar Joshi, "The context of Integral Humanism", in K. C. Sudhir Babu (ed.) Integral Humanism: vision for tomorrow (Thiruvananthapuram, 2017), p. 60.
4. Mahesh Chandra Sharma, *Deendayal Upadhyay: Kartritva Evam Vichar* (A book in Hindi), (New Delhi, 1994), p. 401.

Interest in the Common Man

Pandit Deendayal's thinking in line with Indian ethos gave utmost priority to the enhancement of the wellbeing of a common man. Least wonder, Pandit Deendayal's interest in the wellbeing of a common man got spontaneous expression in his views and policies. He thus opposed both capitalism as well as Marxism because they threatened justice and humanity respectively through exploitative capitalist order and through harsh statism. Pandit Deendayal's concern for the happiness of a common man prompted him to oppose Compulsory Deposit Scheme proposed in Morarji Desai's 1963 budget. "It is inequitable and quite burdensome for small savings of small men". – thus commented Pandit Deendayal. Same concern also led him to make the following pungent comment while reviewing Indian Government's Gold Policy in February 1963.

"As the government's taxation policy and corruption dissuade people from converting 'black' money into 'white', same factors generate among public deep attraction for 'yellow money', that is gold".[5]

We observe the reflection of the same concern for the happiness of the common man in the comment given below:

"The long term needs of development and the short term needs of satisfying the expectations of the people for better standard of living have to be balanced".[6]

Pandit Deendayal's prescription that "ideological considerations should not be imported into the basic question of feeding the people", proved prophetic, as the year 1960 witnessed tragic abortion of state trading in food-grains in India. Pandit Deendayal's retort in the same year to the American justification for the wheat loan to India from America under Public Law 480 deserves a special mention here.

The agreement signed by India in 1960 under the U.S. Public Law 480 for a huge wheat loan from America was justified by Mr. Elsworth Bunker, the then U.S. Ambassador in India on the ground that "India can have both freedom and food".[7] Pandit Deendayal however came out with an apt remark, "what we want is our freedom and our food". Pandit Deendayal was the last person to welcome government – sponsored fanfare or wasteful showy display in 1959 on the occasion of the inauguration of a public sector Jabalpur factory manufacturing

5. *See* the Note no. 1, p. 16.
6. "The Third Plan X-Rayed", in *See* the Note no. 1, p. 19.
7. *Ibid*, p. 26.

trucks because that factory was simply building a wooden body on an imported chassis and engine. He similarly attacked again in 1959 extra ordinary enthusiasm of Jawaharlal Nehru in imposing on farmers one of the most non-pragmatic programmes of cooperative farming. He rightly noted that such sort of dogmatic pursuit of the socialist ideology was most unbecoming for the Nehru Government.

Pandit Deendayal sponsored Integral Humanism aims at re-establishing a common man in his rightful position, wherein he can attain divine heights of his latent personality. Pandit Deendayal sponsored this philosophy in the evening of his life. But throughout his life he gave priority attention to the upliftment of the most downtrodden man. He therefore fought against the programme of cooperative farming as according to him this very programme was bound to make farmers landless. He opposed rationalisation of mills in Kanpur, because he feared that it would make the worker jobless. He similarly decided to fight against eviction notices issued by Delhi Municipal Corporation for driving out hawkers from streets, as the miseries of street hawkers touched his heart. It was again Pandit Deendayal's concern for the homeless residents of Mumbai which prompted him to appeal to Mumbai Municipal Corporation to provide on war footing all the basic amenities to inmates of slum areas.

Third Dimension of the R.S.S. Mission: Investment in Human Capital

Pandit Deendayal's deep, lifelong attachment for R.S.S. was rooted in his realisation that he shared with R.S.S. leaders the prime necessity to awaken national consciousness among Indians. Pandit Deendayal also shared R.S.S. decision to awaken national spirit first among Hindus and later among non-Hindus due to common conviction that India is a Hindu Nation. Hedgewar, the R.S.S. founder following the footsteps of Swami Vivekananda had noted that "Hindu citizens have unfortunately abandoned their basic national virtues and opted for affection in favour of provincial, linguistic, sectarian, castiest loyalties". "They have moreover, failed in acquiring appreciable qualities like collectivity, industriousness, rationality, etc. from Britishers". – added Hedgewar. What must have impressed Pandit Deendayal most was the resolve on the part of Hedgewar to imbibe the very qualities through reviving national consciousness among Hindus throughout India.

The fact that at present R.S.S. has emerged as the only organisation in the world engaged in the task of investment in human capital for 97 years since its inception in 1925 is a widely acclaimed phenomenon. And the fact that Pandit Deendayal had played a lion's role in building R.S.S. inspired political formation is equally undeniable! What is most remarkable is the fact that new incarnation of the very political formation has succeeded since 2014 in forming most popular governments in the centre as well as in several states in India. Leaders as well as cadres of this political party whole heartedly acknowledge their debt to the Herculean efforts of Pandit Deendayal for such a miracle.

Economic Policy of Jana Sangh

Pandit Deendayal's economic thinking, going hand in hand with R.S.S. sponsored development trajectory subsequently became the economic policy of Jana Sangh. One can elaborate tenets of this economic policy in the lines below:

1) First, is the main principle of optimum production, equitable distribution and restricted consumption.
   As far as optimum production is concerned, according to Pandit Deendayal, it must cater not only to the present but also to the limited immediate future needs of the people. In no case, however, it should generate excessive supply over and above demand, as factory managers will then be compelled to induce buyers by hook or by crook to buy more and more goods. Pandit Deendayal Upadhyay thus opposes consumption – oriented production just as he rejects eco-destructive production, as from the perspective of Indian ethos it is milking rather than exploitation of resources which is the most acceptable phenomenon. Equitable distribution should care for accomplishing five basic public needs such as bread, clothing, shelter, education and health. It should also bother to maintain the specific ratio between maximum and minimum income levels of citizens.
   Restrained consumption enables an individual to keep his body fit and fine, though it prohibits him from gratifying lust, greed and temptation. Pandit Deendayal rightly underscores socio-cultural dimensions of production, distribution and consumption, because according to him, it is the disdainful attitude of people towards these dimensions that causes horrible perversions. He therefore, pleads for imparting value education to students.
2) The tenet of trusteeship is equally crucial. Pandit Deendayal elaborates this tenet through the analysis of the issue of the

ownership over property. He opposes capitalism because it facilitates the unfoldment of oligopoly through its endorsement of private ownership of property. He similarly rejects Marxism because it sanctions statist grabbing of property through its endorsement of public ownership of property. He thus rejects limitless individual ownership over property and rejects similarly unlimited state control over property. Pandit Deendayal's analysis of the issue of ownership is really quite unique. He states, "When the society accepts my right over property, it also expects me to use it in the interest of people at large. Private property right thus disallows me from using it unscrupulously. Everybody is therefore supposed to be a trustee of his property. The right to own property is thus the right to use it within limits and that too for using it in the interest of society. Pandit Deendayal's view is thus a very balanced and just approach. It recommends that an individual property owner whether big or small should honour society's interest while using his property. It opposes categorically state ownership over property because even the state-owned property is used by individuals, employed by the state. Therefore, if such individuals become corrupt, unscrupulous and dictatorial, ordinary man and woman will feel totally helpless in front of the Leviathan – state. The institution of the state will then be constrained to use its regulatory power for punishing such corrupt, unscrupulous individuals".[8]

The remedy, in short, lies in making each individual aware of his or her responsibility towards society, in imbibing the imprint of trusteeship on everyone's mindset!

Pandit Deendayal's approach is least utopian, least romantic. It widens and broadens the concept of trusteeship, as it expects not only private property owners but also state officials to treat themselves as trustees of society. It welcomes, moreover, the legitimate use of state power not only against unscrupulous state officials but also against unscrupulous private property owners.

Pandit Deendayal thus sponsors the concept of trusteeship and sanctions in similar vein the occasional, legitimate use of state power for keeping private property owners on the track. Here one comes across one of the most notable maxims or aphorisms through Pandit Deendayal's words:

"State control over individual's satanic instincts and individuals' revolt against devilish statist transactions are the signs of perverted

8. *See* the Note no. 5, p. 268.

society. Control and revolt are the weapons of indispensability. Occasional use of such weapons can be considered legitimate but permanent reliance on them can hardly be treated as rational".[9]

3) *Third tenet*: Decentralised economy is a distinct contribution of India. It mirrors self-employed sector which provides best alternative to the public and private sectors. It provides opportunities of development to common men as in a decentralised economy each one's peculiarities can be taken into account. There is accordingly adequate scope for the display of each one's creativity.

   Decentralised economy is an effective antidote to the spread of exploitative capitalism. When there is small scale production, there is hardly any chance for a producer to collect capital on a huge scale. Such an economy is likely to affect favourably the quantity as well as the quality of goods and services, as small scale cottage industries will boost creativity of producers. The economic democracy that will take roots in villages will be the additional benefit of decentralisation. Decentralised economy will moreover facilitate the emergence and growth of balanced development wherein cottage industries located in villages will provide essential assistance to big industries centred in metropolitan cities. Pandit Deendayal indeed carried ahead R.S.S. sponsored development trajectory for India!

Pandit Deendayal Upadhyay: Builder of Bharatiya Jana Sangh

Dr. Shyama Prasad Mookerjee, a member of Jawaharlal Nehru's first cabinet of ministers, resigned his ministerial post in protest against Nehru-Liaqat pact in the immediate post freedom years of India. He formed a new political party and sought assistance from Shri Guruji Golwalkar, the then R.S.S. Chief in building this party. Shri Guruji was the last person to convert R.S.S. into a political party; he nonetheless deputed Pandit Deendayal to be the right hand of Mookerjee. According to Balasaheb Deoras, the Third Chief of R.S.S., what impressed Shri Guruji most were the three unique qualities of Pandit Deendayal: first, he was capable of thinking in the light of Indian ethos, secondly, he had zero personal ambition and thirdly, he was competent enough to build a team of dedicated party workers.

That Pandit Deendayal proved his mettle is more than obvious. It was on 11th February 1968 that death snatched him away from this world. By that year, all three parliamentary and assembly elections of

9. *Ibid.* p. 269.

Pandit Deendayal's political career from 1951 to 1968 had taken place in India. And the success achived by the Bhartiya Jana Sangh in this period by winning seats in elections inspired Craig Baxter to comment as,

> "Jana Sangh is the only political party in India that has increased its percentage of the political vote and its share of parliamentary and assembly seats in each successive election from 1952 through 1967".[10]

Pandit Deendayal had a very clear and distinct line of thinking.

His views mirrored this thinking. Thus, at one place he stated, "Ours is a party with difference. It springs from the craving of the nation to come into its own. It is the urge of the nation to assert and accomplish what it has been destined to do".[11]

At another place, Pandit Deendayal expressed his thought in the following way:

> "We aim at political power with a view to achieving certain social and national objectives".[12]

It was in the same national spirit that Deendayal vented his party's mission:

> "The Jana Sangh follows the reformist tradition of Dayananda and Tilak, not only in the social field but also in the arena concerned with economic issues".[13]

Pandit Deendayal thus tried to imbibe in the minds of party workers that their party has emerged for accomplishing our nation's craving and this is why we can't afford to be worshippers of naked powerism".

The Jana Sangh workers were thus asked by him to pursue principled politics, to honour ethical values in all transactions, and to respect justice as well as humanity. No wonder, under Deendayalji's leadership Jana Sangh not only grew in strength but also emerged as a distinct party of dedicated workers.

Akhand Bharat

For Pandit Deendayal the issue of Akhand Bharat was the article of faith. He mentioned time and again throughout his life that India is one nation, one culture, one civilization, one people and one state. And as he was a friend, philosopher and guide for the workers of Jana Sangh, this newly emerged political party also remained committed to the

---

10. Craig Baxter, A Biography of an Indian Political Party: Jana Sangh (Bombay, 1971), p. 2.
11. Deendayal Upadhyay, "The Mission of Jana Sangh", *Organiser* (New Delhi), Diwali Issue, 1964, p. 187.
12. *See* the Note no. 1, p. 115.
13. *Ibid.* p. 131.

implementation of the pledge of Akhand Bharat! That was why Pandit Deendayal and Jana Sangh always pleaded for geo-cultural nationalism of India. For the same reason, they fought in favour of unity and integrity of India and against discretion on the part of any religious community or province to decide about geographical borders on India. One and the same article of faith led them to argue against Nehru-sponsored transfer of Berubari to Pakistan. The mammoth historical rally of five lakh workers in New Delhi on 16th August 1965 organised by Jana Sangh against Kutch – Treaty with Pakistan was also the most effective articulation of the faith in Indian unity.

Pandit Deendayal's write up, titled 'Can we afford to compromise on Kashmir' in general and the two paragraphs from this write-up in particular are worth serious consideration for ever. The very paragraphs are given below:

I. **"We demand a categorical assurance from the Prime Minister that he would not in any way agree to any infringement of the sovereign rights of Bharat in Kashmir**. In this connection attention must be drawn to the Canal Water Treaty which is reported to contain a clause with regard to the Mangla Dam in Pak-occupied Kashmir. The Prime Minister should not sign the treaty unless this clause is deleted. If he accepts Pakistan's right to construct a dam in that area, our earlier protest in this regard will have no meaning. It will mean a virtual abdication of our claim on that part of Bharat's lawful territory".[14]

II. "People should also be watchful. At a time when the government is out to offer lands in bhoodan, they alone are the protectors of the unity and integrity of the country. Let us very clearly tell the Government that no betrayal of the nation's trust shall be tolerated. Be it Berubari or Kashmir, Aksai Chin or Barahoti, the Government has to protect and preserve, and not to pawn and part with, national territory".[15]

It is quite obvious that the emphasised portion of the extract (I) quoted above has acquired immense relevance today.

The historical satyagraha launched by Jana Sangh under the captainship of its first President Dr. Shyama Prasad Mookerjee for putting an end to "two vidhans (constitutions), two Pradhans (Prime Ministers) and two nishans (flags) in the jurisdiction of Jammu-Kashmir evidenced people's faith or conviction in One nation, One culture and One people. Most vocal and aggressive stance on the part of

14. *Ibid.* p. 44.
15. *Ibid.*

Jana Sangh for the liberation of Goa similarly mirrored one and the same conviction. Joint statement issued by Pandit Deendayal and Lohia with a view to creating a confederation of India and Pakistan equally ventilated firm faith of nation in Akhand Bharat".

Pandit Deendayal's faith in the unity and integrity of India led him to articulate his urge that no Indian province be called 'A State'. Same faith guided him to request Hindu residents of Punjab to consider Punjabi language as their mother-tongue. It was in the light of the same faith that Pandit Deendayal opted for divorce between Jana Sangh and Swatantra Party.

"How can Jana Sangh shake hands with Swatantra Party which favours and welcomes United Nation's intervention for resolving Kashmir-conundrum?" – thus questioned Pandit Deendayal. As Pandit Deendayal considered entire India as a single entity, he was eager to disseminate Jana Sangh – work in all nooks and corners of India. That was why, impressive all India sessions and training classes of Jana Sangh held in South India made Pandit Deendayal immensely happy. The Calicut session of Jana Sangh held under the presidentship of Pandit Deendayal was the victorious culmination of his dedicated efforts. Tragically, he breathed his last in the immediate aftermath of the All India Session of Jana Sangh held at Calicut!

Pandit Deendayal Upadhyay: Inimitable Ideal Organiser

A mention has been made above that according to Craig Baxter, amongst all political parties in India, it was the Jana Sangh alone which made most remarkable progress in its march in the first three post freedom decades of India. A mention has also been made in the same vein that the same period witnessed the rise and very effective ascendancy of Pandit Deendayal as the architect of Jana Sangh. Thus, it has been pointed out how Pandit Deendayal Upadhyay had demonstrated his inimitable organisational skills. The present section is devoted to elaborate Pandit Deendayal's organisational skill and acumen.

Pandit Deendayal, basically being a full time R.S.S. activist, treated entire India as his home and all Indians as his kith and kin. What was unique was the fact that he never deviated even for an inch from the mission of R.S.S. He thus saw that Jana Sangh contributed through its policies and practices to the process of reconstruction of Indian nation. Realisation on his part that the lack of collectivists had caused a great damage to Bharat Varsha prompted him to chalk out essential 'dos' and 'donts' for party workers. He accordingly expected decision makers in the party to take into account all dimensions of the decisions to be taken. He felt that free and fair discussion among workers regarding all pros and cons of all issues was 'a must' before arriving at the final decision. Similar, rather, priority attention, according to him, was to be paid to the well-being of marginalised and vulnerable sections of Indian society. He insisted that fair, equitable representation be given to Scheduled Castes and Scheduled Tribes at all levels of the organisational structure of the party.

Pandit Deendayal was well aware of lingering socio-economic problems faced by India. He was equally eager to see the end of such problems and the unfoldment of expeditions reconstruction of India. He accordingly, condemned the widespread prevalence of meaningless rituals, superstitions, fatalistic tendencies and status-quoist instincts. Some specimens of his views are worth quotation here.

a) "We do honour our past. But we oppose condonation of unjust and inhuman customs and traditions".
b) "Order is appreciable, status-quo-ism is condemnable".
c) "There is a clear line of demarcation between Ram Rajya Parishad and Jana Sangh. If the former is no-changer, Jana Sangh is changer".
d) "Our goal is not merely to protect our culture but to revitalise it so as to make it dynamic and in tune with the times".
e) "We shall have to end a number of traditions and set in reforms which are helpful in the development of values and of national unity in our society. We shall remove those traditions which obstruct this process".
f) "We condone no discrimination based on colour, caste, creed, religion, and gender. Whoever is competent and willing to walk in tune with universal welfare (that is 'Lok-Samgraha') deserves our welcome".

Pandit Deendayal Upadhyay and Organisation of Political Democracy

Elaboration of Pandit Deendayal's views and practices pertaining to his role as an inimitable organiser will remain incomplete, if we fail to analyse his thoughts in connection with Indianisation of Democracy. This is why, I have decided to do some justice to Deendayal's thoughts on democracy in India.

It is a fact, quite inspiring for all of us that India has been marching ahead uninterruptedly on the democratic path. Pandit Deendayal has rightly stated that our culture and civilizational ethos have strengthened the roots of our democracy. He therefore, put forth valuable thoughts by referring to our past. He moreover practiced what he preached. Impressive integrity throughout his life between contemplation and action, supplemented by his transparency used to make deep impact on anybody who came in his contact. One can classify his thoughts on democracy into three types: normative, empirical and prudential. Analysis of these thoughts under the relevant three headings will enable us to delve deep into Pandit Deendayal's mind.

Normative Thoughts: It is the honest pursuit on the part of a politician of certain norms that makes his life meaningful and when such politicians lead people, democracy takes solid roots. Pandit Deendayalsponsored norms are, no doubt, quite thought provoking. One may here refer to the following four norms:

(i) Let the principled politics replace power politics. We know that power corrupts and absolute power corrupts absolutely, because when there is a competition among politicians for grabbing power by hook or by crook, people cast aspersions not only on these politicians, but also on the democratic form of government. When, however, politicians pursue principles and values and refuse to run after pelf and power, democracy obtains public acclaim. From the perspective of Pandit Deendayal principled politics also connotes 'Lok-Niti', that is, pursuit of policies conducive to nation's sentiments. Thus, in the immediate post freedom years of India, the Nehru Government initially refused but subsequently accepted the public demand of restoring Somnath Temple in Saurashtra. Lok-Niti accordingly defeated Raja-Niti!

(ii) Let representative democracy get transformed into participatory entity. People's representatives are accordingly expected to give voice to the voiceless, to articulate public grievances with a view to finding solutions. Common masses would then realise that the legislative and executive wings are doing justice to them. In democracy, it is through elections that people send their representatives to the legislative assembly. This is why, very representatives must have regular interactions with voters. They should moreover, respond to the voter's legitimate expectations.

(iii) Let socio-economic democracy underpin political entity. Democracy offers everybody a right to vote, as a result of

which, each voter is able to register his or her vote. If however, every voter remains deprived of bread, clothing and shelter, if handful 'Haves' continue to exploit innumerable 'Have-Nots', the latter, would suffer acute alienation and the dream of participatory democracy would remain unaccomplished. Dr. Ambedkar rightly underscored the urgency to supplement the right to vote by the right to food as well as the atmosphere of equality. The philosophy of Integral Humanism reminds us of the ancient Sanskrit saying which brings to our notice the basic significance of bread through the rhetorical question:
"Which sin is not committed by a starving man?" Success of democracy thus depends on the fulfilment of basic needs of masses. Hence socio economic democracy is 'a must' for the successful unfoldment of political democracy.

(iv) Let every political party be wedded to certain ideals. Pandit Deendayal was a reluctant politician. He never gave undue importance to 'Artha' and 'Kama', the material goals of a human life. As has been stated above, he had zero personal ambition in his life. That he was known for his ability to think in the light of Indian ethos and that he had the competence of forming a team of dedicated workers of a missionary zeal has also been mentioned in the lines above. Pandit Deendayal therefore, rightly concluded that the R.S.S. inspired political formation must be wedded to sublime ideals. If democracy nurtures political parties, busy in the pursuit of shameless powerism, it is sure of digging its own graveyard. Let therefore, there emerge and grow, according to Pandit Deendayal, such political parties in India which intend to pursue distinct ideologies, principles and thoughts.

Empirical Thoughts: Pandit Deendayal was a very pragmatic thinker and activist. He knew that no one can afford to ignore ground realities. Hence, his writings and speeches have drawn certain caricatures of the then existing political parties and leaders. We observe mirrors of his empirical thoughts in certain specimens given below:

(i) "Today politics has ceased to be a means. It has become an end in itself. We have today people who are engaged in power politics. There are elected representatives who squabble for power and jockey for positions and leave the purposes of the state to be fulfilled by fits and starts".

(ii) "In a system where there is no provision for recall, the party alone can regulate the behaviour of the legislature after his election. The people are helpless till the next elections".

(iii) "Most of the political parties today have no grass-roots. The Congress which one day was a mass party in real terms has now ceased to have any hold on the masses. The newer parties have yet to work hard to endear themselves to the masses".

(iv) "Election alliances develop a sense of negativism in the people. It is not proper. They invariably involve a compromise of principles and to some extent help the opportunist elements in our country".

Pandit Deendayal's writings and speeches, in short, inform us of the ugly spread of power, negativism and opportunism in the Indian polity. They also bring to our notice that there are signs of challenges through mobocracy, plutocracy and so on.

Prudential Thoughts: Pandit Deendayal was really a very unique political leader of post freedom India. Once R.S.S. leadership gave him the responsibility of organising a political party befitting Indian ethos, he pondered not only over norms and over the circumstances in which these norms were supposed to be achieved, but also over sensible ways and means to be adopted for achieving such norms.

One can begin the elucidation of Pandit Deendayal's prudential thoughts by referring to the following paragraph penned by him:

"Democracy requires a high order of non-attachment with power. Like Lord Ram, the politician in democracy should always be prepared to accept power, if called upon, and also to relinquish it without feeling in the least the great loss it might involve. Like a sportsman, he would fight for a victory but be prepared for a defeat. If he cannot take defeat with good grace and refuses to congratulate his opponent, he is not a democrat".[16]

This paragraph is autobiographical, in the sense that Pandit Deendayal was the epitome of non-attachment in every respect. He moreover demonstrated consummate or incomparable calmness of mind in the aftermath of his unfortunate defeat in the Jaunpur parliamentary by-election in 1963. This is why Pandit Deendayal's views articulated in this paragraph impress us even today! This is why, again, the view that 'politician's non-attachment with power is a cornerstone of democracy' deserves further analysis. Following subsection is towards such an analysis.

16. *Ibid.* p. 111.

(a) ***Indianisation of Democracy***: Pandit Deendayal's diagnosis of the origin and growth of democracy in Europe is quite revealing. It informs us that Europeans opted for democracy when they underwent horrible pains and strains due to autocracy in the respective nation state. They thought it indispensable in reaction to guarantee certain basic rights to each individual with a view to guarding him from the onslaught of the state. They therefore, paid extraordinary attention to forms, procedures and 'dos' as well as 'don'ts'. They thus framed certain rules and regulations pertaining to issues such as separation of powers, election proceedings, relations between rulers and opponents, etc. Pandit Deendayal points out in this connection that Europeans decided to guarantee human rights not because of their affirmative faith in human divinity and dignity but because of their fear that without these rights, an individual would prove to be helpless creature in front of a Leviathan state. He similarly points out that European's reliance on external forms and procedures is also an articulation of their disregard for the role played by human mind – behind physical activities. Deendayal's comment in this context is immensely significant. It is as follows-

> "Mere creation of a Parliament and / or the fact of its being an elected body do not mean the existence of a parliamentary democracy. **These are but the outward forms, which lose all significance if the inner attitude needed for the successful working of democracy is lacking in those who offer themselves as candidates and are chosen as their representatives".**[17]

It is essential to point out that the emphasized portion of this extract informs us of Pandit Deendayal's conviction in the supremacy of mental attitude of functionaries in democracy. One and the same conviction prompted Swami Vivekananda first and Mahatma Gandhi later to launch attack on British democracy. Both of them observed that the lack of proper inner attitude in British parliamentarians had converted British democracy into plutocracy. And very conviction goaded Pandit Deendayal to plead for Indianisation of democracy. Indians believe in human divinity and dignity. They therefore, wish to go beyond reliance on outward or external forms or procedures, beyond acceptance of majority – rule in democracy. They, in short hanker after enhancement of social capital, whereby entire society and not mere majority enjoys the fruits of genuine harmony and trust.

17. *Ibid.* p. 110.

(b) *Education of Voters*: Deendayal has expounded a very innovative concept known as 'Lokamat Parishkar' (Education of voters). He has actually prescribed through the elaboration of this concept certain ways and means for making democracy meaningful. Such a prescription is in tune with Pandit Deendayal's pleading for Indianisation of democracy as he informs us that in the ancient Indian polity, *Rishis* and *Munis* used to engage themselves in educating masses and at present genuine Karma-Yogi elites should come forward to carry the legacy of such ancient sages. That this prescription is most vital and notable contribution made by Pandit Deendayal in the deliberations over Indian polity needs to be underscored here. As stated earlier, Pandit Deendayal was quite perturbed over ground realities in our polity. His prescription that at present unattached elites are required to initiate the process of educating voters is really worth due attention. Pandit Deendayal's prescription appeals to same elites to educate rulers as well, because in a democratic set up, rulers are likely to articulate views of majority only. Pandit Deendayal, however expects such rulers to go beyond majority – minority syndrome and do justice to the public will. This is why, he underscores the necessity to educate rulers as well through the agency of unattached elites. He gives priority to the education of voters, as they are the master decision – makers in democracy. Deendayal lucidly points out that it is the strength of common voters that can bend or mend the fate of rulers in democracy. His reminders and appeals to voters are quotable in verbatim:

(i) The voter should see that he votes for a principle and not for a party, that he votes for a party and not for a personality, that he votes for a person and not for the purse.

(ii) Let him pay attention to the cause and not to the caste, go with the worthy rather than with the winner. Choose the right man and see that the man you choose wins, that will be your victory.

(iii) Vote is a matter of conscience. Do not sell it. Do not destroy it. When you vote, take a momentous decision, please do not take it just on the spur of the moment.

(iv) Vote is an individual right to be exercised socially. It symbolizes your freedom, use it freely. If you are a democrat do not be dictated by anybody but your conscience.[18]

---

18. *Ibid.* p. 123-124.

(c) Distinct Salient Features of Jana Sangh

We have discussed so far Upadhyaya sponsored two important prescriptions for making our democracy meaningful. What impresses everyone most is the fact that Pandit Deendayal built a new political party – 'Bhartiya Jana Sangh in the light of these prescriptions. He built this party literally from scratch, that too within around one and half decades. World thus noticed Pandit Deendayal's life mission aptly articulated and accomplished in the distinct salient features of Jana Sangh. It is therefore, intended to elucidate these features at the end of the present write-up. Such an elucidation is accordingly a respectful and humble homage to the life mission of Pandit Deendayal Upadhyay, a great architect of Jana Sangh, a political party that emerged for accomplishing the craving of modern India!

Jana Sangh indeed proved to be a party with a difference. It was wedded to the distinct ideology conducive to Indian ethos. Its workers were disciplined and dedicated activists. It disseminated its message throughout India through several, constructive, agitational, and organizational programmes. Subsequently, Jana Sangh acquired the new title: 'Bharatiya Janata Party'. As the B.J.P. has achieved unalloyed majority in parliamentary elections first in 2014 and later in 2019, India is lucky to have rulers whose policies and practices are presently shaping Indian polity in full consonance with Indian culture and civilization.

Respectful Pranam to Pandit Deendayal Upadhyay!

PART - I

3

Pandit Deendayal Upadhyay and Mahatma Gandhi

It was the respectful homage paid to Mahatma Gandhi and to Pandit Deendayal Upadhyay as well by Honourable Ramnathji Kovind, former President of India in the first presidential speech that triggered the thought in my mind to pen this paper. This thought got further boost when Shri Gulam Nabi Azad, a leader of the Congress Party expressed his displeasure over the respectful Presidential homage paid to two leaders in the same vein. As I went on reading speeches delivered and the essays written by Mahatmaji and Pandit Deendayalji, the commonalities noticed between the viewpoints of both of these architects of Modern India left a deep indelible impact on my mind. I also came across certain write ups wherein the respective thinkers underscored very commonalities. Recently I had an opportunity to peruse certain books and essays published during post-cold war years and it became obvious to me that all these publications have endorsed or lent their credence to appropriateness of the Indian philosophy and culture in contemporary years. The implicit as well as the explicit references made in these publications to the views of Mahatma Gandhi reminded me of the similar opinions expressed by Pandit Deendayal Upadhyay. No wonder, these very references led me to notice how the present global thinking has recognised the relevance of the views of both votaries of Indian philosophy and culture. This paper is thus a logical culmination of several events, comments and observations.

It is essential, of course, to begin the articulation of this paper first by referring to the above-mentioned Presidential Remark as well as to Gulam Nabi Azad's reaction, elicited by this remark. Later I would highlight commonalities between viewpoints on the part of Gandhiji and those of Pandit Deendayal Upadhyay. Third section will be devoted to elucidate how the Indian culture expressed through Gandhiji's and Pandit Deendayalji's viewpoints is immensely relevant at the present juncture. When the world in general and the affluent West in particular have lent imprimatur on the precepts and practices of Gandhi and Pandit Deendayal, India, the land of the origin of these two stalwarts must pay urgent attention to the issues which happened to be of deep concern to these two dignitaries. Elucidation of the very theme will mark the end of this paper.

Assessment of the Critique of the Presidential Remark

As has been mentioned above it was the Presidential Remark in grateful appreciation of Gandhiji and Pandit Deendayalji which elicited a critical reaction from Gulam Nabi Azad that triggered the genesis of this paper. One must therefore first take into account what has actually been stated by Honourable President of India before undertaking critical analysis of the reaction it elicited.

Relevant Presidential Remark can be presented here in the following paraphrase form: "All of us should come together and endeavor to make our nation strong and prosperous. We all aspire to see the blossoming of fully egalitarian order in India through the building of well-educated, morally sound, upright and homogeneous society. Both Mahatma Gandhi as well as Pandit Deendayal Upadhyay not only shared this viewpoint, but also imbibed the significance of such perspective on mass scale through interactions with several people. Ler us march ahead in the light of the guidance of these stalwarts."

What astonished me most was the critique on the part of Gulam Nabi Azad in reaction to the Presidential Remark. One can, of course give certain benefit of doubt to Mr. Azad, because no previous Indian President ever referred to Pandit Deendayal Upadhyay and that too while paying homage to Mahatma Gandhi. Mr. Azad must have felt astonished to read in Presidential speech the simultaneous mention of Pandit Deendayal and Gandhi! The fact that Pandit Deendayal was a full-time worker of R.S.S. and a founder member of Bhartiya Janta Sangh, whereas Mahatma Gandhi happens to be the father of Indian Nation cannot be ignored. That our former President still dared to place these leaders in the same bracket or category must have perhaps irritated Gulam Nabi Azad. Secondly, Pandit Deendayal Upadhyay never belonged to the so-called Gandhian school of thought. He actually followed the footsteps of Ekalavya, learnt the inimitable Adhyatmic Vidya from Gandhiji from a remote corner and succeeded in overtaking contemporary counterparts of Arjuna, affiliated to Congress. We cannot thirdly forget the time-distance between Mahatmaji and Pandit Deendayalji. It was the latter half of the decade 1930s which blessed the beginning of the public life of Deendayal in the capacity of the full-time worker of R.S.S. and incidentally, very years witnessed the last decade of the life of Gandhiji. Fourthly, the criticism levelled during these years by Deendayal against certain policies and practices of Gandhi cannot be brushed aside lightly. It is a fact that from the perspective of Deendayal, roots of Muslim separatism are deeply entrenched in the history of India, whereas Gandhiji blamed only British rule for the separatist tendencies among Muslims. Deendayal differed with Gandhi not only in terms of the diagnosis of the problem, but also in respect of remedial measures. He favoured affirmative (and not reactionary) consolidation of Hindus in India as a first step towards Hindu-Muslim unity, whereas Gandhiji relied on wooly Ram-Rahim approach as well as on involving Muslims in the political fight against British Raj. Tragically enough, Gandhiji failed in resolving Muslim problem and confronted the emergence of Pakistan at the cost of Akhand Bharat. And in the immediate post partition years, when Pakistan invaded Jammu and Kashmir state, Gandhiji had to bless the dispatch of Indian army to that state for defeating Pakistan. We, in short do accept certain differences between Deendayal and Gandhi. What is essential is to point out however, that there are striking commonalities which overcome contrasts between these two leaders. The so-called contrasts or differences were also those of degree and not of kind. Deendayal was thus in favour of Hindu-Muslim unity, though he considered it indispensable to consolidate Hindus as a condition precedent to march toward genuine unity between Hindus and Muslims. Deendayal as well as Gandhi believed in the geo-cultural nationalism of India; they also shared the viewpoint that Hinduism is the core of Indian nationalism. The Hinduism that was pursued and liked by Deendayal was however as militant as tolerant, as assertive as large hearted and as selective as all accommodative! Deendayal has, of course, pointed out in this connection that Hinduism is basically tolerant, large hearted and accommodative, though on occasions it does exhibit militancy and assertiveness. He shares with Gandhi strong reservations about the institution of the state, as according to him, coercion or compulsion is not liked by Hinduism. He, again like Gandhi considers state as one of the social institutes. He refuses to offer supremacy to state over society; although he underscores the primacy of the state. Least wonder, he honours Shivaji Maharaj as one of the great inheritors of Prabhu Ramchandra, whereas Gandhiji declared Raja Shivaji as a misguided patriot.

I have elaborated so far how apparently, Deendayal does appear to be different from Gandhi, how one may observe a seeming gap or a distance between Deendayal and Gandhi. I have thus justified how Gulam Nabi Azad does deserve to be given a benefit of doubt. I have, however pointed out in the similar vein that the differences between the viewpoints of the two stalwarts are actually those of degree only. Bhagavad Gita is thus a common fountainhead for both. But Deendayal asks us to keep in mind the militancy-oriented import of Gita, because like Vivekananda and Tilak he takes into account that householders who predominate the world can't afford to ignore pragmatic, worldly affairs. Gandhi, however is insistent on proffering such content of Gita which glorifies spiritually brave and courageous dignitaries. He states in other words that the esoteric import of Gita lies in the message of equanimity. Gandhiji unfortunately ignored that unlike Hindus who have undergone renaissance particularly since 19th century, Muslims have remained bereft of the fruits of similar transformation. Least wonder, he failed in eliciting favourable response from Muslims. Leaders of post independent India refused to draw due lessons from history. They opted not only for dogmatic projection of Gandhi-sponsored one-sided profile of Hinduism, but also for enthusiastic indulgence in launching anti-Hindutva tirade. Pandit Deendayal Upadhyay was therefore constrained to criticise the 'so-called' Gandhi-Bhaktas. He, however did take into account eternally valuable dimensions of Gandhian thought. He noted that Gandhiji was interested in converting India's freedom into independence, in the sense that the latter desired to facilitate the articulation of Indian ethos, of course with due adaptations to modern conditions. Pandit Deendayal Upadhyay rightly averred that all such dimensions of the Gandhian thought were worth sincere pursuit. His speeches and writings spontaneously mirrored very dimensions. It is essential to pay due attention to this sort of the USP of Deendayalji's world of thought. Gulam Nabi Azad seems to have forgotten the very U.S.P. of Deendayal. He is of course not alone. Some other leaders and intellectuals who do not share the positions, policies and practices of Sangh-Pariwar have also resented Presidential clubbing of Deendayal and Gandhi. All of them need to be reminded that truth cannot be monopolised by a party or an organization and that untouchability whether in social or in political transactions is the most condemnable phenomenon.

One more factor that can also be held responsible for the bitter reaction over Presidential Remark is the hatred entrenched strongly among pseudo-secularists against protagonists of Hindutva-ideology. It is essential to bring to the notice of present pseudo-secularists that leaders of non-RSS formations particularly during the first three post freedom decades were immensely sensible and mature, that they were too prone to transcend party affiliations to honour persons devoted to the highest good of Bharat Mata. Dr. Sampurnananda, former Chief Minister of U.P. and a former Chancellor of Kashi Vidyapeeth was one of the stalwarts of that era, whose foreword to the 'Political Diary' of Pandit Deendayal Upadhyay contained due appreciation of Panditji. The most relevant extract of the foreword runs as follows:

> "This Diary informs readers of the ideas of one of the most notable political leaders of our time, a man devoted to the highest good of his country, of a person of unimpeachable character, a leader whose weighty words swayed thousands of educated men".

Dr, Sampurnanand found it essential to mention at the outset of his foreword that as he belonged to Congress Party, whereas Deendayal happened to be a leader of Bhartiya Janta Sangh, it was inappropriate on his part, from the perspective of some people to draft a foreword to Deendayal's compilation of essays. His comment, in this connection is worth quotation here:

> "As a matter of fact this foreword is only a simple expression of that great virtue of tolerance which we all must learn to practice if democracy is to take roots in our country".

Dr. Sampurnanand, actually transcended tolerance and extended a hearty welcome to Deendayalji's views, which according to him were found akin to those of Mahatma Gandhi and Dr. Bhagwan Das. Our former President has, indeed enriched the legacy of Dr. Sampurnanand. I am tempted to refer in this context to the heartfelt homage paid by Barrister Nath Pai, the then President of the Praja Socialist Party to the life and mission of Pandit Deendayal Upadhyay. Mr. Nath Pai stated that Deendayalji had concretised the 15th stanza of the 12th Chapter of Bhagavad Gita. How apt was the homage as this stanza informs us of the following content:

> "One who is not disgusted by anybody and who personally disgusts nobody, who is equipoised in happiness and distress, fear and anxiety is very dear to me".

Deendayal's wisdom and several saintly qualities prompted Shri Charan Singh, a Janata Party leader to walk hand in hand with Upadhyay when the latter launched a successful campaign against Nehru-sponsored Cooperative Farming in India. These very qualities cemented a bond of friendship between Deendayal and Dr. Rammanohar Lohia who jointly co-authored a statement in favour of creating a confederation of India and Pakistan. Bitter reaction over Presidential grateful remembrance of Deendayal and Gandhi in the same vein is indeed most unjustifiable and in fact condemnable!

Striking Similarities and Commonalities

Let us now pay attention to similarities between the two leaders. While elaborating similarities and commonalities between Deendayal and Gandhi, one must first note that Pandit Deendayal Upadhyay begins his lecture series on Integral Humanism by referring to the affirmative stance of 'Hind Swaraj', the magnum opus of Mahatma Gandhi. It seems that in pre-independence years, when most of Indian leaders were busy in driving Britishers out, and as a result when the general thrust or stance was negative, great stalwarts like Tilak and Gandhi gave priority to think about post-independent India's march in the light of its culture and civilization. Deendayalji has thus appreciated Gandhiji's affirmative vision based on Indian ethos.

During the course of lecture series, Deendayal informs us that in India, "we have placed before ourselves the ideal of the fourfold responsibilities of catering to the needs of body, mind, intellect and soul, with a view to achieving the integrated progress of man".[1] The elaboration of this topic made by Deendayal in this connection reminds us of the elucidation of civilization attempted by Gandhi in "Hind-Swaraj". Integral Humanism invites our attention to the fact that body is treated in Indian civilization as an instrument of Dharma, whereas Westerners regard human body and the satisfaction of its desires as the aim of life. Gandhiji's 'Hind Swaraj' attacks Western or modern civilization on the same ground. It points out that in the modern civilization, rooted in the West, one observes a shift in the balance between the four aims of life favourable to Artha and Kama, discrediting Dharma and Moksha. Gandhiji thus informs us that Western civilization is engrossed fully in pampering human body. He in fact challenges Westerners:

> "When you concentrate your full attention on obtaining material prosperity (Artha) and on satisfying sensual urges (Kama) and

1. *See Ekatma-Manav Darshan* (Hindi-version), New Delhi 2012, p. 26.

throw into oblivion two lofty aims such as Dharma (sustaining society) and Moksha (liberating oneself from all bonds) how can you call your life as civilized and cultured?

Tamer Soyler of Humboldt University rightly comments:

> "from Gandhi's perspective, modern civilization has caused a distortion in people's perception of life and time has come for all to get rid of this perversion to have a more human life".[2]

The attack launched in Integral Humanism on six lower human tendencies is also in full consonance with similar criticism levelled in Hind-Swaraj against Darwinian principle: 'Survival of the fittest'. Deendayal reminds us that our culture has called such tendencies: desire, anger, greed, temptation, insolence and jealousy as six enemies (Shadripus) in human life and this is why everyone of us is expected to defeat these enemies with a view to obtaining real victory in the moral warfare. It is revealing to juxtapose this sort of Deendayal's viewpoint with the following commentary on Gandhism – "According to Gandhi, the Gita enjoins the duty of a moral warfare against wickedness".[3] In the above-mentioned list of six enemies, desire or 'Kama' stands first. Befitting English word for 'Kama' happens to be 'lust' and therefore Swami Vivekananda gave utmost importance to the abstinence or forbearance from lust and gold. (Kamini-Kanchan-Viraha) Dr. Ramnath, a Mauritian Gandhi-Scholar has made a very notable remark in this connection:

> "Suppose in the place of God, we put Gold as the goal we would then develop a certain competition by having recourse to hate and violence to grasp that Gold. Gandhi advised us to remove lust from our life – the 'L' which, I think could be deleted from the Gold to make it become God, through certain spiritual disciplines".[4]

Both Deendayal as well as Gandhi opposed the operation of the Darwinian principle: 'Survival of the fittest', because this principle sanctions the victory of a strong being over the weak counterpart. Neither Integral Humanism, nor Hind-Swaraj justifies this principle as it honours the law of the jungle. 'Hind-Swaraj' refuses to call Euro-Americans as civilized, as they salute this law of the jungle.

Deendayal and Gandhi advise us, of course, in the light of the prescription of Indian philosophy to worship higher or divine human

---

2. Tamer Soyler, "Gandhi, Civilization, Non-Violence and Obama", in *Journal of Alternative Perspectives in Social Science*, v.2, no.1, 2010, p. 437.
3. M. Yamunacharya, "Gandhi and the Gita" in M. K. Grover (ed.) *Political Thinkers of Modern India: v.7*: Mahatma Gandhi (Delhi, 1994), p. 140.
4. D. B. Ramnauth, *Mahatma Gandhi: Insight and Impact* (Mauritius, 1989), p. 16.

tendencies like love, sacrifice, renunciation, compassion, empathy etc. as it is their conviction that only through the genuine worship of these divine tendencies that civilization and culture will unfold themselves.

If the worship of just mentioned divine tendencies will facilitate the unfoldment of civilization, a surrender to satanic instincts like desire, greed, temptation, etc will expedite the perversion in human society. Deendayal like Gandhi considered Isha-Upanishad as the perennial source giving guidance to all of us in our march towards the goal of civilization. Gandhiji was more explicit; as according to him, the secret of his life could be put in three words: "Ten tyakten bhunji thah"; the words of Isha Upanishad. Gandhi himself translated this Mantra as: "Renounce and enjoy". The literal translation of this Mantra however runs as follows:

> "Protect or support yourself (bhunji thah) through renunciation or detachment" – (Ten tyakten). According to the remark made by Madan Mohan Mathur over this topic, Gandhiji used the verb 'enjoy' in the place of 'protect', because after renouncing unreal or surplus whatever remains at one's disposal is real and that is enjoyable.

Next comment given below underscores the significance of renunciation, one of the divine tendencues:

> "Renunciation is an eternal maxim in ethics as well as in spirituality. There is no true enjoyment except what is purified by renunciation".[5]

Deendayal as well as Gandhi have insisted on a war against lower human instincts, whereas Marx underscored the importance of a class-war. They have argued that the instincts such as desire, greed, temptation goad and guide capitalists to amass wealth at the cost of labour, whereas according to Marx, it is dialectical materialism which compels capitalists to be exploitative grabbers of wealth. Same analysis leads Marx to plead that the very dialectical materialism will trigger a class-war for replacing capitalism by socialism. Deendayal and Gandhi do not deny the role of industrial revolution as well as that of technological and scientific advancement – in the widening of the rift between the 'Haves' and the 'Have nots'. They however consider instincts such as lust and avarice on the part of the capitalists as crucially and basically important factors for the 'Great Divide'. Prof Vishwanath Prasad Verma has rightly pointed out that "the

5. Madan Mohan Mathur, "Gandhiji's Secret Mantra. Renounce and Enjoy", in *Times of India* (Mumbai) 29 November, 2017, p. 18.

sophisticated technological, secularistic, aggressive and lustful aspects of modern western civilization repelled Gandhiji".[6] If the Gandhian diagnosis of the 'Great Divide' in capitalism differs from the Marxian analysis of the same scenario, the remedial measures suggested by Gandhi are also at variance with those prescribed by Karl Marx. As Deendayal and Gandhi share the same viewpoint, the commentary of Prof. V. P. Verma given below is appropriate for comprehending Deendayal's analysis as well in this regard.

> "Gandhi is a moral and spiritual individualist. The individual seeking to better his character by moral technics is the starting point of Gandhian ethics. Marx however avers that not an appeal to the sentiment of justice by individual self-sacrifice but organized expropriation by the armed proletariat of the expropriators would destroy the evils of society. Gandhi thinks that the root of the malady is deeper. Not individual wealth but the individualistic propensity towards the acquisition of wealth is the central devil. Not the elimination of the actual amount of the quantities of commodities but the suppression of the drive towards the avaricious accumulation and monopolistic possession of things that may be and are needed by others, would bring the millennium. He did not oppose structural changes, but he felt that such changes are never sufficient. Gandhiji, in short felt that along with structural changes, man's moral faculties must be ennobled".[7]

Deendayal and Gandhi have in other words expressed very strong reservations about Marxian strategy of the exclusive reliance on structural changes through labour led statist grabbing of production-forces! Both of them thus emphasise how the war against satanic instincts is crucial, if compared to the class-war.

Holistic Indian Culture

Neither Deendayal nor Gandhi entertains the concept of class-war in society because Indian culture, the basic fountainhead for both of them is holistic, it believes in the fact that divinity is immanent as well as transcendent. As it is immanent, everyone is steeped in sanctity. Each one should however remember that he or she must rise over and above one's being in order to feel divinity as it is transcendent. The society should therefore honour each one and the latter must also worship society. Human beings should nurture close relations with society.

---

6. Prof. V. P. Verma, "Gandhi and Marx', in M. K. Grover (ed.) *See* the Note no. 3, p. 93.
7. *Ibid.* pp. 95-96.

Pandit Deendayal Upadhyay has reminded us that whereas human beings do remember family relations, animals forget very contacts. He has commented further that human beings use family relations for constructing a more harmonious order in life, to establish other relationships flowing from these basic relationships, so as to knit the whole society, as a single unit of cooperation. Thus, various values and traditions are built. Standards of good and bad are determined accordingly. Affectionate brotherly relations are thus considered as good and worthy, enmity is however disapproved.[8]

That Deendayal shares this outlook with Gandhi can be substantiated through the following comment: "Gandhi believed in the doctrine of man's oneness with God and humanity. The moment a man awakens to the spirit within, he cannot remain violent; the passions, selfishness and violence do not belong to the immortal spirit of man. 'Since all men', argued Gandhi 'partake in divine essence, they are ultimately one'.[9]

Deendayal's Integral Humanism, as well as Gandhiji's Hind-Swaraj logically underscore that it is cooperation and not conflict which is the basis of human relationships and it is the spirit of cooperation only which will enable us to march towards world peace.

Jay Prakash Narayan has lucidly explained how the moral solvent sponsored by Gandhi can resolve the problem pertaining to inter relationship between individual and society. He thus points out that just mentioned moral solvent has been prepared by Gandhi through assigning mutual moral responsibilities to individual as well as society. Gandhiji has thus asked individuals to be altruists, to serve society in the spirit of Karma-Yoga, he has similarly expected society to bother for the interests of individuals. Individuals should remember, in other words that they can perceive transcendent divinity only through unselfish transactions and society must also note that immanent divinity can be perceived only through the genuine concern for everybody's wellbeing. J. P. Narayan offers here the famous quotation of Mahatma Gandhi: "The future world society of men will be an oceanic circle whose center will be the individual, always ready to perish for the villages, till at last the whole becomes one life composed of individuals never aggressive in their arrogance, but ever humble, sharing the

---

8. *See* the Note no. 1, p. 20
9. Quoted in M. P. Dube (ed.) *Social Justice: Distributive Principles and Beyond* (Jaipur, 2017), pp. 70-71.

majesty of the oceanic circle of which they are integral units."[10] This quotation is a clear endorsement of the Indian faith in spiral circles mirroring symbiotic links between individual and society at large.

Gandhiji, relying on symbiotic relations between and among various castes in Hindu society opted for social remorse for the sin of the development of untouchability in history and prescribed social service towards the larger community as repentance for this sin.[11] He moreover appealed to upper caste Hindus to demonstrate empathy through accommodating the demands of the poor, underprivileged members. He similarly called the latter to treat 'savarna Hindus' with brotherly trust.[12]

Deendayal, like Gandhi relied on Dharma, as according to both of them, it strengthens the silken bonds in society. Prof Vamsee Juluri informs us that if Deendayal calls Dharma as a universal ethical ideal, Gandhi considers Dharma as that religion that underlies all religions. "Barring such nuances, their views on religions universalism are incredibly similar".[13] They thus share the view that 'Dharma' is wider, broader and deeper than religion which is akin to a sect; a creed. Both of them aver that 'Dharma' sustains universe through proffering basic eternal values. When Deendayal points out that whereas Indian civilization worships Dharma for its intrinsic importance, Westerners honour it for its instrumental significance, he merely echoes Gandhian thought.[13A] Both of them accordingly refer to the English saying: 'Honesty is the best policy' and juxtapose Indian view that 'Honesty is a principle'. They point out in this connection that it is 'Dharma' which provides standard for deciding the propriety of behavior in different situations. Logically they insist on values. Gandhiji's insistence on

---

10. *See* J. P. Narayan, "Gandhi and the Politics of Decentralisation" in *See* note no. 3, p. 674. J. P. Narayan has relied on Gandhiji's letter from Panchgani dated 21 July 1946. The letter titled "Swaraj-Freedom and Self-Rule" contains Gandhiji's idea of an oceanic circle. Immediately after the paragraph quoted in note no. 10, one comes across the following extract which is equally valuable: "The outermost circumference will not wield power to crush the inner circle but will give strength to all within and derive its own strength from it".
"If Euclid's point, though incapable of being drawn by human agency, has an imperishable value, my picture has its own for mankind to live. Let India live for this picture."
11. R. Srivatsan, "Impasses around contemporary Hinduism" in *Economic and Political Weekly* (Mumbai), 23 March 2019, p. 27.
12. S. V. Pande and Archana Srivastava "Social Development through Social Justice" in M. P. Dube (ed), *See* the Note no. 9, p. 128.
13. Vamsee Juluri (a professor at the university of San Fransisco) "ahimsa has no political hue", in *The Hindu* (Chennai), 2 October 2015, p. 15.
13A. *See* the Note no. 1, p.27 Also see Gandhi's speech on Ashram Vows at the YMCA Madras on 16 February 1916: Raghavan Iyer (ed) *The Essential Writings of Mahatma Gandhi* (New Delhi, 2005), p. 283.

avoiding following seven sins is naturally shared by Deendayalji: 1) politics without principles, 2) wealth without work, 3) commerce without morality, 4) knowledge without character, 5) pleasure without conscience, 6) science without morality and 7) worship without sacrifice.

As Deendayal is convinced that Dharma is mirrored in the pursuit of principles and values, he rightly appreciates such non-Hindus as well who are keen on the honest implementation of principles. The following extract from Deendayal's lecture-series on Integral Humanism evidences Deendayslji's firm conviction in Dharma:

> "In 1939, Shri Hafij Mohammed Ibrahim was elected on the Muslim League ticket. Later on, when he joined the Congress, he gave up his post in the U.P. Assembly, in pursuance of the healthy principles of public conduct, sought re-election on the Congress ticket and was again elected".[14]

Deendayal, in short, refused to discriminate against non-Hindus. He actually respected value-worshipping non-Hindus; his genuine pursuit of Dharma was in full consonance with Indian civilization.

It is well known that Gandhiji amended famous Ram Dhun by inserting the line "Allah-Ishwar Tero Nam" immediately after reciting "Raghupati Raghav Raja Ram" This type of Gandhi-sponsored amendment in Ram Dhun is generally mentioned as a specimen of Gandhiji's faith in genuine secularism; a faith in Sarva Dharma Samabhav! What is relatively unknown is the fact that Deendayalji also held the same view. Deendayalji thus stated on one occasion that we pay our obeisance to Lord Vishnu through reciting one thousand names of the Lord.

> "We shall be too glad if we add Allah's name as well in the list of one thousand names". He respected each and every Indian irrespective of caste, colour creed and religion!

As Deendayal as well as Gandhi believed in holistic society shaped by symbiotic, spiral relationship, and as from their perspective, 'Dharma' is the fountainhead for such relationship, they remarked that if people pursue Dharma in public as well as private transactions no external agency in the form of state or government is required to keep law and order in society. Such a line of thinking is quite different from that rooted in the West. One may here refer to the Human Development Report 2016 published by the United Nations Development Programme, wherein, government is expected not only to keep law and

14. *See* the note no. 1, p. 6.

order in society, but also to strengthen bonds of relations between individual and society.

Some elucidation regarding the genesis and growth of state is thus called for in this context. As per Indian philosophy, there had prevailed in the hoary, ancient era in India a stateless society. Again, as per the same philosophy, once people deviated from the path of Dharma, once interruption and disorganization took roots in our land, there had emerged the institution of state for establishing law and order. Deendayal following Gandhi informs us that it was the contract signed between the King and the masses which shaped the emergence of the state.[15] Joan Bondurant informs us that Gandhiji not only endorsed ancient Indian view pertaining to the contract between the King and the people but also made his own contribution to this view. As per this contribution if the King assured people that he would take care of their well-being, the people also assured the former in return that they would never fail in rendering mutual help to each other whereby there would emerge ideal society.[16]

A study of the political views expounded by Deendayal and Gandhi enables one to claim that the roots of the successful implementation of democratic norms in post independent India are traceable in the ancient Indian polity. Both of these stalwarts are worried over the morphing of democracy into plutocracy and mobocracy. Both of them therefore prescribe that conscious and constant efforts must be put in for nurturing genuine democratic values in society.

What is most astonishing and pleasing is the fact that Deendayal as well as Gandhi found the book titled 'Daishik Shastra' penned by Badrishah Tooldharia as immensely inspiring, as a treasury of perennially guiding principles for shaping Indian polity. We can't afford to ignore this commonality between these two leaders. Pandit Deendayal Upadhyay expressed his affection for Daishik Shastra in the write up in one of the issues of 'Panchajanya' in the year 1959. The most relevant extract from his write up runs as follows:

> "It is in the book titled Daishik Shastra that one comes across analysis of the basic theories pertaining to the code of conduct of Indian nation. That Lokamanya Tilak appreciated this book is notable. One can comment that 'Karma-Yoga Shastra' and 'Daishik Shastra' are the books most complementary to each other. Each one

15. *Ibid.* p. 40.
16. Bondurant, Joan V., Conquest of Violence: The Gandhian Philosophy of Conflict (Mumbai, 1959), pp. 167-168.

> busy in the task of national reconstruction must find time to study these books".[17]

We all know that 'Daishik Shastra' played a crucial role in shaping Deendayalji's Integral Humanism. As for Gandhiji's appreciation in favour of 'Daishik Shastra' one can refer to the preface penned by Shri Giriraj Shah (the grandson of Badrishah Tooldharia) to the English version of 'Daishik Shastra'. Gandhiji's appreciation referred to by Giriraj Shah is worth quotation here:

> "Shri Badrishah Tooldharia of Almora deserves congratulations of all the patriots and Hindi lovers for beautifully explaining the tenets of Dharma (that which sustains) and spiritualism in terms of politics".

Present relevance of Deendayal and Gandhi

I have stated in the first paragraph of the present paper that quite a few publications of the post-cold war years have acknowledged the debt owed by the present era to the Indian culture. One must take a note of certain extracts from these publications, because they inform us of the relevant 'do's and dont's' prescribed by Indian culture and substantiate them through the pertinent quotations from Gandhian literature. Resembling extracts from Deendayal's writings and speeches buttress the similarities and commonalities between Deendayal and Gandhi.

Role of Culture in the Development Process

The book titled 'The world is Flat' written by Thomas Friedman reviews the trajectories of development pursued by various nations in the post-cold war years. It is full of appreciation for India, and makes laudatory remarks while writing about Indian culture, because according to Friedman, (the author of this book) the adaptability as well as adoptability of Indian culture have enabled India to come out with flying colours during globalization-years. The notable remark is quotable here:

> "Indian culture has made it possible for India to absorb best global ideas and practices and also to weld them with its traditions. No wonder, full advantages of globalization have been reaped by India".[18]

Such a remark reminds us quite automatically what has been stated by Pandit Deendayal Upadhyay regarding our culture:

---

17. Quoted in Mahesh Chandra Sharma, *Deendayal Upadhyay: Kartritva evam Vichar* (New Delhi, 1994), p. 344.
18. Thomas Friedman, *The world is flat* (London, 2006), p. 422.

"It adapts old, eternal values to present circumstances and adjusts modern values to the indigenous conditions.[19]

Thomas Friedman also refers to certain Indians' virtues like tolerance which have propelled them to reach impressive heights in economic activities. He substantiates his point by inviting our attention to the content of the June 21, 2004- essay written by Paul Johnson, a British historian for Forbes:

"Hindu religion is tolerant and permissive. When left to themselves, Indians always prosper as a community. Take the case of Uganda's Indian population, which was expelled by Idi Amin and received into the tolerant society of Britain. There are now more millioners in this group than in any other recent immigrant community in Britain. They are a striking example of how far hard work, strong family bonds and devotion to education can carry a people who have been stripped of all their worldly assets".[20]

I have stated above that according to Deendayal as well as to Gandhi, our Indian culture teaches us to absorb divine tendencies and to efface satanic instincts. And the fact that present global thinkers trace the origin of contemporary Indians' economic achievements in the tenets of Indian culture must be quite endearing and pleasing to these two stalwarts.

Global Endorsement of Symbiotic Relationship

While writing in the lines above, about holistic thinking in the Indian culture, I have mentioned that Westerners continue to believe in compartmentalist approach. This is why when we Indians believe that an individual can broaden and widen his or her vision with a view to getting merged in the cosmos, westerners expect an external agency like government to strengthen the bonds between individual and society. If we believe in spiral circles linked to each other between an individual and society; Westerners draw concentric circles totally separate from each other between in individual and society. I have also stated in the same context that the Human Development Report 2016 does expect government to facilitate the linking between individual and society. One should not, however forget that the same HDR 2016 gives us hints that Westerners presently happen to be in a mood to accept the existence of spiral circles between an individual and society.

19. *See* the Note no. 1, p. 16.
20. *See* the Note no. 18, p. 425.

The following extract (relevant in this connection) of the HDR 2016 needs to be interpreted properly:

> "The government's role is to ensure a balance between the protection and the empowerment of the individual and the concentric circles of security providers which are either extensions of the individual or, if they are malfunctioning, the threat to the individual".[21]

This extract points out to us that the individual is separate from constituents such as family, society, nation, etc. It also informs us that clashes are likely to arise between the individual on the one hand and encircling constituents on the other-and that the government is expected to ensure a balance on such occasions. The HDR 2016 thus mirrors fragmentary or compartmentalist approach. When, however, one and the same extract calls constituents like family, village, society, etc. as extensions of the individual, one comes across a hint of the change in the typical Western approach. The word 'extension' gives us to understand that each individual is linked with family, village, society, and so on. The same extract, of course, does inform us that in case, the individual is threatened by family, village, etc, it is the responsibility of the government to ensure smooth relations between individual at the centre and encircling constituents on the other. This type of a mention, no doubt, reminds us that the Euro American line of thinking continues to believe in fragmentary approach relying on the assistance from external agency of the government. Astonishingly enough, however, the same HDR 2016 conveys to us on another page that if the goal of universal human development faces barriers through deprivations among groups like women, ethnic minorities, indigenous people, persons with disabilities, etc, reliance on divine tendencies and not on external agencies is the best possible antidote. The extract given below is quite suggestive in this regard:

> "Overcoming of such barriers will require putting empathy, tolerance and moral commitments to global justice and sustainability at the centre of individual and collective choices. People should consider themselves part of a cohesive global whole rather than a fragmented terrain of rival groups and interests".[22] (emphasis is added)

That this extract is reflective of Western endorsement of the views on the part of Deendayal and Gandhi is crystal clear. The emphasized

21. *Human Development Report 2016* (New York, 2016) p. 128.
22. *Ibid.* p.6.

portion of this extract is extremely important as it mirrors global rejection of fragmentary approach. The HDR 2016 moreover denotes that contemporary thinking puts its foot down in opposing the operation of the Darwinian principle of survival of the fittest, that it advocates how we must take care of downtrodden and destitute masses.

Eco-Destructive Consumerism

Integral Humanism, like Hind Swaraj resented Euro American culture as it encourages perverted industrialism which causes environmental degradation through extravagant, wasteful use of resources. Pandit Deendayal Upadhyay, for example condemns consumption oriented, eco-destructive industrialism. He argues that the Mantra "to throw away the old one and to buy a new one goads industrialists to create fresh demands for his products". Manufacturers accordingly opt for producing such products which are least durable. They thus show interest in prompting people to go on accomplishing varieties of wants one after another. Resultant extravagant use of resources causes massive degradation of environment. Mahatma Gandhi had expressed similar views through Hind-Swaraj. The solution suggested by Deendayal through the following paragraph also echoed Gandhian thought only:

> "Keeping in view the aim of human life, we must endeavor to see how, with the minimum of fuel, man proceeds to his goal with the maximum speed. Such a system alone can be called civilization. This system will not think of merely a single aspect of human life, but of all its aspects, including the ultimate aim. This system will be constructive rather than destructive."[23]

This system sponsored by Gandhi and Deendayal thus advocates a well-regulated use of resources with a view to causing least harm to ecology; it pleads for initiative on the part of business corporations to extend help to community at large, it appeals to all to opt for austerity.

Quite a few write ups, books, etc published during post cold war years have picked up or endorsed the views mentioned above. One may thus allude to the interview granted by Jill Stein, Green Party candidate for the U.S. Presidency in 2016, wherein one comes across a very appreciable commitment to expedite world march toward just and sustainable development process. The extract given below from this interview is more than suggestive:

---

23. *See* the Note no. 1, p. 64.

> "We need to put people, planet and peace over profit for facilitating transformational change, so that we can survive into the next century".[24]

Jill Stein has underscored here that an industrialist or a businessman should bother more for the interests of entities like people, planet and peace than for considerations of personal profit. She has, in other words articulated the necessity of holistic thinking. One can interpret her thinking as pondering over Vyashti (profit), Samashti (people), Srishti (planet) and Parameshti (peace), where considerations about Vyashti are to be kept aside in the interests of broader entities.

One may also refer to the views of Vikram Mehta, Chairman of Brookings India, who has offered a very laudable, comprehensive interpretation of the implementation of the Corporate Social Responsibility Act 2013. He thus points out that Indian companies and corporations are at present under obligation due to the CSR Act to spend at least two percent portion of their profit for complying with social responsibility. Corporations are thus expected to discard Milton Friedman's dictum: "the business of business is business" from their public vocabulary. Mr. Mehta welcomes this trend. He however appeals to corporations to start spending portions from their profits not because of compulsion, but out of conviction; not because such expenditure is mandatory, but because of their commitment to the society at large. He also requests these corporations to adopt intra-corporate partnership approach whereby corporations such as Wipro, L&T, Unilever, etc. would help each other with a view to putting in joint efforts for uplifting society to higher levels.[25] The following paragraph quoted by Vikram Mehta from Jeremy Rifkin's book: 'The Zero Marginal Cost Society' is quite thought provoking:

> "Social entrepreneurs look for returns not through the 'invisible hand' of the market but through the helping hand of collaborative partnerships between their social enterprise and the community. While they accept the importance of people, planet and profits, they would rank people, and the planet ahead of profits if push came to shove".

Another paragraph from Vikram Mehta's write up is equally quotable here:

> "The corporations should develop intra-corporate partnerships in the sense that if one company gives assistance for constructing a

24. *See* Vijay Prashad, "The power to create a new world is ... in our hands", in *Frontline* (Chennai), 15 April, 2016, p. 64.
25. Vikram S Mehta, "CSR: Corporates should reach out", in *The Indian Express* (Mumbai), 4 August, 2015, p. 13.

school-building, another corporation should help the same school for improving the quality of education imparted there. What the corporations should do is to take a holistic approach".

One of the quotations mentioned above informs us that at present companies and corporations rely on helping hand of corporate partnerships and not on the 'invisible hand of the market'. We are thus given to understand that the concept of invisible hand of the market sponsored by classical economists like Smith and Ricardo is no longer acceptable among entrepreneurs. David Hawkins states that another concept: 'self-interest' sponsored by these economists with equal enthusiasm is also no longer appreciated, as the power of 'self-sacrifice' demonstrated by Mahatma Gandhi seems to have taken roots in the world".[26]

Prof Vamsee Juluri, whose write-up has already been referred to in the lines above informs us that Deendayalji succeeded in presenting a manifesto for decolonialization on the lines of Hind-Swaraj, because he like Gandhiji happened to be the genuine epitome of high thinking and simple living.[27] Rajiv Malhotra's appreciative remarks in favour of Mahatma Gandhi can therefore be reproduced here for highlighting Deendayalji's life and mission as well. "Gandhi noticed that the ever-increasing consumption in an industrial economy depletes the natural resources and destroys the self-sustaining villages which comprise the social fabric of India. In response to this problem he advocated and embodied a simple lifestyle".[28]

It was during 1950s and early 1960s that Pandit Deendayal Upadhyay presented his views on economy, polity and society. His views were quite resembling with propositions of Gandhi. He thus pleaded for family farming in the place of cooperative farming, he advocated the necessity to provide gainful employment to each individual, he insisted on the economics of austerity, he always favoured affirmative and constructive politics. During those years, however, when even the Gandhian ideas were sidetracked by the Indian leadership, Deendayal's views were bound to be neglected. Last three decades however seem to have acknowledged the relevance of very views. The recent welcome extended by the West in particular to Gandhian ideas is simply notable. Here we remember the prediction made in 1969 by Prof. A. K. Dasgupta. The extract of this prediction is as follows:

26. David Hawkins, Power vs Force (London, 2012), p. 156.
27. *See* the Note no. 13.
28. Rajiv Malhotra, *Being Different* (Noida, U.P, 2013), p. 348.

> "Marxian revolution, let us recall, was originally meant for the industrialised West, but was actually adopted, against Marx's own prediction, by the underdeveloped East. Can it not be that this reversal of venue will be repeated in the case of Gandhian revolution too? It may well happen that it will catch the affluent West sooner than one would imagine. May be that the suitable soil for a peaceful revolution such as Gandhi envisaged is an affluent society and not an immature one".[29]

The Debt we owe to Deendayal and Gandhi

Just concluded section of this paper has informed us that according to Prof Dasgupta it would be the West and not India which would revive the legacy of Gandhi. I have also mentioned in the same section that the HDR has sanctioned, of course, to some extent the Gandhian thought of the symbiotic relationship between the individual and the society. One may add one more evidence in the lines below for substantiating the point that the Westerners have come close to accept India-sponsored holistic paradigm of development. Joseph Stiglitz, a recipient of the Nobel Prize in Economics and one-time chairman of Bill Clinton's Economic Advisory Council has thus approved the quite comprehensive definition of development in the following paragraph: "It is an enhancement of the totality of a nation's four fold capital stocks: the capital of material goods, natural capital such as soil, water, forest, fish, human capital including health, education, employment, and social capital comprising mutual trust and social harmony".[30]

If the West has given us signs of its approval of the line of thinking originated in India and articulated by Gandhi and Deendayal, we Indian must also pay back the debt we owe to these architects of modern India.

We must accordingly implement appropriate interpretations of spiritualism. First, we must treat every being as an embodiment of a spark of divinity. It is obvious that there should not be any discrimination against anybody on the basis of colour, caste, creed and religion. We must secondly worship justice and equality not because of compulsion but out of conviction. We must thirdly remember that individual salvation depends on collective emancipation. Unattached service of downtrodden sections is therefore a must!

---

29. *See* Pulin B. Nayak, "A.K. Dasgupta on Gandhi and the Economics of Austerity", in *Economic and Political Weekly* (Mumbai), 16 December 2017, p.45.
30. Quoted in Madhav Gadgil, "Development as a people's movement", in *The Hindu* (Chennai), 01 December, 2014.

Pandit Deendayal Upadhyay, following the footsteps of Mahatma Gandhi always fought for serving the interests of landless farmers, jobless workers, shopless hawkers and homeless residents. It is therefore 'a must' for us to put an end to every sort of alienation.

Gandhiji as well as Deendayalji were men of action. They thus translated their ideas in practice. They never gave precedence to office over ideas. Neither they opted for knowledge without character, nor did they pursue politics without principles. Seven social sins mentioned during the course of argumentation in the lines above deserve to be avoided very scrupulously.

Survival of democracy during post freedom years of India is a matter of pride for all of us. Last seven decades have witnessed regular elections at national, provincial and local levels. During these years we have preserved the sanctity of institutions like free press, independent judiciary, election commission, etc. That people at large observe basic norms as well as dos and don'ts is also quite appreciable. But still our democracy suffers from certain inadequacies and problems. Money-power and caste power thus continue to dominate our polity and society. People's representatives bother more for power than for peoples' interests. Writings and speeches of Pandit Deendayal Upadhyay provide us due guidance to keep us on the right track. One can refer to quite a few recommendations made by Deendayalji for transforming representative democracy into the participative entity. i) Defections from a party on ideological grounds can be justified. But the parties should not encourage defections on other grounds. ii) It is necessary for a party to have grass roots – if it wants to exercise its authority in peoples' interests, iii) The voter should see that he votes for a principle and not for a party, that he votes for a party and not for a personality, that he votes for a person and not for the purse. iv) Discipline is to a party what 'Dharma' is to a society. v) A sense of negativism is quite harmful for polity and society. Let the political parties therefore pursue affirmative and constructive policies as well as programmes. Gandhiji died unfortunately within six months after India gained freedom. But He would have surly approved just mentioned prescriptions and recommendations; as they aim at scientific ordering of polity and society.

Deendayal like Gandhi aimed at elevating 'nara' to 'Narayana' or the human to the divine. No wonder, his Integral Humanism and Gandhi's Hind-Swaraj are valuable guides for us. We all are indebted quite deeply to the lives of these nation-builders. This is why, we should repay the debt we owe to them through the observance of principles in our transactions.

Elite Sponsored Line of Thinking during Immediate Post Freedom Years in India

> "The main elements of the then prevalent development paradigm were: the emphasis on economic growth, capital intensive technology and centralized planning. Underdevelopment, according to this paradigm was mainly the result of internal factors such as traditional ways of thinking, outdated land tenure systems, caste bound immobility and the deep-rooted rural bias of the population" (p.388)
>
> "Steel mills in the place of spinning wheel, Central Planning Commission in New Delhi in the place of an oceanic circle of autonomous village panchayats and Harold Laski in the place of Ruskin and Tolstoy had overruled then the mindsets of leaders and thinkers." (p. 388)

It was in 1978 that Ivan Illich informed Indians that whereas they were suffering from defeatism, from inferiority complex, Western scholars were coming up with Gandhian ideas and concepts. Curiously enough, the year 1928 had heard Gandhi's assessment of the West through the following anxiety:

> "God forbid that India should ever take to industrialism after the manner of the West. The economic imperialism of a single island Kingdom (England) is today keeping the world in chains. If an entire nation of 300 millions took to similar economic exploitation, it would strip the world bare like locusts". (p. 392) See Detlef Kantowsky (Prof. of Sociology at the University of Konstanz, Germany)" in B. R. Nanda, (ed.) Mahatma Gandhi: 125 Years (New Delhi, 1995).
>
> "When Gandhi considered all religions as equal, he gave premium to religions which make the state theocratic. He did not understand Muslim psychology and the fear complex arising out of apprehensions about their perpetual domination by the Hindus"
>
> Madhuri Wadhwa, *Gandhi between Tradition and Modernity* (New Delhi, 1991), p. 31.

4

Pandit Deendayal and Dr. Ambedkar

Two Architects of Modern India

The title of this paper is bound to startle scholars, researchers and political activists as it contains juxtaposition of Pandit Deendayal and Ambedkar. These scholars and activists may question the writer of this paper about the rationale and legitimacy of this venture. It is a fact that Pandit Deendayal and Ambedkar belonged to two generations, that they never had any interaction with each other, that they represented apparently two different schools of thought. And still both of them have been clubbed together in the present venture as architects of modern India.

It is, thus, essential to explain, at the outset of this write up, the rationale behind this exercise. A study of the speeches and writings of these two stalwarts has prompted the writer of this paper to observe that Pandit Deendayal carried forward, in fact enriched the legacy of Indian reformers, including Dr. Ambedkar. As the present paper intends to highlight how Pandit Deendayal enriched the legacy of Indian reformers in general and that of Dr. Ambedkar in particular, second section in this essay will be devoted to elucidate Dr. Ambedkar legacy. Through the third section titled "Deendayal Upadhyay's life Mission and Vision", readers will be informed of certain happenings and anecdotes of Pandit Deendayal's life with a view to substantiating Pandit Deendayal's sincere concern for downtrodden masses. Unique commonalities between the viewpoints of Pandit Deendayal and those of Ambedkar will also be highlighted through the same section.

As for the fourth and the last section, some elaboration (little lengthy) is required. We all know that Bharatiya Jana Sangh, the political formation which was nurtured with utmost care by Pandit Deendayal in the capacity of its General Secretary since its emergence till a few months before his death acquired Number Two position in the life span of Pandit Deendayal. Such a great organizer was, however assassinated on 11thFebruary 1968. Nonetheless, the inspiration provided by Pandit Deendayal to the workers at large made Bharatiya Jana Sangh a formidable political formation. Subsequent years witnessed the genesis and growth of Bharatiya Janata Party, the new incarnation of Pandit Deendayal led Jana Sangh. It was Pandit Deendayal's bunch of thoughts that continued to guide B.J.P.'s trajectory to the pinnacle of glory in the 2014 parliamentary elections in India. B.J.P. thus succeeded in 2014 in getting absolute majority and in forming its own government in the Indian Parliament under the Prime Minister-ship of Narendra Modi. The 2019 parliamentary elections again gave clear, absolute majority to the NAMO-led B.J.P.

The Modi government has accordingly acquired a crucial role in the development process of India. What is most remarkable is the fact that workers of BJP including Narendra Modi consider themselves as disciples of Pandit Deendayal. They moreover take inspiration from Dr. Ambedkar as well, as the role played by Babasaheb Ambedkar in the history of social reforms in India is simply unique.

It is a matter of conviction not only for B.J.P. but also for entire Sangh-Parivar that social and religious revolutions must precede political transformation. The concept of justice which makes you acknowledge your limits and goads you simultaneously to appreciate others' merits is also an article of faith for the workers of Sangh-Parivar. They thus echo the views of Pandit Deendayal and Ambedkar. Their colleagues have got a chance to form the central government in India. Several state governments have also come under the control of the B.J.P. People naturally expect the Modi-government in the center to facilitate social, religious and economic transformation in India with a view to uplifting marginalized masses. Fortunately, Modi-government is trying its best to fulfil these expectations. Last section under the title "Policies and practices of the Narendra Modi-government" is thus meant to narrate how the present Indian rulers are implementing the guidance of Pandit Deendayal and Ambedkar, the two architects of modern India!

The Rationale behind this Essay

The writer of this essay knows that whereas Dr. Ambedkar was born in 1891, Pandit Deendayal's birth year was 1916. Pandit Deendayal was, thus, quite younger if compared to Ambedkar. No wonder when the United Nations celebrated one twenty fifth birth anniversary of Babasaheb Ambedkar in 2016, Indians commemorated birth centenary of Pandit Deendayal in the same year. It was in the latter half of 1930s that Dr. B.R. Ambedkar had emerged as the most effective spokesman, an all India leader of Dalit citizens. Those were the immediate post Poona Pact years and Dr. Ambedkar's decision to renounce Hinduism announced in 1935 had created historical commotion throughout India. Mahatma Gandhi had then started a campaign with a view to generating among caste Hindus divine tendencies like compassion, sympathy and attachment for the depressed Dalit brethren. Then Pandit Deendayal happened to be a bright, promising college student studying in Kanpur. His sensitive heart must have grasped then that the adamant stance on the part of the orthodox, status quoist Hindus was posing a big challenge for the votaries of the justice, equality and unity. Pandit Deendayal had by that time become a devoted swayamsevak of Rashtriya Swayamsevak Sangh, the organisation founded by Dr. K.B. Hedgewar with a view to organising Hindus irrespective of affiliations linked with caste, creed, language, etc. Pandit Deendayal must have then felt that R.S.S. activities under the leadership of Dr. Hedgewar, oriented towards rebuilding India through the reorganisation of Hindus would ultimately succeed in homogenising our society, in ending inequality and hierarchy. This line of thinking inspired him to be a full-time worker of R.S.S. One can indeed point out that though Pandit Deendayal belonged to the generation next to that of Dr. Ambedkar, he did realise the significance of the role played by the latter and his own decision to devote his whole life for the R.S.S. work shaped his patriotic activities. He accordingly underscored social dimension of Hindutva throughout his life.

We must similarly take into account the age gap of twenty-two years between Mahatma Gandhi and Dr. Ambedkar, if 1869 was the birth year of the former, the latter was born in 1891. But several scholars have penned research papers for juxtaposing their views, for comparing and contrasting their contributions and for assessing the impact of their roles on Indians. Such a comment on the author of this paper's part is likely to trigger somebody to invite attention to the interactions between Mahatma and Dr. Ambedkar face to face as well as through letters and write ups. One must therefore accept that if such interactions between these two stalwarts offer a solid ground to scholars to juxtapose them, the absence of very interactions between Ambedkar and Pandit Deendayal denies us an opportunity to club them together. Is it not a fact, however that a student of history may take initiative in comparing and in fact in harmonising the viewpoints of the two heroes of the past, even when there is no record of any interaction between them? And does this not endorse such initiative as legitimate and worthy enough on the ground that proper lessons must be drawn from the past? This write up is thus a very humble exercise to demonstrate that Pandit Deendayal, being an exponent of Integral Humanism tried to integrate and harmonise the stances and the roles of the two national heroes: Mahatma Gandhi and Dr. Ambedkar. Pandit Deendayal, in fact, never deviated from underscoring social dimension of cultural nationalism.

One should now take into account the third question posed to the writer of this paper. He must, in other words address the challenge whether and how far Pandit Deendayal and Ambedkar being leaders of two different schools of thought deserve to be clubbed together in the same vein as the architects of modern India. It is simply obvious that those who pose this challenge assume that Pandit Deendayal and Ambedkar had led two schools of thought which were totally opposite to each other. This is why they hold the view that such types of two swords cannot be placed or inserted in one and the same scabbard. They opine that whereas Dr. Ambedkar renounced Hinduism after subjecting it to harsh attacks, Pandit Deendayal remained throughout his life a staunch votary of Hinduism. They, therefore, argue that it is simply unjust and totally unfair to place Pandit Deendayal and Ambedkar in one and the same rank of the architects of modern India. Such sort of argument is frankly speaking simply prejudiced. Dr. Ambedkar, no doubt, did formally renounce Hinduism and opted for Buddhism. It cannot, however, be forgotten that the Indian constitution drafted by him had declared quite categorically in the decade just preceding to his embrace of Buddhism that the Hindu Code is applicable not only to Sanatanis, Lingayats, Arya Samajists, Jains and Sikhs but also to Buddhists. Dr. Ambedkar's decision to embrace Buddhism was, indeed, in tune with his unalloyed attachment for and faith in the broad Dharma -family. One must moreover remember that Pandit Deendayal also shared Ambedkarian attacks on outdated unjust and inhuman customs as well as conventions. Thus opinion cannot be subscribed that

Ambedkar and Pandit Deendayal had belonged to two camps or schools of thought totally opposite to each other. And even if it is perceived that Pandit Deendayal and Babasaheb were occupants of two poles opposite to each other, one can think of harmonising them in the light of Vivekananda's teaching. The letter written by Swami Vivekananda to Mohammad Sarfaraz Hussain of Nainital on 10th June 1898 contains the following dream:

> "I see in my mind's eye the future perfect India rising out of this chaos and strife, glorious and invincible with Vedanta brain and Islam body".[1]

An attempt to comprehend contributions of Pandit Deendayal and Ambedkar to the development process of India is thus apt and befitting to the syncretic Indian tradition. Dr. Dhananjay Keer has rightly stated that the life of Ambedkar was a phase in the Indian renaissance that was inaugurated by the Upanishads with their stream of new thoughts when the gods, priests and sacrifices receded into the background.[2]

Dhananjay Keer has further added:

> "Dr. Ambedkar was the first great revolutionary leader who rose for the first-time form among the oppressed people during the history of over two thousand years of their slavery. He wanted reorganisation of the Hindu social order on the basis of liberty, equality and fraternity. If the Hindus acted upto his principles, they would be a free people, a living, movable race, a moving society".[3]

As for Pandit Deendayal's contribution to the development process of post Independent India, one must refer to the foreword penned by Dr. Sampurnanand, the then Chancellor of Kashi Vidyapith, Varanasi to Pandit Deendayal's collection of paper titled "Political Diary" in 1968. Dr. Sampurnanand has placed Pandit Deendayal in the galaxy of political thinkers involved in the scientific ordering of Indian society, the galaxy inaugurated in ancient times by Bhishma Pitamaha and enriched in modern times by Mahatma Gandhi and Dr. Bhagwan Das. The inimitable appreciation articulated by Dr. Sampurnanand in honour of Pandit Deendayal deserves to be reproduced here:

> "These words of Political Diary clothe the idea of one of the most notable political leaders of our time, a man devoted to the highest

1. *See* Selections from Swami Vivekananda (Calcutta, 1981) p. 535
2. Dhananjay Keer, *Dr. Ambedkar: Life and Mission* (Bombay,1971) pp. 465-466
3. *Ibid.*

good of his country, of a person of unimpeachable character, a leader whose weighty words swayed thousands of educated men".[4]

The writer of this essay indeed feels confident that readers will endorse the rationale behind his venture.

Dr. Ambedkar's Legacy

Preceding section of this paper has pointed out how Pandit Deendayal had found it essential to emphasise social dimension of nationalism and how he had incorporated in the treasury of his thoughts the legacy of Dr. Ambedkar. One must therefore elaborate unique dimensions of the legacy of this Bharat-Ratna. That Dr. Ambedkar was interested in reorganising Hindu social order on the basis of liberty, equality and fraternity has also been mentioned in the preceding section. Dr. Ambedkar's legacy accordingly comprises as its first dimension the dream of an ideal society assuring social endosmosis. Dr. Ambedkar pursued this dream or this vision throughout his life, as it was his conviction that only genuine social endosmosis would emancipate depressed masses. Inclusive discourse of emancipation can be considered as the second dimension of Ambedkar's legacy. If the reliance on the institution of Dharma was the third dimension, faith in psychological transformation of society was the fourth one. Let us elucidate these dimensions in this order only.

Ideal Social Order

The biography of Dr. Ambedkar informs that Bhimrao took a vow during his student years only to devote his life for uplifting Dalit brothers and sisters. The goal of replacing unjust, graded society by the ideal social order based on liberty, equality and fraternity thus fascinated him in his youth. Bhimrao rightly felt that Hindu social order resembles with a multi-storey house without a staircase. Residents residing in bottom level flats cannot climb up. They thus remain confined to their castes for the whole lifespan. He therefore aspired to reconstruct the social order wherein people can move freely from one level to another. His use of the metaphor of social endosmosis in this context is quite apt.

"Endosmosis ensures the passage of fluid through a membrane to an adjoining cell in the body".[5] And social endosmosis facilitates the

4. *See Political Diary* (Bombay,1968), p. ix
5. Krishna Kumar "The curriculum taboo" in *The Indian Express* (Mumbai), 7 July 2018, p. 11

flow of ideas and knowledge through interactions and contacts in society. Members of the ideal social order in Ambedkar's vision thus reap full benefits of liberty, equality and fraternity.

It was the deep contemplation of Ambedkar over such ideal society that shaped his lifelong efforts towards emancipation of depressed masses. The institutes formed by him, the agitations launched by him, the campaigns organised by him, and the testimonies as well as memoranda submitted by him to various commissions and committees were imbued with his perseverance to emancipate Dalits of India! The commissions and the committees approached by him during years from 1919 to 1949 with a view to seeking justice for depressed masses included Southborough Commission, the Simon Commission, the Round Table Conference, the Cabinet Mission and the Minority Sub-Committee of the Constituent Assembly. Dr. Ambedkar's vision was, of course quite broader than that of John Rawls, who expounded later in 1971 the theory of distributive and retributive justice. His vision thus sought, besides Rawls-sponsored justice an assurance of communitarian practices congenial to the emancipation of Dalits!

Dr. Ambedkar realised that the caste system in Hinduism has imposed on depressed masses various bans, as a result of which millions of people have remained deprived of various freedoms. He feared that the prevalence of hierarchical caste system in post independent India would continue to torture depressed masses. That was why, he set before him the goal of creating socio-economic order in India wherein each other would enjoy the fruits of liberty, equality and fraternity. He accordingly insisted that post independent India should distribute due gains of development among depressed people as well. He actually pleaded for compensatory discrimination in favour of Dalits and retribution or punishment to that extent for caste Hindus for their wrongs for centuries in the past. Dr. Ambedkar thus argued for distributive justice, actually for compensating justice in favour of Dalits with a view to reducing or balancing their pains due to caste system. He similarly pleaded for retribution or vengeance to that extent for those who reaped exclusive benefits of caste system. Uniqueness of Ambedkarian line of thinking lay in the fact that it went beyond Rawls-sponsored distributive and retributive justice. This line of thinking thus gave precedence to social revolution over political transformation. We observe uniqueness also in its insistence on social and economic dimensions of democracy. One may as well refer in this connection to Ambedkar's viewpoint that principles of liberty, equality and fraternity form an inseparable trinity and that the crucial principle of fraternity has got religious connotation.

Inclusive Discourse of the Emancipation of Dalits

That Dr. Ambedkar believed in associative, accommodative or inclusive discourse of the emancipation of Dalits is crystal clear. He, no doubt did opt for confrontation on occasions. That he launched anti Gandhi, anti-Patel and anti-Nehru Campaigns in the decade from 1935 to 1945 is also a well-known fact. We cannot moreover ignore that the language used by him in his interactions with these leaders was sharp and accusatory. And still one can legitimately comment that Babasaheb preferred coexistence to conflict. He thus involved various persons belonging to different castes and strata in the institutions formed and the agitations launched by him in the upliftment-mission of depressed masses. He appealed to Gandhians engaged in the Harijan Sevak Sangh -activities to facilitate cordial, friendly contacts between caste Hindus and Dalits, although he disliked the patron-protege paradigm of this organization.

It was in 1935 that Dr. Ambedkar announced his decision to renounce Hinduism. But even in the aftermath of such announcement he considered mission of organising Hindus as sacred and urgent. That was why, he offered best wishes to the leaders of Jat Pat Todak Mandal, the organization engaged in organising Hindus. One comes across at the end of his book titled "The Annihilation of Castes" the most revealing message to the leaders of this organization:

> "Yours is a national cause. It is more important than Swaraj. There is no use having Swaraj, if you cannot defend it. More important than the question of defending Swaraj is the question of defending the Hindus under the Swaraj....
>
> ...Without such internal strength, Swaraj for Hindus may turn out to be only a step towards slavery. Goodbye and good wishes for your success".[6]

Later in 1956, Dr. Ambedkar embraced Buddhism along with five lakhs of followers. He found it essential to explain to his followers the rationale behind the Initiation ceremony (Deeksha Samaroha). And, it was on 15 October 1956 that he delivered the speech, titled "The Great Conversion" for spelling out the logic behind this historical exercise. Just at the outset of the speech he said:

---

6. Quoted in Sheshrao More, *Dr. Ambedkaranche Samajik Dhoran* (Pune,1998), p. 187

"Some people believe that I have purposely chosen Nagpur because this city is the center of R.S.S. activities and that I wanted to do something spectacular right in front of their eyes. Well, that is not true. I have no such motive. I have no desire to irritate or to provoke anybody by scratching his nose nor, do I have time for this kind of childish pranks".[7]

This extract categorically points out that Dr. Ambedkar decided to hold initiation ceremony at Nagpur not in reaction or in opposition to the R.S.S. the leading Hindu organisation. During the course of his speech, Babasaheb Ambedkar elaborated the significant role played by human mind in shaping human life. He referred in this context to the valuable counsel given by Samarth Ramdas, a Marathi saint poet. We can thus observe that Dr. Ambedkar remained fascinated by Hindu organisation and by the Hindu philosophy.

As for the impact of Hindu philosophy on Dr. Ambedkar, one must recollect that Dr. Ambedkar always had a very deep affection for the Upanishadic theories of Brahma and Brahmaism. He has in fact defended these theories quite forcefully through his book "Riddles in Hinduism", published in 1954. He has thus stated that two objections raised regarding 'Brahma' and 'Brahmaism' are fully groundless.

"It is thus stated that Brahmaism is piece of impudence. For a man to say: 'I am Brahma' is a kind of arrogance"[8]

After calling this objection as totally wrong Ambedkar has argued that in a world where humanity suffers so much from an inferiority complex such an assertion on the part of man is to be welcomed...... thus the charge of selfish arrogance cannot stand against Brahmaism.[9]

He has also taken into account another objection that Brahma is unknowable. He has put forth his defence in this connection in the following way:

"All the same this theory of Brahma has certain social implications which have a tremendous value as a foundation for democracy. If all persons are parts of Brahma then all are equal and all must enjoy the same liberty which is what democracy means. Looked at from this point of view Brahma may be unknowable. But there cannot be

7. B.R. Ambedkar, "The Great Conversion" in Verinder Grover (ed.) *Political Thinkers of Modern India*, Vol.16: B.R. Ambedkar (New Delhi),1992), p. 74
8. *See* the Note no.6, p.462
9. *Ibid.*

slightest doubt that no doctrine could furnish a stronger foundation for Democracy than the doctrine of Brahma".[10]

What hurt Ambedkar most was the fact that though the theories of Brahma and Brahmaism provided foundation for equality, Hindu's social order demonstrated unjust inequality in practice. Babasaheb therefore felt that caste Hindus should accept that there is discrepancy between their philosophy and their practice, between what they think and what they transact. He moreover realized that Mahatma Gandhi also shared his views. Prof. Gopal Guru invites our attention in this context to one of Ambedkar's letters to a colleague in London. It is essential to understand the background of this letter. During freedom struggle, Gandhiji fasted in protest against British government's decision to disallow Appasaheb Patvardhan, a Gandhian to undertake scavenging work in Ratnagiri Jail. Ambedkar's comment over this issue in the just mentioned letter runs as follows:

> "I read Gandhi's letters published from Yerwada Jail. I have read in Daily Hearld that Gandhi fasted for Ratnagiri's Appasaheb Patvardhan. Gandhi's stand was correct whereas British authorities were wrong. How can they perpetuate hereditary occupation in one caste?"[11]

Here Dr. Ambedkar appreciated Gandhiji's stand, as it revolted against outdated social convention of confining scavenging only to untouchable castes. He thus found Gandhiji as well as Appasaheb as truthful, in the sense that they practiced what they preached."Truthfulness, as Ambedkar would see it, is nothing but truth performance. For him, grasping the truth through action is more important than approaching it through theoretical operation. Truth performs through action and autonomous initiative".[12]

Gopal Guru rightly remarks that Ambedkar was a path finder and not a fault finder. No wonder, Ambedkar was prepared to shake hands with reformers like Gandhi as the goal of removing untouchability was a silken bond tying former with the latter. Second dimension of Ambedkar's legacy informs us in short that cooperation and coordination are to be preferred to clashes and conflicts! Emancipation of Dalits is facilitated through inclusive and not through exclusive discourse.

---

10. *Ibid.*
11. Quoted in Gopal Guru, :Ethics in Ambedkar's Critique of Gandhi", in *Economic and Political Weekly* (Mumbai, April 15, 2017), p. 98
12. *Ibid.*

Reliance on the Institution of Dharma

It was the year 1924 which observed the beginning of Ambedkar's uninterrupted public life. Dr. Ambedkar spent the first eleven years of his Public life reforming and reorganising Hindus. His efforts however failed in getting favorable response from caste Hindus.He in fact faced violent reactions from them. His decision to give up Hinduism, announced in 1935 at Yeola, in Nasik District, Maharashtra, was indeed a logical outcome of all such bitter experiences undergone by Babahsaheb. India witnessed at least for the decade after 1935 the most angry and confrontationist profile of Dr. Ambedkar. The Speeches delivered and the write ups penned by Ambedkar during these years were full of attacks on Hinduism. Unique peculiarity of Dr. Ambedkar however lay in the fact that his faith in the institution of Dhamma remained evergreen throughout his life. The deep imprints of character and of noble virtues received in the childhood years shape the life of a human being. The life of Dr. Ambedkar informs us of the impact of such childhood imprints imbibed on his mind.

Such imprints probably prompted Ambedkar to make the following comment in his speech titled 'The Great Conversion', delivered at Nagpur on 15 October 1956:

> "For the progress of mankind religion—or to be more precise 'Dhamma' is absolutely necessary".[13]

Dr. Ambedkar stated further in the course of his speech that a human being is not a beast, and therefore "he must develop mind side by side with the body". Religion acquires importance in the human life, as it fills mind with pure thoughts. It is the religion which is based on Truth as well as on the principles of justice and equality and which is imbued with rational way to eradicate suffering that shapes the human mind.

Still later Ambedkar argued:

> "Poor, downtrodden masses rather than well-to-do, happy go lucky classes need religion badly, the former sections are required to stand on their feet and to march ahead confidently. And religion provides essential energy to unfortunate masses".

Here Ambedkar expressed his disagreement with Marx who had condemned religion by calling it an opiate. Ambedkar here attacked

---

13. *See* the Note no.7, p.79

caste system and Hinduism based on such system as well, because according to him they sponsor injustice and inequality. From the perspective of Ambedkar Buddhism being superior to Hinduism due to its reliance on Truth, Justice, Equality and Rationality, is bound to provide genuine salvation to depressed masses, and this is why, he decided to revive and propagate the gospel of Buddhism! I have mentioned above that Dr. Ambedkar aspired to reorganise Hindu social order based on the principles of liberty, equality and fraternity. The parallelism between these principles and those of Buddhism such as prajna (understanding as against superstition and supernaturalism), Karuna (love) and samata (equality) is quite clear. It seems, such parallelism must have also prompted Ambedkar to embrace Buddhism.

The fact that though Ambedkar was fed up with Hinduism, he continued to have deep attachment for Bharatiya culture was also a crucial factor that shaped Ambedkar's decision to embrace Buddhism. Dhananjay Keer informs us that Ambedkar opted for Buddhism, as this 'ism' is a part and parcel of Bharatiya culture.[14]

He moreover provides the following quotation from Ambedkar's interview:

> "I have taken care that my conversion will not harm the tradition of the culture and history of this land". [15]

Third dimension of Ambedkar's legacy thus underscores the importance of religion in the human life in general and in the lives of depressed masses in particular. It conveys to us moreover Ambedkar's concept of ideal religion. As Buddhism, from the viewpoint of Ambedkar happens to be the ideal religion and as it belongs to Indian ethos, Ambedkar decided to be a Buddhist along with half a million of his followers. The initiation ceremony (Deeksha-Samaroha) that took place at Nagpur on 14 October 1956, in fact mirrored Ambedkar's deep faith in India's Dharma-family.

Faith in the Psychological Transformation of Society

It was a conviction on the part of Ambedkar that law alone cannot transform socio-economic order. The letter dispatched from Port Said on 14 November 1932 by him to Thakkar Bappa, the General Secretary of the Anti-Untouchability League vividly articulates his viewpoint. The relevant content runs as follows:

---

14. *See* the Note no. 2, p. 498
15. *Ibid.*

"The touchables and untouchables cannot be held together by law, certainly not by any electoral law substituting joint electorate for separate electorate. The only thing that can hold them together is love. The salvation of the Depressed Classes will come only when the caste Hindu is made to think and is forced to feel that he must alter his ways. I want a revolution in the mentality of the caste Hindus".[16]

This extract is immensely important. First, it informs us of Ambedkar's conviction that mental or psychological transformation of society is basic. Secondly, it conveys to us his opinion that in a human life it is the mind rather than the body which plays a crucial role. Thirdly, it mirrors Ambedkar's viewpoint, in full consonance with Indian ethos that Descartes-sponsored mind-body dichotomy was least acceptable to him. It also underscores fourthly, that cordial, brotherly relationship between touchables and untouchables is the genuine promissory note assuring a healthy social order.

We can legitimately comment that Babasaheb Ambedkar was the genuine son of the Indian Soil. Least wonder, he aspired to build relations-based social order congenial to Indian culture rather than the Euro-centric contract-based society. If he expected love, compassion and empathy for Dalits from caste Hindus, he urged Dalits to educate, organize and agitate! His insistence on character building is well known to all. It was he who called Indians in one of his speeches to give up parochial, narrow identities in favor of broad Indian identity.[17]

He stated on one occasion that the concept of justice requires each one of us to give priority to neighbor's interests over one's selfish ends.[18]

All these views of Ambedkar demonstrate in short, his faith, his conviction in the psychological transformation of society. They thus take him away from Karl Marx and link him with Herbert Spencer. Karl Marx thought that the institutional transformation through the replacement of capitalist government by the proletarian one would transform society. He was confident that such institutional change would facilitate the unfoldment of socialist society. Herbert Spencer however had strong reservations about Marx-sponsored paradigm. He therefore challenged Karl Marx through the following content in his

16. *See* the Note no. 2, p. 221
17. Raosaheb Kasbe, Ambedkarvad, Tatva aani Vyavahar (A book in Marathi, Pune 1989), pp. 62-63
18. Quoted in Gopal Guru, " Shifting Categories in the discourse on Cast and Class", in *Economic and Political Weekly* (Mumbai) November 19, 2016, p. 24

book: 'Man and the State' published in 1881:

> "Mr. Marx, you may think of changing the society, revolutionizing the society exclusively relying on the institutions of the State. I am afraid, whether you will succeed in your venture because so long as the mindset remains one and the same, mere change in the State Government and the ruler will not deliver the goods". [19]

Ambedkar's legacy in brief expects all of us to devote ourselves to construct the socio-economic order founded on liberty, equality and fraternity. It asks every one of us to build bridges with others, as cooperative spirit enables us to construct the above-mentioned socio-economic order. It calls us to engage ourselves in righteous transactions, as the institution of Dhamma guarantees our march towards our goal. Lastly, it underscores the importance of imbibing due imprints on mindsets of people with a view to shaping desired socio-economic order!

Having thus discussed different tenets of Dr. Ambedkar's legacy; one must highlight Pandit Deendayal's life-mission and vision. Next section of this paper is meant to do this only!

Deendayal Upadhyay's Life-Mission and Vision

Pandit Deendayal Upadhyay played a crucial role in post independent India. It was he who started his public life as a full-time worker of Rashtriya Swayam sevak Sangh in the latter half of 1930s. In the immediate post independence years, the leadership of R.S.S. decided to form a political party under the captainship of Dr. Shyama Prasad Mukherji and directed Pandit Upadhyay to render full assistance to Dr. Shyama Prasad in this venture. It is a fact that Deendayal Upadhyay not only became an assistant to Shyama Prasadji but also put in his energy fully for nurturing this formation with a view to creating a solid alternative to Indian National Congress. And he succeeded in this venture within only fifteen years! Pandit Deendayal was unfortunately put to death by an assassin in February 1968. It so happened however that the inspiration given by him and the lessons imbibed by him on his colleagues enabled Jana Sangh to capture power not only in New Delhi, but also in several state capitals of India. Jana Sangh, of course acquired the title Bharatiya Janata Party in subsequent years. Pandit Deendayal Upadhyay can therefore be called quite legitimately as one of the architects of modern India.

---

19. Quoted in Ashok Modak, *Dr. B.R. Ambedkar's Vision and Mission* (New Delhi, 2016), p. 29

Even a cursory perusal of the biography of Pandit Deendayalji informs us of his firm commitment to justice and humanism. He was fully aware of the hierarchical Indian caste system. He was also in the know of inequalities in India and of the agonies caused to the depressed masses. Least wonder, he was eager to reform and modernise Indian society. He, of course, wished to do this, in conformity with India's age -old ideals such as simplicity and cultural nationalism,renunciation.[20]

Here I intend to elaborate how Pandit Deendayal Upadhyay pursued justice and equality quite spontaneously on several occasions. Later, I also intend to highlight notable commonalities in such pursuit between Upadhyay and Ambedkar!

Pandit Deendayal's Pursuit of Justice and Equality

Deendayalji decided during his college years only to be a full-time worker of Rashtriya Swayamsevak Sangh, because he felt that this organisation's mission of uniting Hindus was the best antidote to the unjust cast hierarchy! He must have noted that common Hindu masses still believe in unjust customs and conventions and consider themselves as 'righteous'. He must have accordingly concluded that the gap between Hindu precepts and practices needed to be bridged on war footing. And his realisation that R.S.S. was engaged in bridging this gap must have prompted him to devote himself to the cause of Hindu Unity. Later he got an opportunity to groom and nurture a political party and the above-mentioned eagerness on his part to reform and modernise Indian society in the light of the values of Bharatiya culture inspired him to articulate his viewpoint in the following extract:

> "Both the Jana Sangh as well as the Ram Rajya Parishad have faith in the eternal values of Bharatiya culture and life. Of these two, the Ram Rajya Parishad represents the more orthodox type and is opposed to all sorts of social and economic reforms. The Jana Sangh follows the reformist tradition of Dayanand and Tilak, not only in the social field but also attempts to extend it to economic issues".[21]

Pandit Deendayal was least status quoist and most enthusiastic to reform our society with a view to doing full justice to downtrodden and destitute sections. Biography of Pandit Deendayal informs us that he always showed deep and transparent concern for vulnerable persons

20. *See Political Diary* (Bombay, 1968), p. 5
21. *Ibid.* p.131

like jobless youths, shopless hawkers, landless farmers and homeless residents. One can refer to several occasions which evidence Pandit Deendayal's divine instincts like compassion, sympathy, love and affection for ignorent, poor and weak citizens. On one occasion, for instance, Pandit Deendayal purchased vegetables from an old, ignorant lady and inserted in her hands, inadvertently a fake coin. Once however he realised his mistake, he rushed back to the vendor, spent his precious time in searching the fake coin and felt happy only after replacing it by the valid one. On another occasion, he promptly retaliated a policeman when the latter was found beating an old female. On the third occasion, Pandit Deendayal observing during his train journey that a bearer of food-plates, who bothered least to comply with the earnest appeals of ordinary third-class train passengers, literally rushed to accomplish the order issued by a first-class train passenger. Pandit Deendayal's counsel to the bearer of food plate is a quotable quote:

> "Serve food, dear brother, to a railway train passenger and not to the railway train compartment!"

These happenings lead one to comment that according to Pandit Deendayal ji, neither an educated fellow should cheat an illiterate vendor, nor a person representing power should exploit a powerless person, nor a rich fortunate be preferred to a poor, ordinary person. Least wonder, Pandit Deendayal fully shared Marx's angst against capitalism. He thus expressed his agony over alienation and fetishism during the course of his lecture-series on Integral Humanism in April 1965 in Mumbai. One can thus allude to the relevant extract in the following lines:

> "In a capitalist economy no one is prepared to give a helping hand to the weak who is left behind, nay, elimination of the weak is considered just and natural".[22]

Deendayalji's determination to create an alternative to capitalism and Marxism with a view to putting an end to the alienation of a common man articulated in his lectures of Integral Humanism is equally worth reproduction here:

> "We shall be required to produce such institutions as will kindle the spirit of action in us, which will replace the self-centeredness and selfishness by a desire to serve the Nation, which will produce not

22. *See Ekatma Manav Darshan* (New Delhi, 2012), p. 71

only sympathy towards our brethren, but a sense of affection and oneness with them. Such institutions can truly reflect our Chiti". [23]

One can legitimately comment that Pandit Deendayal Upadhyay never ignored the social dimension of nationalism.

While elaborating Pandit Deendayalji's stance as a staunch votary of social justice, we will have to be extraordinarily alert and cautious. We must keep in mind that during pre and post freedom decades of India, shrewd opponents of Hindutva-ideology have purposefully launched an anti-Hindutva campaign and disseminated the view that all adherents of 'Hindutva' are hard core obscurantists, proud of outdated customs, interested and engaged in the spread of Brahminism, least sensitive of the agonies of depressed masses, advocates of feudalism and capitalism, blind critics of the so called 'Leftism' etc. In actuality, Deendayal Upadhyay was neither a blind worshipper of our ancient legacy, nor a thoughtless critic of modernism. He, in fact happened to be a pro-reform thinker and activist. He always sided with Daridra-Narayan and pursued sublime instincts such as kindness, sympathy, compassion and so on. Such inimitable qualities enabled him to shape an influential political formation in India. Present B.J.P. leaders who have been marching ahead with flying colors as rulers in India since 2014 rightly trace the roots of their success in Pandit Deendayal's pursuit of social justice.

As Pandit Deendayal Upadhyay was a prolific writer and speaker, we must read the essays and books written by him. We must also go through the speeches delivered by him for picking up gems of his thought. Very gems will enable us to substantiate the comment that Pandit Deendayal spent his life as a worshipper of '*Insaaf*' and '*Insaniyat*' (Justice and Humanism).

Notable Commonalities Between Pandit Deendayal and Ambedkar

I have noted above that Dr. Ambedkar being fascinated by the Hindu concepts: 'Brahma' and 'Brahmaism', showed enthusiasm in defending them. I have also mentioned that Babasaheb attacked Hinduism when he observed among Hindus unbridgeable gap between theory and practice. Such discrepancy in Hinduism caused irritation and anger to him and he took the decision to say good-bye to Hinduism. Dr. Ambedkar felt it necessary to vent his irritation when he got an opportunity to speak in November 1956 at Banaras Hindu University.

23. *Ibid.* pp. 77-78

While speaking on Shankaracharya's philosophy at B.H.U. he stated:

> "If the Brahma pervaded all, a Brahmin and an untouchable were equal. But Shankara did not apply the doctrine to social organization and kept the discussion at the vedantic level. Had he applied it on social level and preached social equality, his proposition would have been profound and worth consideration..."[24]

The legitimate expectation on the part of Dr. Ambedkar that Hindus should apply Brahmaism in practice got a pleasant response from Pandit Deendayal. We thus come across in one of the lectures delivered by Pandit Deendayal a very pungent critique of the perverted interpretation of Hindu Dharma. Deendayalji's lecture elaborated at the outset the ideal of the R.S.S and during the course of the elaboration invited the attention of his audience to the perversion of Hindu Dharma. The crux of the relevant extract of this lecture is worth reproduction here.

"The ideal of the R.S.S. is to carry our nation to the pinnacle of glory through organising the entire society and ensuring the protection of Hindu Dharma. We indeed underscore the significance of Hindu Dharma in the pursuit of our ideal. This is why, we must beware of right and wrong notions of Dharma with a view to doing away with the totally perverted notions prevalent in the name of 'Dharma!'. I remember here a conversation that took place between a well-known pleader and his client. The latter informed the former through such conversation that he had committed so far, several crimes including thefts, molestation and murders even, but "have kept myself away from doing even a single unrighteous act!" The pleader being shocked to hear such a horrible claim from the criminal client insisted on getting from the latter the rationale behind the horrible claim. And the rationale provided by the client ran as follows:

> "Sir, I have not so far drunk even a single drop of water from the glass given by an untouchable person and therefore I claim that I have not done so far even single unrighteous act. "Friends, such sort of perverted notion and interpretation of Dharma needs to be thrown out!"[25]

24. *See* Dhananjay Keer, *Dr. Ambedkar: Life and Mission* (Mumbai, 1971), p.509
25. *See* Mahesh Chandra Sharma, (ed.) *Deendayal Upadhyay: Sampoorna Vangmaya*: Vol. 15 (New Delhi, 2016), pp. 35-36

Deendayalji's subsequent narration of the right notion of 'Dharma' reminds us of golden viewpoints articulated by Vivekananda and Dayananda. Swami Vivekananda, has thus taken us to task for converting our 'Dharma' into 'Don't-Touch-Me-ism'. And Swami Dayananda has asked us to note that 'ones's dealing with all should be regulated by love and justice in accordance with the dictates of 'Dharma'.[26]

Pandit Deendayal Upadhyay found it indispensable to elucidate the proper meaning of Dharma during the course of his lecture series on Internal Humanism. The extract given below is the befitting specimen:

> "Dharma is a fundamental principle of civilized life as its attributes such as honesty, restraint, truthfulness, etc. underpin healthy social life".[27]

Pandit Deendayal Upadhyay, the exponent of Integral Humanism seems to have grasped Dr. Ambedkar's conviction that the religion needed by marginalised and vulnerable masses must be based on equality and justice.[28] Several views articulated by Pandit Deendayal in his lectures on Internal Humanism mirror his closeness to Dr. Ambedkar. One may thus refer to the following statements:

> "Even a modest meal served with dignity and affection, tastes better than the best delicacies served with disrespect. It is therefore necessary to take note of mental happiness as well".[29]

> "In democracy, everybody has got a right to vote, but what can he or she do with this right, when all other rights are diminished".[30]

Pandit Deendayal's grateful remembrance of Dr. Ambedkar in one of the lectures is quite categorical and therefore worth quotation here:

> "The late Dr. Ambedkar had said that our Gram Panchayats were so strong that we neglected the throne of Delhi. We did not remain alert as regards the State, as much as we ought to have done, thinking that Nation's life did not depend on the State. We forgot that though it may not be central, the State is definitely an important institution...[31]

---

26. *See* S.W. Bakhle (ed.) *Hinduism: Nature and Development* (New Delhi, 1991), p. 84
27. *See* the Note no. 22, pp. 22-23
28. *See* Vasant Palshikar, "Gandhi and Ambedkar" in Verinder Grover (ed.) See the Note no. 7, p. 84
29. *See* the Note no. 22, p.23
30. *Ibid.* p.24
31. *Ibid.* p.43

Pandit Deendayal's fourth lecture on Integral Humanism which also deals with the role of the State in Nation's life again reminds us of Dr. Ambedkar's comments quite resembling with Pandit Deendayal's remarks. Pandit Deendayal mentions at the outset of this chapter that Maharshi Bhishma's historical statement pertaining to the role of a king needs to be interpreted in the proper perspective. Bhishma Maharshi's statement that king shapes the circumstances (Raja Kalasya Karanam) is quite known to all. Pandit Deendayal Upadhyay's interpretation is quite interesting. It informs us that according to Bhishma, the king resembles with the executive in a parliamentary form of government. The king in ancient India used to be accountable to the Rishi-Mandal, in the sense that the former was supposed to execute the laws framed by the latter! [31A]

Pandit Deendayal, thus underlines the view that the king in India was not above all, although he was quite influential. Pleasantly enough, Dr. Ambedkar's argumentation in this connection is quite similar to Pandit Deendayal's interpretation of Bhishma Maharishi's statement. Dr. Ambedkar's argumentation runs as follows:

> "In the parliamentary form of democracy, the executive is responsible to the parliament, and this us why, members of parliament assess the responsibility of the executive through questions, Resolutions, No-Confidence Motions, Adjournment Motions, etc".[32]

Pandit Deendayal and Ambedkar thus shared the view point that we must expedite social transformation in India in the direction of equality and justice. Both of them, of course insisted in this connection that democratic procedure be followed for transforming our society. Both of them thus shared the faith that very democratic procedures would enable us to successfully pursue equality, justice and unity! We thus observe Pandit Deendayal's conviction in democracy duly expressed in the lines below:

"In India, democracy and national unity are closely linked to each other. If democracy withers away in India, our national unity will also be endangered! Even those of separatists who opt for democratic procedures will gradually march towards nationalism. Even those who take recourse to casteism and regionalism and win elections in

---

31.A. *Ibid.* p.59

32. Quoted in Sandipto Dasgupta, "Parliamentarism and Not Presidentialism…." in *Economic and Political Weekly* (Mumbai), 18 August 2018, p. 45

democracy will have to pursue inclusive course, as they cannot do anything on their own. This is why, the Dravida Munnetra Kazhagam is also undergoing a gradual transformation in the right direction".[33]

The mention of D.M.K. in this extract prompts me to point out that neither Pandit Deendayal nor Ambedkar compromised on national interest, neither of them relied on negative or reactionary stance. Least wonder, both of them disliked D.M.K. sponsored principles of anti-religion, anti-Gandhi, anti-Brahminism, and so on.

Incorporation of the Poona Pact into Indian constitution, no doubt mirrored reconciliation between Gandhism and Ambedkarism. Pandit Deendayal extended a hearty welcome to compensatory discriminatory measures of our constitution as they aim at redressing disparities in our society. He moreover tries his best with a view to making the oppressed brethren feel that they are part and parcel of our society. He pursued the principles of justice and equality throughout his life. The notion of equality in fact became a central idea in his exposition of Internal Humanism. And the booklet based on his lectures on Integral Humanism is presently considered as the ideological statement of the sangh-parivar.[34]

Policies and Practices of the Narendra Modi Government: *Sabka Sath Sabka Vikas*

I intend to begin the elaboration in this section by referring to the editorial of the Guardian-newspaper published on 18 May 2014, as it analysed the victory of the B.J.P. in the 2014 Parliamentary election in the most innovative way. The editorial inaugurated such analysis through the following remark:

"Today, 18 May 2014 may well go down in history as the day when Britain finally left India". Further it informed readers that for around seven decades a relatively small English speaking elites ruled over India. These rulers went on exploiting voiceless masses. And the very masses offered thumping majority votes to B.J.P. in the parliamentary elections of 2014. The readers came across during the course of the editorial the most revealing comment. The comment is given here:

> "The core constituency of the B.J.P. wants an India where its version of Hinduism has unchallenged primacy".

33. Quoted in Mahesh Chandra Sharma, *Pandit Deendayal Upadhyay* (New Delhi 2004), p. 75
34. Quoted in Anderson and Damle, *The RSS: A View to the Inside* (Gurgaon-India, 2018), p. 82

The editorial actually referred to three significant points. First, it stated that during post-independence decades Euro-centric, rootless elites ruled over India. It also mentioned secondly, that the sons and daughters of the soil, who had remained marginalised and alienated in these decades offered in reaction unadulterated majority in India parliament to the B.J.P. under the leadership of Narendra Modi. The third and the most important point raised in the editorial was pertaining to the expectations from Narendra Modi, the new Prime Minister. It expected first that NAMO would pursue such policies and practices which vent most apt version of Hinduism. It also hoped that NAMO would march ahead with great circumspection, that he would try his best to satisfy popular aspirations and would simultaneously do away with perversions of Hinduism. The expectation expressed by the Guardian-editorial that NAMO would accordingly take the most acceptable nationalist way out is equally notable here! I have stated above that members of the present government take keen interest in the viewpoints of Pandit Deendayal Upadhyay. This is why, whole India hoped in 2014 that it's further trajectory would be guided by the do's and don'ts prescribed by Pandit Deendayal Upadhyay.

Astonishingly enough, quite a few English-speaking Indian elites have expressed in the post 2014 years the views and opinions similar to those articulated by the Guardian-editor. They have actually opted for honest introspection, as BJP's victory in the 2014 parliamentary elections vis-a-vis most miserable performance of the so called progressive and left formations in the same election made them upset and distraught. Mr. Dileep Padgaonkar, the then editor of the Times of India thus came ahead to vent candid confession. "What we need is to acknowledge the flaws in our idea of secularism, as it has been perceived by voters as a hostile attitude to even the most uplifting traditions of India's myriad religious and spiritual practices. And by that token, it has been equated with an indulgent attitude to Muslim extremism. A course correction is in order". [35]

One may also refer to similar, in fact very harsh commentary made (on the results of 2014 parliamentary elections) by Prof. Shiv Vishwanathan in his write up in the issue of The Hindu, dated 22 May 2014. Prof. Shiv Vishwanathan thus stated that for around seven decades, secular formations in India treated Muslim voters as privileged members of the Orwellian Club. If Ramachandra Guha remarked that "Left has allowed the Right to say: "only we are patriots",[36] Yogendra

35. *See Times of India* (Mumbai), 31 May 2014, p. 18
36. *See The Indian Express* (Mumbai), 24 September 2016, p. 19

Yadav found it indispensable to advise non-BJP formations to get in tune with India's culture, civilization, traditions and ethos..."[37]

I have elaborated in the lines above how political leaders and thinkers in India pursued for seven decades quite perverted notions regarding secularism and Hinduism and how such perversions prompted Indian voters to offer absolute majority to Narendra Modi's BJP in the 2014 Parliamentary elections. Incidentally, remarkable upheavals and somersaults unfolded in Indian economy during post-independence years also caused bewilderment to Indian voters. For around three decades from 1947 to 1977 India thus suffered from command and control economy. During subsequent fourteen years from 1977 to 1991, Indian economy faced uncertainties and crises. Same economy however enjoyed benefits of several required reforms in the years from 1991 to 2008. Next six years from 2008 to 2014, however, proved to be catastrophic for Indian economy, as the Manmohan Singh-Government opted for freebie culture through sanctioning several subsidies and stimuli. These years also witnessed horrible scams and scandals. The fact that the Manmohan Singh Government lacked in absolute majority in the Indian parliament added to the pains and strains. Indian economy had actually suffered a lot for around three decades preceding to the 2014-parliamentary elections, as no central government in those years ever enjoyed clear majority in the parliament.

The Manmohan Singh-Government tragically proved to be most indecisive. Such incompetent U.P.A. government under the captainship of Manmohan Singh must have reminded Indians of the following prescient statement made in 1993 by Mr. Abid Hussain, India's former Ambassador to the U.S.A.:

> "Our economy is being reformed, but our political system is getting deformed".[38]

Indian voters, perhaps realising the worth of this statement decided to put an end to the deformities in our political system and the 2014 parliamentary elections gave, them a golden chance to implement their decision. B.J.P.'s stunning victory in these elections thus mirrored voters' mindset!

Indian voters, being upset due to distressing deformities in our economy and polity probably found a solace in B.J.P. slogan which

37. *See Times of India* (Mumbai), 14 March 2017, p. 12
38. Abid Hussain, *Towards a New Polity* (Bombay, 1993), p. 1

assured them in 2014- political contest that NAMO and his B.J.P. colleagues would put in all efforts with a view to developing all with participation of all. From the perspective of Anderson and Damle, this slogan was in tune with the R.S.S. goal of social unity, and stability.[39] Same slogan vividly mirrored Pandit Deendayal ji's emphasis on the social dimension of cultural nationalism. As has been mentioned above Pandit Deendayal Upadhyay never forgot the wellbeing of alienated, marginalised persons. He time and again advised workers of Sangh-Pariwar to pursue practical Vedanta through unattached service of Daridra Narayan!

This subsection: "Sabka Sath, Sabka Vikas" must take note of the speech delivered by Narendra Modi as the Prime Minster on 15th August 2014 from the ramparts of the Red Fort in New Delhi, as it elucidated the title of this subsection. Modi thus appealed to the Indians:

> "Let us take pledge today to engage ourselves in the task of enhancing the welfare of the poor and ignorant masses comprising depressed, marginalized and vulnerable brothers and sisters. We must create different skills in everybody, whereby he or she would be able to earn essential livelihood. We must also create in the competent members of such masses the abilities required for running factories and shops. We must provide inspiration and assistance to them, as a result of which they would get well settled in urban areas. We must, in short overcome all challenges pertaining to skill, manufacturing and urbanisation".

The fact that Modi-government changed Indian economy in its first term can be substantiated by referring to parameters such as increase in growth rate, containment of inflationary pressures, strengthening of foreign exchange reserves, curbing of corruption, providing benefits directly to common masses etc. A narration of the performance of Modi -government attempted in the following lines will, no doubt, evidence this fact only.

A review of several policies and practices pursued by the Modi-government during the last eight years enables one to comment that this government shaped Pandit Deendayal ji's counsel to the 'Haves' to be compassionate and empathetic towards poor and unfortunate 'Have Nots'.

---

39. *See* the Note no. 34, p. 73

Once the P.M. Narendra Modi came to know of around one thousand Dalit youths who had under the leadership of Milind Kamble started successful industrial ventures without relying on any assistance from the government, he decided to encourage 'depressed job seekers' to be 'job givers'. The Modi-government thus encouraged Milind Kamble to consolidate his organisation titled 'Dalit Indian Chamber of Commerce & Industry (DICCI).' It was on 29 December 2015 that this organization 'DICCI' held the first all India conference of Dalit entrepreneurs in New Delhi and invited Narendra Modi there to address the audience! The speech delivered by Narendra Modi there contained the following piece of information:

> "Our government has provided during the last fifteen months the loans worth Rs. 50 thousand crores to 80 lakh budding entrepreneurs belonging to depressed masses. Such loans provided without collateral under the MUDRA Yojana (Micro Units Development and Refinance Agency-Yojana) have proved to be a milestone in the trajectory of 'Sabka Sath, Sabka Vikas' on the background of freebie-culture nurtured by the Manmohan Singh–government! Narendra Modi hoped that such loans would enable Scheduled Caste & Scheduled Tribe youths to start small scale industrial units and to give jobs to around 14 crores of citizens. Later it was on 5th April 2016 (the birthday of Babu Jagjivan Ram) that Narendra Modi inaugurated the Start-up India-Scheme, "whereby the loan worth Rs. One Crore without collateral would be provided to each entrepreneur belonging to the so-called backward castes." One can legitimately say that the immediate aftermath of the emergence of the Modi-government witnessed very conscious government initiatives to strengthen Pandit Deendayal -sponsored social content of cultural nationalism! Such governmental initiatives moreover underscored Pandit Deendayal ji's viewpoint that the government should play a catalyst role in the process of development. B.J.P. victory in 75 out of 85 constituencies reserved for S.C's and S.T's during U.P. legislative assembly election held in 2017 was a logical side effect of the just mentioned welcome-initiatives on the part of NAMO-government! What is most remarkable is the fact that as a result of Mudra Yojana and Stand Up India-Scheme, there have emerged so far within six years around two crores of Dalit entrepreneurs in India".

Modi-Government's Success in Assimilating Muslim

Amicable settlement of the Rama Janmabhoomi Dispute is, no doubt a notable event in the periods of eight years since the emergence of the Modi-government in 2014. It was this dispute which harassed India for four centuries and caused political turmoil for the last three decades. That B.J.P. took initiative in awakening masses over this issue and in evolving a solid Hindu-Vote Bank during the last thirty years is well known to all. B.J.P. in fact reaped full benefits of Ayodhya dispute and acquired absolute majority first in 2014 and later in 2019. That was why, the so-called Leftists secularist's rushed ahead to articulate anxiety over the after effects of majoritarian politics. In actuality, extensive outreach efforts on the part of the Sangh-Pariwar as a whole watered the tree of accommodative, syncretic cultural nationalism with a view to bridging the gap between majority & minority communities. One can thus allude to the statement issued by the Mohanji Bhagwat, the R.S.S. Chief in February 2017. The statement deserves reproduction here:

"No one has the right to measure another person's patriotism".[40]

Just mentioned outreach efforts of the Sangh-Pariwar have paid huge dividends to India. The Supreme Court-verdict on Ayodhya-Dispute on November 9, 2019 thus received a placid response from Hindus and Muslims. Last eight years have, in fact witnessed the unfoldment of quite a few landmark governmental policies. One can thus mention the nullification of Article 370 and abolition of Article 35A, the passing of the Triple Talaq Bill, the passing of the Citizenship (Amendment) Act, and so on. The Ayodhya-Verdict must be considered as the culmination of such policies pertaining to Hindu-Muslim relations. Pleasantly enough, several renowned Muslim intellectuals and leaders have come ahead to offer a hearty welcome to such policies and practices. The initiative on their part to motivate Muslims to appreciate such events is worth due attention. Javed Anand, Convener, Indian Muslim for Secular Democracy has thus appealed to Muslims of India to welcome Ayodhya-verdict with a view to winning Hindu goodwill.[41]Salman Khurshid, former Union Cabinet Minister and senior Congress leader has also requested Muslims to honour this verdict and

40. Suchanandana Gupta, " No one has a right to measure other's patriotism",' Mohan Bhagwat', *Times of India* (Mumbai) ,12 February 2017
41. *See The Indian Express*, 14 November 2019, p. 12

join the collaborative endeavor to build our secular fabric.[42] Arif Mohammad Khan, former member of the Rajiv Gnadhi-cabinet and the present Governor of Kerala has candidly stated that, no major riot took place in India in the era of Modi's Prime Ministership.[43]The Modi-government has indeed implemented quite fully the 2014 election slogan: "Sabka Sath, Sabka Vikas".

I have elaborated in the preceding section of the present paper that Pandit Deendayal as well as Ambedkar were interested in the application of the lofty principles of "Dharma", that they were determined to shape inclusive, accommodative and placid paradigm. The slogan "Sabka Sath, Sabka Vikas", implemented by the Modi-government during the last eight years also informs us of the faith of present rulers in inclusive and accommodative nationalism.

Overall Assessment of the Government Performance

To anybody who attempts to assess the performance of Modi government it is discernible that this government has tried its best to implement the guidance of Ambedkar and Pandit Deendayal. I have highlighted above how Dr. Ambedkar favoured inclusive path while dealing with Mahatma Gandhi. The fact that Babasaheb was deeply interested in the multi-dimensional development of India has also been elucidated in the course of this write-up. Pandit Deendayal ji carried forward one and the same legacy. Both of these architects of modern India were staunch votaries of justice and humanism. They moreover never compromised with the unity of India. If Dr. Ambedkar made the central government strong in India's federal structure, for Pandit Deendayal, unity of India was the article of faith. Both of them criticised Jawaharlal Nehru's romantic and wooly foreign policy, as it facilitated Chinese grabbing of Indian Territory.

Innovative development initiatives and policy reforms introduced by the Modi-government in the last eight years since 2014 in different sectors of Indian economy need to be discussed here and such moves pertaining to agricultural sector deserve to be elucidated at the outset as they aim at enhancing the welfare of our farmers, the key players in our economy. Pandit Deendayal has lucidly highlighted the supremacy of our culture through the following statement:

> "Whereas, Western culture emphasises that one must earn his bread, our culture teaches us that the one who earns will feed and every person will have enough to eat".

42. *See The Hindustan Times*, 14 November, p. 12
43. *See The Sunday Express*, 4 August 2019, p. 8

We thus require huge quantity of food and therefore we must pay serious attention to the growth of agriculture![44] I am quite sure that Dr. Ambedkar also held the same view! As the Modi-government shares this stance, it has launched very useful schemes, such as Pradhan Mantri Fasal Bima Yojana (PMFBY), Pradhan Mantri Krishi Sinchayi Yojana (PMKSY), etc. Fasal Bima Yojana intends to provide farmers with better insurance services at cheap rates. As for the PMKSY one can elaborate two valid points. First, it is in full consonance with Pandit Deendayal ji's thinking which reminds us of our age-old concept of Adeva Matrika Krishi (Agriculture, least dependent on the ups and downs in the natural rainfall). Pandit Deendayal Upadhyay informs us that ancient Indian kings used to dig and conserve wells, tanks, ponds and canals with a view to achieving the dream of Adeva Matrika Krishi. The Krishi Sinchayi Yojana also highlights that the present government wants to revive the Manmohan Singh government-sponsored Water Tank Scheme at village level endorsed through the 2004-2005 budget but abandoned soon forever![45]

Second aspect of PMKSY is as follows. Realising that provision of irrigation facilities to farmers need to be supplemented by other unique measures, Modi-government started issuing soil health cards to cultivators, encouraged them to use neem-coated urea, enhanced Minimum Support Price for some crops, set up Cold Chain Projects and Mega Food Parks and so on.

Modi-Government's Unique Decisions and Schemes

Several decisions taken and schemes launched by the Modi-government in the years between 2014 and 2020 need to be highlighted in a separate subsection as they inform us of the rulers' Commitment to Indian ethos. The scheme-'Make in India' launched on 25th September 2014 (Birthday of Pandit Deendayal Upadhyay) with a view to making India a leading manufacturing hub has no doubt produced remarkable results! Thus, India has produced Arihant submarines, tankers and planes as well as world class semi high-speed Train sets: Train 18 and Train 20. If "Skill India-scheme" has started providing a good number of skilled youths to the industry, the other two schemes Start Up India & Stand Up India have given inspiration to the creative youths to launch their ventures. The pride of place deserves to be offered to the scheme: MUDRA (Micro Units Development and Refinance Agency)

---

44. *See* the Note no.22, p. 64
45. Ashok Modak, *Uniqueness of Integral Humanism* (Nashik, 2016), p. 33

as the government gives credit-support through this agency to Microfinance Institutes which further lend money to small businesses and self-help groups and individuals. That the scheme MUDRA has enabled so far two crores of Dalit youths to be job givers has already been mentioned in the lines above!

Modi Government's initiatives in the fields of infrastructure and power are equally praiseworthy. One can thus refer to Sagarmala Project which aims at utilising 7500 km long Indian Coastline as well as at modernising India ports. Bharatmala Pariyojana as well as Setu Bharatam Project have bridged critical infrastructure gaps in India. Development activities launched by the present central government in the National Waterways-sector are equally impressive. As far as the power sector is concerned the UDAY (Ujwal DISCOM Assurance Yojana) launched on 5th November 2015 undoubtedly wants to fulfil Pandit Deendayal ji's dream to provide continuous flow of electricity even to the remotest villages.[46] (DISCOM means Distribution Companies)

Pursuit of Social Justice

It is the pursuit of social justice which is the most endearing normative attribute of rulers. Gandhi, Ambedkar and Pandit Deendayal share this perception. They have rightly criticized a dominant minority which causes injustice to the majority of people. They have moreover supported the latter and asked this majority to uplift itself with a view to coming on par with the so-called superiors. They have, infact endorsed the claims of all humiliated, oppressed and exploited persons like landless labourers, marginal farmers, jobless workers, poor villagers, Dalits and females. These three architects of modern India legitimately expect rulers to enact laws in consonance with these claims. Their major thrust, of course, lies in changing the social consciousness of people. They are thus interested in generating broad social awareness of the goal of rebuilding a just and humanitarian socio-economic and political order. Least wonder, they insist that social democracy must precede political democracy to achieve, the just mentioned goal S.V. Pande and Archana Srivastava, two reputed sociologists of India have beautifully summed up the crux of this viewpoint through the following extract:

> "The real success of the policy of social justice as the crucial indicator of social development depends more on the attitudinal

46. Sharad Kulkarni, *Pandit Deendayal Upadhyay: Ideology and Perception* : Part IV: Integral Economic Policy (New Delhi, 2015), pp. 54-55

changes marked by a sense of fraternity between and among various sections when exhibited spontaneously in the behavioural patterns of both the so called superior and inferior groups, that is when the members of the superior strata start treating the inferior as their natural equals and latter start treating the former with brotherly trust". [47]

The above-mentioned common perception shared by Gandhi, Ambedkar and Pandit Deendayal is in full tune with Indian ethos which honours relations-based society and offers catalyst role to the rulers. Ambedkar and Pandit Deendayal have of course pleaded for the enthusiastic initiative on the part of the government, as they were immensely eager to put an early end to the deeply entrenched unjust hierarchical socio-economic order in India! They simultaneously argued that members of the upper strata should voluntarily come ahead for supporting governmental initiatives and for expediting the upliftment of the downtrodden sections of our society. They thus expected the Indian government to be active enough in providing required succour to the marginalised and vulnerable people and similarly motivate upper strata members to respond positively to outreach initiatives of the rulers.

Modi-government's performance in this context is undoubtedly laudable. In a country like India, rulers are expected to expedite the growth process and to show deep concern for providing benefits of this process to the marginalized and vulnerable masses. The role played by Modi-government's two initiatives: 'the ease of living' and 'the ease of doing business' is quite notable in this regard. Common masses living from hand to mouth existence and fighting daily against all odds badly need relief in their transactions. Modi-government has realised this need and offered direct access to educated youths to central and state services online through portal Umang. Its decisions to give forty million B.P.L. households LPG connections under Ujjwala Yojana and to offer rural households free cooking gas connections and completed electrification have also eased the lives of ordinary families. It's Initiative to provide more and better road connectivity to masses living in remote villages as well as its campaign – "Swaccha Bharat Mission" which has supplied rural households with toilets and made people free from open defecation are simply unique. One may also mention here some other schemes such as Pradhan Mantri Sahaj Bijli Har Ghar Yojana, Pandit Deendayal Upadhayay Gram Jyoti Yojana etc. which

47. S.V. Pande and Archana Srivastava, "Social Development through Social Justice"..... in M.P. Dube (ed.) *Social Justice: Distributive Principles and Beyond* (Jaipur, 2017), p. 128

have eased the living of a common man and tackled issues of inequality innovatively. Modi-government's performance in the light of its initiative: 'Ease of Doing Business Index' has succeeded in improving India's rank within four years from 142 in 2015 to 100 in 2018. No less than World Bank's President Jim Yong Kim has appreciated this feat and offered best wishes to Narendra Modi. This initiative has given relief to the S.C. and S.T, job givers as well, as 'red carpet' has taken the place of 'red tapism' in government-offices.[48]

Two additional dimensions of the above-mentioned government scheme of providing free cooking gas connections to rural households deserve here due elaboration. This scheme announced by Arun Jaitley, the then Finance Minister in the 2016 Budget elicited full applause from Swaminathan S. Anklesaria Aiyar who praised the Modi-government through the following lines:

> "I am not usually a votary of expanding subsidies. But I fully support subsidies for rural cooking gas to save rural lives. At last we have recognized a huge problem neglected for decades". (See the write up: "The key Budget proposal that you probably missed—"In *Sunday Times of India*, 13 March 2016, p. 16".[49])

Swaminathan S. Anklesaria Aiyar has underscored the significance of this scheme through the following extract: "The smoke from cooking chullahs made of clay or stones, fuelled by firewood or dung and used by 700 million Indians cause incalculable indoor pollution. Respiratory diseases caused by this smoke are the second biggest killers after unclean water".[50]

First dimension of the scheme of providing free cooking gas to Below Poverty Line households thus mirrors rulers' concern for the health of females. Second dimension of this scheme is also equally admirable. One comes across this dimension in the extract given below from Arun Jaitley's budget-speech delivered on 29 February 2016:

> "I am happy to inform members of Parliament that 75-lakh middle class and lower middle-class households have voluntarily given up their cooking gas subsidy, in response to the call given by the Honourable Prime Minister. Their gesture is a matter of great pride for the country".[51]

---

48. Quoted in Dr. Vinayak Govilkar, *Modinomics* (Nashik, 2018), p. 246
49. Quoted in Ashok Modak, *See* the Note no. 45, p. 35
50. *Ibid.*
51. *Ibid.*

Arun Jaitley's information to the parliamentarians that the 'Haves' of India responded positively to the Prime Ministerial appeal to give up governmental assistance in the interest of the 'Have Nots' is quite unique. It is crystal clear that present rulers have succeeded in awakening social consciousness among members of the upper strata.

I have referred in the beginning of this section to the fear expressed by Abid Hussain in 1993. Abid Hussain had actually articulated his anxiety that deformities in political system might endanger the implementation of economic reforms in India. I have also stated in the course of the further elaboration that Indian voters who shared this fear or anxiety decided to end deformities in our political system. That the occasion of 2014- parliamentary election gave a golden opportunity to Indian voters and that the latter grabbed it with a view to ending such deformities through ballot box have also been elucidated above. It is a fact that Indian voters gave absolute majority to the B.J.P. in 2014 and the B.J.P. under the Prime Ministership of Narendra Modi has succeeded to the large extent during eight years since 2014 in remedying our political system with a view to doing full justice to economic and social reforms. The Modi-government pursued policies and practices befitting to the thinking of Gandhi, Ambedkar and Pandit Deendayal.

I would like to end this paper by alluding to the most crucial extract of the resolution drafted by Mahatma Gandhi and passed unanimously in the immediate post Poona Pact hours meeting chaired by Pandit Madan Mohan Malaviya. The fact that it mirrored delicate reconciliation between Mahatma and Doctor adds to its eternal relevance.

> "This conference resolved that hence forth, among Hindus no one shall be regarded as an untouchable by reason of his birth and those who have been so regarded hitherto will have the same right as other Hindus in regard to the use of public wells, public schools, public roads and all other public institutions. The right will have statutory recognition at the first opportunity and shall be one of the earliest acts of the swaraj-parliament, if it shall not have received such recognition before to secure, by every legitimate and peaceful means, an early removal of all social disabilities now imposed by custom upon the so-called untouchable classes, including the bar in respect of admission to temples".[52]

52. Quoted in D. G. Tendulkar, Mahatma, *Life of Mohandas Karamchand Gandhis*: Vol. III, p. 213

The whole resolution from which the just mentioned extract has been taken out was on the one hand a sequel to the Poona Pact and on the other a prelude to the Constituent Assembly-resolve to do full justice to the depressed sections of our social order. Our Constituent Assembly, no doubt did emerge as the above mentioned swaraj-parliament and inaugurated India's march towards equality and justice. The parliament, shaped by the 2014 parliamentary elections under the Prime Ministership of Narendra Mode took a pledge to expedite this march only. I have mentioned above that Narendra Modi and his colleagues call themselves as disciples of Pandit Deendayal. It is essential to keep in mind that all of them take equal pride in bringing into practice the guidance of Dr. Ambedkar as well. Narendra Modi has stated quite aptly in one of his write ups that Dr. Ambedkar is a worthy inheritor of the galaxy of great social reformers of India and this is why, we must actualise the principle of self-articulation in practice in honour of Babasaheb Ambedkar".[53]

All of us are deeply indebted to Pandit Deendayal and Ambedkar and the present rulers of India are pursuing policies and practices in the light of the teachings of both of these architects of India!

53. Narendra Modi, "Dr. Babasaheb Ambedkar: Krantikari Samajsudharak" in Kishor Makwana (ed.) *Samajik Samarasata* (Delhi, 2012), p. 35

5

Pandit Deendayal and Dr. Ram Manohar Lohia

A write up on the topic pertaining to commonalities between Pandit Deendayal and Lohiaji is immensely relevant at present because the concern on their part for the well-being of a common man deserves to be revived for countering the phenomenon of social Darwinism fostered today by LPG trends (Liberalization, Privatization and Globalization Trends) Post-Cold war years have, no doubt witnessed how have the capitalist nation states used L.P.G. trends for their benefits. Rich capitalist countries have thus grabbed their third world counter parts for selling goods and services, for exploiting labour power and for pocketing attractive interest amounts over capital investment. Worldwide widening of inequality indeed mirrors the operation of the Darwinian principle: "Survival of the Fittest". Suffering on the part of an ordinary human being in such circumstances is inevitable.

Pandit Deendayal articulated his agony over the pathetic condition of a common man through lectures on Integral Humanism. His articulation is worth quoting here: "Man, the highest creation of God is losing his own identity".[1]

That Dr. Ram Manohar Lohia was equally distressed over the helpless condition of an ordinary person is vividly evidenced in his speech tilted 'A Philosophical Hypothesis', delivered at Hyderabad in August, 1952. The following extract from this speech mirrors his distress:-

1. Deendayal Upadhyay, Integral Humanism (Bombay, 1967), p. 84

> "Many revolutions have taken place in the world, with high and noble aspirations, and their maturing took an ignoble turn. Liberty, Fraternity and Equality have tended to degenerate into all kinds of hierarchies. This civilization, which started out as a noble praise of the individual has already degenerated into one in which the individual is merely a number and a tag".[2]

Vamsee Julury, a professor of media studies at the University of San Francisco in the U.S.A. has rightly referred to the fact that Pandit Deendayal blamed Charles Darwin, an English naturalist for sponsoring the law of the jungle and for justifying the principle "Survival of the Fittest". He has also correctly pointed out that Pandit Deendayal's categorical condemnation of the Darwinian exercise of building whole cultural and social edifice upon lower human tendencies such as lust, anger, greed, etc. reminds us of Mahatma Gandhiji's views expressed in Hind Swaraj.[3]

Dr. Lohia refers in one and the same Hyderabad-speech to the degeneration of lofty principles: Liberty, Fraternity and Equality into all kinds of hierarchies and blames Charles Darwin in the implicit manner. The fact that he was deeply indebted to Mahatma Gandhi for his distress over the just mentioned degeneration is more than obvious. If Sachchidanand Sinha has called Lohia's Socialism as an Underdog's Perspective[4]; Shri. Sunil, national vice-president of Samajwadi Jana Parishad found the roots of Lohia's socialism in the Gandhian assessment of modern capitalist civilization. The extract given below, from Sunil's write up is quite suggestive: "Lohia was not alone in pointing out basic characteristics of capitalism. Gandhi was one who warned against the evils of modern capitalist civilization and called it a satanic civilization at the beginning of the last century. Hind-Swaraj or Indian Home Rule was written by him and published in 1909. Gandhi was clear that industrializing India would require colonial exploitation of others, which was neither feasible nor desirable. But he never cared to theorise in an intellectual or academic fashion. It was left to Lohia to express his ideas in a more intellectual way and join in ideological debates. What Lohia said was essentially Gandhian, clothed in more systematic and intellectual apparel".[5]

2. Rammanohar Lohia, *Marx, Gandhi and Socialism* (Hyderbad, 1963), p.189
3. Vamsee Julury, "Ahimsa has no political hue", in *The Hindu* (Chennai) 2 October, 2015, p.15.
4. Sachchidanand Sinha "Lohia's Socialism: An Underdogs's Perspective" in *Economic and Political Weekly* (Mumbai) 2 October, 2010, p. 51
5. Sunil, "Understanding Capitalism through Lohia" in *Economic and Political Weekly Ibid.* p. 62

I have already mentioned in the lines above how according to Vamsee Julury, Pandit Deendayal also found his source of inspiration in Gandhiji's Hind Swaraj. Mahatma Gandhi who epitomized Indian culture and civilization thus offered an exchange number to both Pandit Deendayal as well as Lohia and this very number facilitated in subsequent years the process of direct dialing between them. It was a sort of conviction on the part of Pandit Deendayal as well as Lohia that in pre independence years, great stalwarts like Gandhi and Tilak had refused to concentrate exclusively on anti-British policies and practices, that such stalwarts had given a serious thought to the face of the new Bharat after independence. The fact that great visionaries like Gandhi and Tilak had pondered positively over the direction to be given to post-independence India on the basis of Indian ethos was also a matter of consensus between Pandit Deendayal and Dr. Lohia.

That Pandit Deendayal was serious infact quite insistent about positive or constructive line of thinking is crystal clear, that he carried forward the legacy of nation builders like Swami Vivekananda is also equally transparent. What is not clear or transparent in Lohia's line of thinking is the fact that he was also fond of positive or constructive viewpoint. His criticism against Marxism that this ideology is Euro centric and his harsh attack on University-professors reflected in the following paragraph have, no doubt shaped his caricature or image in the negative way.

> "Like the team of blinkered oxen in an oil press, they go on and on, researching into sectional conditions with Europe's tools and without a thought that these tools are inadequate and require to be refashioned".[6]

Apparent reading of this type of paragraph does prompt anybody to assess Dr. Lohia in the negative way. We must not, however ignore that Lohia's opposition to the use of European tools was based on the rationale that such tools don't have universal validity. We should therefore conclude that Dr. Lohia expected his contemporaries to create such tools of thought which possess universal validity. Lohia did expect India to pursue modern civilization. He however challenged those who consider the pursuit of modern civilization as equivalent to that of Euro-American civilization. Do we not know that Euro-American Civilization informs us either of capitalist trajectory or of communist

6. Rammanohar Lohia, "Interval During Politics" p. 94 quoted by Yogendra Yadav, "What is Living and What is Dead in RammanoharLohia?" In *Economic and Political Weekly Ibid*. p. 95

path? And are we not aware of the fact that both of these phases of Euro -American civilization have already reached a dead end? If capitalist trajectory gave birth to plutocratic states relying on market fundamentalism, the communist path proved suicidal to the Soviet Union. If capitalism killed equality, communism murdered liberty. No ISM pursued fraternity. According to Yogendra Yadav, "Lohia's critique of the modern civilization appears very much in line with and more subtle and fully developed Gandhi's view of satanic modern civilization".[7]

Lohia's very critique, incidentally reminds us of Pandit Deendayal's assessment of Capitalist as well as communist systems. This assessment runs as follows:

> "Both these systems have failed to take account of the integral Man, his true and complete personality and his aspirations. One considers him a mere selfish being lingering after money having only one law, the law of fierce competition, in essence, the law of the jungle, whereas the other has viewed him as feeble lifeless cog in the whole scheme of things, regulated by rigid rules, and incapable of any good unless directed. The centralization of power, economic and political is implied in both. Both, therefore, result in dehumanization of man".[8]

Both Lohia as well as Pandit Deendayal shared Gandhiji's angst and agony. That was why, they rejected capitalism and communism as well. Both of them were eager to witness the emergence of civilization, totally superior to both isms! Both of them did share a constructive and positive vision, though in the case of Lohia, we are required to delve deep into his writings and speeches with a view to assessing him rightly. We have made an attempt in this direction and pointed out about how his urge to have a new civilization shaped his attack on Euro -Centric perspective. We can similarly state that the 'Angreji Hatao' campaign launched by Dr. Lohia was moulded by his concern to place all Indian languages on the high pedestal with a view to offering them due status. Lohia's fight against the supremacy of English in India was actually a part of his broad cultural strategy of nursing the self-identity of each language group of India.

Lohia's non-congressism in the aftermath of the third general election in India deserves to be explained at length, because it was

---

7. *Ibid.*
8. *See* the Note No. 1, pp. 83-84

rooted in Lohia's urge to shape a new socio-political and economic civilization. His non-congressism actually informs us of the reverse side of his attack on the Nehruvian agenda of modernization and development. Rajaram Tolpadi's assessment of Dr. Lohia in this connection deserves quotation here. It is as follows:

> "Lohia's critical attitude towards modernity and development particularly reflected in his critique of Nehru and Indian communists deserves sympathetic consideration. He believed that socialism was not merely a just economic arrangement aimed at equitable distribution of wealth, but also an enabling cultural setting that helped people achieve freedom, equality and justice. Therefore, Lohia considered the above mentioned Nehruvian agenda as a mad rush for modernity without being aware of its darker side. He, infact envisioned an alternative socialist civilization that attempted to arrive at a critical, democratic and open ended paradigm of modernity deeply engaged in the historical and cultural context, in which it has to be practiced".[9]

Just quoted extract conveys to us that Lohia had a vision of an alternative socialist civilization, that he was fond of a democratic and open-ended paradigm of modernity and that he was prone to locate such paradigm in the historical and cultural context of India. Lohia himself informs us of his viewpoint to weave the vision of an alternative socialist civilization through the threads picked up from Gandhi's life and philosophy. From his perspective, "Gandhiji's action may well act as a filter through which socialist ideas flow and get rid of their dross".[10]

It was the very fascination on the part of Lohia to build an alternative socialist civilization on the foundation of Gandhian philosophy that prompted him to attack Nehruvian model of development which relied on a leviathan state. Lohia's historical speech titled, 'The Doctrinal Foundation of Socialism', delivered at Panchmarhi, in May 1952 contains the most relevant and apt extract in this context:

"The new world must go beyond capitalism and communism if for no other reason than that the techniques of mass production are inapplicable to two thirds of the world. Communism only alters the

---

9. Rajaram Tolpadi, "Context, Discourse and Vision of Lohia's Socialism", *Economic and Political Weekly* (Mumbai), Note No. 4, p. 77.
10. Ram Manohar Lohia "Gandhism and Socialism" in *Marx, Gandhi and Socialism*, Note No. 2, p. 121.

capitalist relations of production and seeks to reproduce its forces; socialism must alter them both. This is no rejection of the machine but it is a rejection of the situation in which the heavy machine and its counterpart, of the Leviathan State, predominate".[11]

Lohia's faith in Gandhiji's life and philosophy led him to prefer indigenous model of development over Euro-centric model. Same faith prompted him to give precedence to civil society over the institution of state. It was in the light of the same faith that Lohia discarded Communist strategy of ending capitalist production relations through the statist means such as centralized control and apparatus in which everything gets done to the detail according to a master-plan. It was a conviction on the part of Lohia that such communist strategy entails the sacrifice of general aims-such as pursuit of truth, observance of democracy and worship of individual freedom. Lohia's unique insistence on the pursuit of the aim of immediacy also mirrored his faith in Gandhian philosophy. As per this aim, Lohia refused to justify a present lie by future truth, an immediate bureaucratization by remote democracy, a present sacrifice of individual freedom by a remote human wellbeing, etc.[12]

Lohia, in short believed in the purity of means for achieving the end of stateless society. That was why, Lohia's Economics after Marx not only challenged ruthless Stalinist means but also endorsed his conviction that the Soviet Union would fail in achieving the end of the stateless society and in actualizing the formulation: "from each according to his capacity to each according to his needs". Uniqueness of Lohia's prediction lay in the fact that it was made in 1943, in the heyday of the Soviet era!

If Lohia attacked the predominance of the Leviathan state due to his faith in Gandhian philosophy, Pandit Deendayal did the same with additional rationale. Pandit Deendayal's conviction in the Indian ethos found ventilation in the following comment: "We had not considered the state to be the sole representative of the nation. Our national life continued uninterruptedly even after the state went in the hands of foreigners".[13] It was the same conviction that inspired Deendayalji to make a generalized, quotable comment: "Those nations whose life centered in the state were finished with the end of the state. On the

---

11. "The Doctrinal Foundation of Socialism" in *Marx, Gandhi and Socialism* (MGS) Note No. 4, p. 328
12. *Ibid.* p.331
13. *See* the Note No. 1, p. 50

other hand, where state was not believed central to its life, the nation survived the transfer of political power".[14]

It is needless to state that the first half of this comment contained the prediction about the Soviet Union. And the uniqueness of Pandit Deendayal's prediction lay in the fact that it was made in the years from 1947 to the early 1970s, the heyday of statism, which witnessed the dynamic growth of Western nation states and persuaded Jawaharlal Nehru to rely quite heavily on the institution of the state. Lohia recommended as an antidote to the Nehru-sponsored Leviathan state, the entity of the four-pillar State. He also advocated the use of small-unit machine.

If the major portion of the paragraph above informs of Pandit Deendayal's diagnosis of the pursuit of statism, last section of the same enables us to understand Lohiaji prescription of the antidote! Such sort of intermingling merely brings to our notice how Pandit Deendayal and Lohia shared the same line of thinking.

Amongst all socialist thinkers, Lohia was unique in the sense that he understood the problems which would crop up as a result of the mechanical application of the development model pursued elsewhere! He therefore asserted that each and every society should evolve its own authentic model of development based on its own historical and cultural ethos. Lohiaji's assertion reminds us of Pandit Deendayal's comment that according to Ayurveda, a disease in each place needs to be ended through the remedy suitable to that place only.

यद्देशस्य यो जन्तुः तद्देशस्य तस्यौषधम्।*

Pandit Deendayal's book titled "The Two Plans: Promises, Performance and Prospects" attempted a very penetrating critical analysis of India's first two five year plans and made the appropriate comment: "We can't afford to sacrifice our democratic humanist and cultural values for achieving economic welfare".[15] Pandit Deendayal walks hand in hand with Lohia and condemns the pursuit of economic aims at the cost of general aims. He thus prescribes again like Lohia to achieve full integration in practice of economic aims like mass production, offering of decent living standards to all etc. with general aims like charter of human rights, democratic representation, workers' control and so on.

---

14. *Ibid.* p. 51
    *This is the brief or concise expression of the content in *Bhava Prakash Sanhita*
15. *See* Mahesh Chandra Sharma (ed.) *Deendayal Upadhyaya: Sampoorna Vangmaya* - Vol. Six, p. 18

Yogendra Yadav has invited attention to Lohia's response to the question: "What is modernity?" posed by Rabi Ray in September 1962 at a Socialist Party Camp held in Nagarjun Sagar. Dr. Lohia's response equated modernity with a forward-looking worldview.[16] It distinguished between side looking world view and the forward looking counterpart by referring to the former as Euro-centric outlook. It has already been explained how according to Lohia as well as Pandit Deendayal side looking or Euro-centric view would cause harm to India. One must, however underline the following advice given by Lohia, as it contains the replica of similar suggestion on the part of Pandit Deendayal "Whatever is suitable or rational in the side looking or the backward looking people-adopt that". Does not this advice remind us of the following suggestion made by Pandit Deendayal through the Mumbai-lecture series? "We must absorb the knowledge and gains of the entire humanity so far as eternal principles and truths are concerned. Of these the ones that originated in our midst have to be clarified and adapted to changed times and those that we take from other societies have to be adapted to our conditions".[17] Pandit Deendayal has, in short asked us to absorb that portion of the side looking world view which is suitable to Indian ethos, and that section of our backward looking perspective which is suitable to the present era. Rationality shared by both leaders is thus a notable specimen of commonality.

One of the most significant comments made by Dr. Lohia in his essay titled 'The Meaning of Equality' deserves a special treatment in my write up as it has prompted Yogendra Yadav to refer to Vivekananda's perspective. And a deep reflection on my part over this reference makes me realize close kinship between Lohia and Pandit Deendayal. Let me first quote Lohia's comment: "The ancients in India seemed to have sensed that inward equanimity and out ward equality were two sides of the same coin for alone in India's languages does a single word samatvam stand for both meanings. 'Samata or samatvam is the word".[18] According to Yogendra Yadav, the link established by Lohia between the idea of equality and the inner self or that between modern egalitarian thinking and Indian intellectual. traditions must be considered as the most interesting contribution. The footnote added here by Yogendra Yadav is equally revealing — "Lohia was, of course, not the first one to establish this link. Some of the 19th century thinkers

16. Yogendra Yadav, See the Note No. 6, p. 95
17. *See* the Note No. 1, p. 22.
18. "The Meaning of Equality" in M.G.S. *See* the Note No. 2, p. 240

such as Vivekananda took this for granted". Dr. Lohia actually goes much ahead. He not only establishes a linkage between inward equanimity and outward equality, but also makes a solid recommendation to the modern man. "Man must strive to feel an inward equality between contrary conditions of pleasure and pain, heat and cold, victory and defeat" Last paragraph of Lohia's essay, which culminates his outlook on equality deserves to be reproduced in full: "Equality is thus found to be inward and outward as well as spiritual and material. Equality must therefore be grasped in all its four meanings. Material equality must mean the outward approximation among nations as well as the inward approximation within the nation. Spiritual equality must mean outward kinship as much as it means inward equanimity. Only an integrated concept of these four meanings of equanimity, kinship, material equality within the nation and among nations is worthy to become a supreme aim of life and its purpose".[19]

Lohia's sorrow, mirrored in the lines subsequent to the just quoted extract is quite exemplary as it informs us of Vivekananda's distress over our deterioration. Lohia conveys to us that we Indians have abandoned our legacy and begun to confine ourselves to our families only, whereas our ancient forefathers were immensely broad and large hearted enough to consider entire universe as our family. According to Swami Vivekananda genuine spirituality teaches us to treat everybody as the incarnation of divinity. No wonder, it imbibes in *me self—hood rather than brotherhood -for every being. Swamiji's guidance to the world to build socialism on the basis of spiritualism is therefore highly memorable! Dr. Lohia's elaboration of the meaning of equality through the special essay indeed informs us of his obeisance to Swami Vivekananda and to the ancient Indians.

It seems that Lohia as well as Pandit Deendayal shared Vivekananda's agony over the deterioration that has crept in Indian society. They launched therefore an attack on untouchability. It was this agony that inspired both of them to ask people to synthesize Asian contemplativity with European activity. Their guidance to combine the Indian emphasis on the change of heart with the Western stress on the change through law was also triggered by the same crucial agony. Their denial to allow the institution of the state to be an overpowering Leviathan and their simultaneous acceptance of the state as a very crucial social institution were again reflective of their distress over deterioration of India!

---

19. *Ibid.* pp. 240-241

The spirit of nationalism, in fact, the spirit of Indian Nationalism is another silken bond which ties close kinship between Pandit Deendayal and Lohia. Both of them share the conviction that nationalism continues to be relevant in the present world. The view that Indian Nation is ancient, is also a matter of consensus between them. They are convinced about the purpose of our nation in the sense that according to them India has come into existence not in reaction or in opposition to any power, but in response to the positive, inherent urge on its part. From the perspective of both of them, Indian Nation is neither territorial nor political as it is basically cultural. Both of them consider that every inch of our motherland is sacred and that is why, each one in India irrespective of caste, class, creed and party to which he or she may belong must respect our nation. Elaboration of all such views is a must here, as it highlights very interesting commonalities between Panditji and Doctorji.

All of us know that Rashtriya Swayamsevak Sangh (RSS) played a crucial role in Pandit Deendayal's life. It is a fact that Pandit Deendayal became a full time worker of RSS during his college years and devoted his whole life for the cause of RSS. As the name of the organization suggests it has come into existence with a view to reawakening our nation,through the band of dedicated workers throughout India. Least wonder, Indian Nation was an article of faith for Pandit Deendayal. He suggested time and again through speeches and writings that each nation in the world has emerged with a view to accomplishing a mission suitable to its intrinsic identity, that every nation has been contributing to the world treasury and that the existence of a nation has got permanent relevance! The case of Lohia is however different. From the perspective of the so called 'progressives' in India, Lohia's attachment to the Indian Nation is mysterious because they consider attachment to the nation as contemptuous, despicable and preposterous. The commentary on the part of Yogendra Yadav in this connection is worth consideration here: "With 'nationalism' becoming a dirty word in progressive politics, we cannot even recognize Lohia's brand of nationalism which combined a sharp response to Chinese aggression with a visionary Himalaya policy".[20] It is essential to remember here that Dr. Lohia's 'Economics After Marx' published in 1943 proudly proclaimed the relevance of nation in the whole world. His articulation is inimitable: "From Peking to Kahira and beyond, over Calcutta and

---

20. Yogendra Yadav, "On Remembering Lohia" in *Economic and Political Weekly* (Mumbai) 2, October, 2010, p. 47. 21. *See* the Note No. 2, p. 38

Bombay, Nationalism at least, with regard to consumption of goods is becoming the dominant spring of action".[21] Lohia's book in fact endorsed through supportive sentence that "nationalism is likely to grow and ramify .with the passage of time".[22] Genesis and growth of fifteen independent, sovereign nations on the cemetery of the artificial nation-state titled Soviet Union provide solid proof of the relevance of nation in the 21st Century. Present world, no doubt does endorse Pandit Deendayal and Lohia. Pandit Deendayal's pride in the ancient roots of India is again least astonishing, as like all Hindutva protagonists, he used to quote a particular shloka from ancient Vishnu Purana which informs us of the fact that the conviction prevails in India from centuries together whereby we call the land located in the north of the Indian Ocean and in the south of the Himalayas as Bharat and the progeny born in this land as Bharatiya!

What is most pertinent in this connection in the case of Lohia is the fact that he articulates quite spontaneously his fascination for ancient India. He for instance, informs us through his essay on the meaning of equality that for ancients in India the sensation of inward equanimity and that of outward equality were two sides of the same coin.[23] If Lohia conveys to us while elaborating anecdotes of Mahatma Gandhi that there are three belts of worship predominant in our country, the Ram Belt, the Krishna Belt and the Shiva Belt, mirroring fundamental realities of the Indian situation.[24] He points out similarly in the essay titled: 'Abstract and Concrete', that "the laws of Manu and Yajnavakya must at one time have given life and concrete meaning to the generalized principles to which they corresponded".[25] His essay: 'A Philosophical Hypothesis', gives transparent vent to his fascination for ancient years of India. See the specimen:

"This debate between the desirable and the pleasurable, the Preya and the Shreya, which Nachiketa and Yama hold in the Kathopanishad's probably the earliest debate of that kind which human history knows, and a debate which is entrancing in some of its verses". How fascinating they and similar verses are".[26]

As for the positive or constructive origin and unfoldment of our nation, Pandit Deendayal's conviction in this aspect can be juxtaposed with Lohia's implicit belief in the same notion. Pandit Deendayal is in

21. *See* the Note No. 2, p. 38
22. *Ibid.*
23. *Ibid.* p. 240,
24. *Ibid.* p. 174,
25. *Ibid.* p. 213,
26. *Ibid.* p. 184

agreement with the spiritual definition of the nation coined by Ernest Renan, a French thinker. This definition has got two dimensions; if the first one informs of the desire on the part of the residents there to share the memories of the rich legacies of the nation, the second one mirrors their determination to live together with a view to carrying forward very legacies. One must also allude to Pandit Deendayal's thought that the general mission of humanity is fulfilled by each nation through the pursuit of its own unique mission. According to Pandit Deendayal, each nation has got its own soul, which is called 'Chiti' in the Indian terminology and this 'Chiti' shapes the mission of that nation!

That Lohia was fond of ancient India has already been pointed out. One must also refer to Lohia's deep interest in Nachiketa of the Ishopanishad, as according to him without Nachiketa's disdainful rejection of gold, Marxist dream of abolishing private property will remain unfulfilled. How beautifully has Lohia stated: "As long as the emotional lure of private property exists, Marxism or any similar social doctrine will be continually at war with its own handiwork".[27]

Lohia conveys that present Indians, Hindus and non-Hindus as well do have strong affection for Rama, Krishna & Shiva, that they are fascinated by the stories of Yajnavalkya and Nachiketa and that they can be inspired by references to such lofty examples. He accordingly endorses Pandit Deendayal's conviction in the origin and unfoldment of Indian Nation.

Lohia's implicit support to Deendayal's faith in geocultural nationalism of India must also be taken into account. We cannot afford to ignore Lohiaji's viewpoint that in India cultural symbols and practices strengthen the threads of national integration. The comment made by Yogendra Yadav in this connection is of great relevance. "The targets of Lohia's attack were clear and obvious. Side looking, imitative and shallow modernists or cosmopolites — he had the brown sahibs, their political patrons and opponents like the communists in mind — were the prime objects of his contempt".[28] Lohia has coined two interesting adjectives:' Side-looking' and 'imitative' for attacking bureaucrats and communists for their Euro-centrism and also for their renunciation of cultural and religious symbols as well as practices prevalent in India. Sachchidanand Sinha's remark is indeed quite noteworthy; it runs as follows: "India to Dr. Lohia was not merely a

27. *Ibid.* p. 117
28. Yogendra Yadav, "What is living and what is Dead" in Ram Manohar Lohia in the Note No. 6 p. 102

political entity limited by its physical boundaries. It was a cultural and spiritual awareness, which suffused him with the aura of the epics".[29]

Lohia's boundless love for Indian culture found expression in several avenues like his worship of Rama, Krishna and Shiva, his belief that if Prabhu Rama symbolized unity between the north and the south, Bhagavan Krishna epitomized that between the east and the west of India, his faith in the sublime Indian values such as Truth, Ahimsa, Aparigraha etc. and his love for Indian rivers, and so on.

If Pandit Deendayal worshipped the indivisibility of India on the ground that each inch of our motherland is sacred, Lohia had also possessed the same feeling for Mother India. Least wonder, Jana Sangh under the leadership of Pandit Deendayal articulated time and again its faith in Akhanda Bharat, launched effective agitations to retain Berubari and Kachcha in India and attacked Nehruvian policies compromising with Indian borders. Several instances in the life of Lohia evidence quite transparently how this leader was quite faithful at the feet of indivisible India. One may thus take into account the amendment suggested by Lohia to the resolution passed by the Congress Working Committee in July 1947 at New Delhi. The amendment ran as follows: "Geography and the mountains and the seas fashioned India as she is and no human agency can change that shape or come in the way of her final destiny".[30] Lohia's book: "Guilty Men of India's Partition", gives us to understand how Nehru's indifference and unconcern regarding East Bengal at the time of India's partition on the pretext that the marshy and muddy land of that region does not deserve due defence caused anger to Lohia. Later, it was Jawaharlal Nehru again, whose question: "why to fight for the Himalayan land where does not grow a single blade of grass" caused equal pain and irritation to Lohia. An extract a reader comes across in the lengthy preface at the outset of Lohia's "Marx, Gandhi and Socialism" can very well be attributable to Pandit Deendayal. Such is the commonality between these two leaders. Following lines present the very extract. "Since the commencement in right earnest of India-China battles, I have been compelled to advocate ardently the use of weapons. In order to leave no room for misunderstanding, I have deliberately exaggerated my position. I have asked for the bomb, if it were available. I may not use the bullet for victory over another's home, but when my country is attacked, I would not hesitate to use any weapon that is necessary and available".

---

29. *See* the Note No. 4, p. 55
30. Indumati Kelkar, *Dr. Rammanohar Lohia: His life and Philosophy* (Pune, 1997), p. 109

Thorough and deep study of Lohia's writings and speeches is indeed a must, as it enables one to arrive at the right image of Lohia. Such a study moreover helps one to underscore close kinship between Lohia and Pandit Deendayal. I thus intend to recapitulate that Lohia's thoughts were basically constructive and positive, that he found inspiration for his views in the Indian ethos epitomized in the Gandhian philosophy, that the same source of inspiration led him to attack capitalism and communism, that he was a staunch nationalist, that he was a votary of cultural nationalism, that he was a devotee of the indivisibility of our Motherland.

Similar fresh efforts to analyse Pandit Deendayal's views from a different perspective will, hopefully enable us to comprehend a correct image of Pandit Deendayal. Even a cursory glance at Mumbai-Lectures on Integral Humanism prompts one to comment that Pandit Deendayal did not have any prejudice against European ethos. He in fact appreciates quite candidly that it was the urge to honour workers' rights that had triggered socialist revolutions in Europe. Next statement on his part is equally noteworthy. "Even where socialism was not accepted, the politicians had to accept the rights of workers. Welfare state was accepted as an ideal".[31] Pandit Deendayal mentions in the same paragraph that the ideas or doctrines such as nationalism, democracy, socialism or equality which have dominated European social and political thinking are good at origin. What hurts him most is the degeneration which has crept in subsequent years in the implementation stage in Europe. Pandit Deendayal perhaps purposefully excludes capitalism from the list of lofty ideas or doctrines, because he accepts implicitly, of course, Lohia's viewpoint that capitalism being a twin of imperialism walks hand in hand with the latter.

Pandit Deendayal thus seems to be in agreement with Lohia, as both of them rightly invite our attention to the subsequent degeneration of sublime doctrines. One cannot, of course ignore subtle differences between their approaches. According to Pandit Deendayal, it was the lack of holistic approach which resulted in degeneration. He thus states that Europeans imposed imperialism on Asians, Africans and Latin Americans as they were totally unconcerned about the interests of Third world countries. He commented that capitalists' mad rush for pocketing more and more profit widened socio-economic and political inequality in society because of capitalists' apathy for the wellbeing of workers. He also pointed out that socialism degenerated into statism, because the

31. *See* the Note No.1, p. 15

sponsors of socialism concentrated their attention exclusively on pursuing economic growth. Such a pursuit was bound to cause great damage to public welfare! Resultant alienation of common man perturbed both Pandit Deendayal and Lohia as well.

Lohia's analysis of the degeneration of above mentioned lofty ideas is equally interesting. Lohia blamed Marxian analysis of capitalism on the ground that such analysis threw into oblivion capitalists' ventures in the third world countries. He in fact accused apathy not only on the part of the 'European Haves' but also on that of the 'European Have-Nots' towards the black coloured natives of third world countries. He thus stated how the colour conscious and status conscious Europeans bothered least for the happiness of non-Europeans. Sachchidananda Sinha invites our attention to Lohia's attack on Arnold Toynbee on the ground that the latter assured redemption to Christians only.[32] He also refers to Lohia's criticism of Hegel on the ground that the latter considered. Prussian state as the final or terminal station for the unfolding World Spirit.[33] Lohia no doubt shares Pandit Deendayal's statement that it was the lack of holistic approach which resulted in the degeneration of original ideas. Lohia's analysis blames categorically Europeans and White coloured people for their indifference towards non Europeans and non-whites. Same analysis criticizes Toynbee and Hegel respectively for the apathy towards, non-Christians and non-Prussians. Deendayal's attack on the absence of holistic approach can legitimately be juxtaposed with Lohia's attack on the Europeans as well as Christians' and Prussians' partiality in favour of respective groups.

Pandit Deendayal's Integral Humanism speaks at length about Dharma and as the term Dharma is considered equivalent to religion, so called progressives in India have levelled several charges against votaries of Dharma. Pandit Deendayal plainly states that all those principles which bring about harmony, peace and progress in the life of mankind are included in the term of Dharma.[34] He has refused to opt for Euro-centric approach, he has similarly opposed to embrace all customs and conventions rooted in India, because both approaches would disturb harmony, peace and progress of Indian Nation. He similarly recognizes the role of 'Artha' as well as that of 'Kama' in the light of Dharma because only such sort of a pursuit assures us of harmony, peace and progress. As according to Pandit Deendayal, Dharma comprises do's and don'ts' essential for the sustenance of human life, he brings to our

---

32. *See* the Note No. 4, p. 53
33. *Ibid.*
34. *See* the Note No. 1, p. 29

notice that no culture or civilization ever honours any of the six lower human tendencies such as desire, anger, greed, temptation, insolence and jealousy. His criticism against capitalism and communism on the ground that if the first ism relies on desire greed and temptation; the second ism builds its paradigm on the plinth of anger, insolence and jealousy, accordingly deserves full appreciation. No follower of Lohia will disagree with this line of thinking on Pandit Deendayal's part.

In the opinion of Pandit Deendayal, Dharma sustains society or nation. He has therefore stated that the laws which help manifest and maintain Chiti' or 'Soul' of a Nation are termed Dharma of that nation. Dharma is the repository of the nation's soul. It is in this respect that Dharma is supreme.[35] Such a rationale leads Pandit Deendayal to comment that the institution of state should always be subservient to society or nation. This very rationale brings him close to Lohia; both of them unanimously condemn a Leviathan State overpowering society.

Pandit Deendayal, like Lohia of course does recognize the significance of the state in the life of a nation. He reminds us of our fault in the following manner: "We forgot that, though it may not be central, the state is definitely an important institution, serving some needs of the nation, just as a limb of the body".[36] He expresses his gratefulness toward Dr. Ambedkar in this context. "Late Dr. Ambedkar had said that our Gram-Panchayats were so strong that we neglected the throne of Delhi. We did not remain alert as regards the state, as much as we ought to have done, thinking that nation's life did not depend on the state".[37] Pleasantly enough, Dr. Lohia also laments over our negligence of the state. Pleasantly, because this viewpoint also strengthens the kinship between these two leaders. Lohia's lament over the long absence of statehood in India is expressed as follows: "For over ten centuries India had no state. As soon as an occupying power prepared to turn native, it was overpowered by yet another invader. The cauldron was set simmering again. It was not allowed to settle down into a native and vigorous statehood".[38]

Pandit Deendayal has rightly differentiated between Dharma Rajya and a theocratic state. As per Pandit Deendayal's analysis, if in Dharma -Rajya the state remains aloof from any religion and guarantees that everyone is free to worship the religion as per his choice, a theocratic state offers freedom of worship to the people belonging to the particular

35. *Ibid.* p. 52
36. *Ibid.* p. 51
37. *Ibid.*
38. *See* the Note No. 2, p.

religious sect only, thus treating all other citizens as secondary. Pandit Deendayal and Gandhiji thus sail in the same boat. As Dharma denotes certain principles which sustain human life, anybody who leads a principled life deserves due respect. One must thus go beyond any consideration pertaining to caste, colour, creed, religion or gender while thinking about a person of principles. Pandit Deendayal's reverential remembrance of Hafij Mohammed Ibrahim is quite relevant and apt in this context. Pandit Deendayal informs us of the fact that Shri Hafij Mohammed Ibrahim who got elected in 1937 to U.P. Assembly on Muslim League ticket resigned as M.L.A. before joining Indian National Congress and accordingly followed healthy principles of public conduct. Pandit Deendayal showers equal reverence on socialists who left Congress and founded Socialist party in 1948, as they also first resigned and later fought elections on Socialist tickets. I am sure, no Lohiate will disagree with such type of interpretation of the concept of 'Dharma'.

Pandit Deendayal's interpretations of age old shlokas and maxims are equally noteworthy, as they are in tune with Lohia's line of thinking. He, for example states that the age old Sanskrit line राजाकालस्यकारणम् needs to be interpreted in the right spirit. Although, it does mean that the king shapes circumstances, one should not forget the fact that he is expected to shape circumstances in the light of Dharma; in the light of certain principles. Secondly, according to Pandit Deendayal, the Indian king is quite akin to the executive in the setup of parliamentary democracy, wherein the laws enacted by the legislature are supposed to be implemented by the executive. And people expect quite legitimately that each minister, a member of the executive must set right precedent through his transactions in the light of the laws enacted. “This is”, in the opinion of Pandit Deendayal, “the right interpretation of the statement' that the king shapes circumstances”. Similarly, according to Pandit Deendayal another Sanskrit line बुभुक्षितः किम् न करोति पापं? deserves due interpretation. This line which contains a rhetorical question: “What sin is not committed by the fellow who is starving?” must be interpreted as a mandate for the government to see that nobody in the state remains starving and hungry. In similar vein, Pandit Deendayal presents a revealing interpretation of shloka from the Raghuwansha of Kalidas.

The shloka is as follows:

प्रजानांविनयाधानात् रक्षणातभरणादपि ।सपितापितरस्तासां ।केवलंजन्महेतवः ।

(Being responsible for the maintenance, protection and education of his subjects, King Dilip was the true father of citizens.)

Pandit Deendayal's addendum to this narration is fully quotable. Let me submit it here: "The description of King Bharat after whom our country has been named Bharat also runs similarly: by maintaining and protecting his subjects, he was called Bharat. This is his country, Bharat. If in this country maintenance and protection are not guaranteed, then the name Bharat is meaningless".[39]

The concern for the common masses articulated by Pandit Deendayal in this narration needs to be elaborated as in the lines preceding to this narration, Pandit Deendayal points out that it is the responsibility of the society to take care of the downtrodden. The lines quoted below are self-explanatory: "In a society even those who don't earn, require food to eat. There are, for example, children and the old, diseased and invalids. Society is supposed to take care of such human beings. Parameter of man's social concern and his culture is his promptness to take care of the downtrodden".[40]

Nuanced approach on the part of Pandit Deendayal is really quite enlightening. As per this approach, the state or the government is the guardian of the downtrodden and destitute in the sense that it keeps a watch on welfare oriented social initiatives. The line drawn by Pandit Deendayal between the state or the government on the one hand and the society on the other is highly significant. This line gives us to understand that in the opinion of Pandit Deendayal, neither market fundamentalism, nor crude statism is the genuine antidote to end socio-economic and political inequalities. Pandit Deendayal recommends in other words managed social initiatives, managed, of course, by the government elected by the people. Pandit Deendayal calls that society as cultured and civilized wherein 'well to do people' engage themselves on their own in several public welfare activities and the government facilitates such social initiatives. Similar expectations on the part of Dr. Ram Manohar Lohia from the workers of the socialist party and from the middle class members at large are indeed in tune with Pandit Deendayal's dream.

I have stated in the beginning of this write-up that in the current post-cold war years, when the social Darwinism seems to have taken roots, the lives spent and the philosophies sponsored by Pandit Deendayal and Ram Manohar Lohia would give us due guidance essential for overcoming the challenges of inequality and poverty. The

39. *See* the Note No. 1, pp. 74-75
40. *See Ekatma Manav Darshan* (A book in Hindi) New Delhi, 2012 p. 65 Also quoted by Ashok Modak, Uniqueness of Integral Humanism (Nashik. 2016), p. 37

delineation of the positions and the views of both of the leaders attempted in the lines so far have perhaps substantiated my claim. It was the common concern for the wellbeing of the common masses that inspired these worthy souls to articulate similarly on issues such as capitalism, communism, Euro-Centrism, Congressism, Indian nationalism and so on. It is my conviction that a perusal of these positions and views will give us adequate strength to walk towards the goals of equality and affluence in our society.

PART - II

6

Integral Humanism

Unfoldment of Vivekananda's Vision

It was in the year 2016 that we celebrated the birth centenary of Pandit Deendayal Upadhyay, the sponsor of Integral Humanism. This very year reminded us of the completion of Twenty Five years of the post-cold-war era. We all know that it was the collapse of the Soviet Union in 1991 that marked the beginning of this era. Leadership of the U.S. (United States) did feel relieved then because of the disappearance of the opposite pole in the form of the S.U. (Soviet Union).

Soviet Union was the first laboratory in the world, started for experimenting the operation of Marxism-Leninism. The demise of this laboratory naturally caused a tremendous shock to the leftist advocates of the Marxism. The above mentioned relief on the part of the American leaders of course proved to be a short term phenomenon. Subsequent years witnessed sub-prime and Lehman crises and the world at large came to know of the bankruptcy of capitalism as well. The publication of the book 'Great Divide' in 2015 informed us how the mad rush for derivatives in the capitalist world had caused historical tragedies to common masses there.

Joseph Stiglitz the author of the book accordingly endorsed with solid evidence the thesis of Thomas Piketty that capitalist markets do create major divides. If the demise of the Soviet laboratory of Marxism

Leninism demolished the romantic dreams sold to common masses there, the financial meltdown in 2008 in the capitalist world mirrored the implementation of the sarcastic hoarding,

> "Big Five have been bailed out and the ordinary masses have been sold out".

Twenty Five years of the post-cold war era, in short, presented the irrelevance of both paradigms of development throwing the interests of common masses to the wind.

Commemoration of Pandit Deendayal's birth centenary and the dissemination of his Integral Humanism through seminars, etc. in 2016 indeed acquired historical relevance against the insolvency of both Marxism as well as capitalism.

It was in 1965 that Pandit Deendayal elaborated through four lectures in Mumbai about the philosophy of Integral Humanism. He stated that if the reliance on statism would cause an existential threat to the Soviet Union, the mad rush after greed would endanger the relevance of capitalism. He also expressed his confidence in the development-paradigm built on the basis of Indian culture. This very confidence in fact prompted him to elaborate the philosophy of Integral Humanism. In 2016, the astonishing coincidence between Pandit Deendayal's birth centenary and the exposure of the western paradigms startled all.

It is essential here to point out that Vivekananda's interpretations of Indian Culture had a deep impact on Upadhyaya. Therefore the Indian Culture which he accepted as the basis for the projection of Integral Humanism was a version duly filtered through Vivekananda's Vision.

Incidentally, India's achievements in polity and economy during post cold war years, particularly against the downward march of the Euro-American world elicited appreciative articulations from several leaders and thinkers. Kuldeep Nayar revealed how Margaret Thatcher became fascinated in 1991 by the perception of the contrast between united India and sinking Soviet Union[1]. One may also refer to the resolution approved unanimously at a UNESCO sponsored meeting of experts on interface of Cultural Identity and Development held at New Delhi on 19-23 April, 1993 as it showered praises on India's organic pluralism. The fact that the delegates assembled at the Sixth Dialogue of Civilization held in the Greek island of Rhodes in 2008 arrived at a

1. Kuldeep Nayar, "Violence does not pay" in *Gulf-News*, (Dubai), May 3, 2008, p. 11

consensus over the topic of Indian unity in diversity equally deserves to be noted[2].

One may also allude to the speech delivered by Pakistani Scholar Prof. Muhammad Jamail Qalaundar at the SAARC Lit Fest held in New Delhi in March, 2016. It underscored the significance of cultural and civilizational unity inherent in the Indian subcontinent[3]. Such a review of the worldwide applause of India's uniqueness will remain incomplete if we ignore the address of Ahmed Badreddin Hassoun, the Grand Mufti of Syria at the World Sufi Conference held alongwith SAARC Lit Fest in New Delhi. The Grand Mufti of Syria made the most memorable comment:

"India's pluralist society is an inspiration for conflict prone countries of the West Asian region".[4]

As for the Indian achievements in the field of economy during post-cold war years, the comments made by two renowned personalities are worth quoting. Paul Krugman has thus cited Indian economy as the model for the world. (Quoted in S. Gurumurthy, India's Time has Come, p.117)

From the perspective of Christine Lagarde the IMF Managing Director, India has emerged as a bright spot on a cloudy horizon. (Quoted in *Times of India*, March 18, 2015, p. 16)

Whoever probes into well acclaimed Indian Miracles witnessed in post cold war years will find the roots of them in the pursuit of Indian-centric practices. S. Gurumurthy informs us that all these practices are self-reliant, humanistic, family oriented frugal common-sensical, rooted in millennia of learning and faith in universal brotherhood. (See the blurb, India's Time has Come)

Through such practices we Indians have actually implemented Vivekananda's guidance to forsake Euro-centric approach and opt for practices conducive to Indian ethos. During post cold war years, several Indians along with community clusters such as Patels, Nadars, Gaundar, Jatavs etc. started marching on autonomous economic paths. Family values have shaped their relation based transactions. India has accordingly enjoyed cumulative benefits of the reliance on its ethos. An attempt to elucidate how Integral Humanism is the apt unfoldment of Vivekananda's vision is indeed relevant in the present context.

---

2. *See* S. Nihal Sing, "Speed-dating civilizations: courtesy the new Russia" in *Asian Age* (Mumbai) October 16, 2008, p. 4
3. *See* The speaking Tree a *Times of India publication* (Mumbai), March 13, 2016, p. 3
4. *See The Hindu* (Mumbai), March 14, 2016, p. 13.

It is important to comprehend the typical background scenario against which Vivekananda expressed his views and positions. Swamy Vivekananda noted that William Wilberforce had initiated in 1793 a campaign of the Christianization of Indians on the ground that only the Philosophy of Jesus Christ would save Hindus who were drowned in the ocean of ignorance, inequality and superstitions. He also grasped that the book, titled 'History of British India', penned by James Mill in 1817 had presented Indians in general as dissembling, treacherous and uncivilized. He moreover took into account Macaulay's colonial arrogance venting deep intellectual hatred of the Indian ethos. Vivekananda, moreover perceived that the British Government in India had decided in the light of Charles Travelian's guidance to impart such type of education to Indians that they would consider themselves as protegees and Britishers as their Patrons.

What hurt Vivekananda most was the fact that educated elites in India had also started feeling themselves as inferior, wretched and downtrodden. The fact that Indians began to imitate Euro-Americans also caused equal hurt and irritation to Swamiji. Vivekananda therefore felt it essential to delve deep into Upanishads and Vedas with a view to arriving at the crux of Indian ethos. He also decided to study the treasury of Euro-American scriptures. Such a perusal on his part, which also prompted him to compare and contrast Indian ethos with its Euro-American counterpart was accompanied by his interactions with elites in India. Vivekananda's keen eyes observed through his wanderings in all parts of India that beneath poverty and ignorance there lay precious civilizational and cultural traits. Vivekananda did not, of course, fail to notice poverty and inequality in India. He actually underscored that India should walk on the path of prosperity, that wealthy Indians should take initiative and revive on their own the ancient spiritual principles with a view to enjoying through renunciation.

His decision to visit the U.S.A for addressing the World Parliament of religions and for having interactions with American elites proved transformative in several respects. It transformed some, if not all arrogant and abusive Americans into introspective souls. It changed the views of certain opinion makers there, as they began to consider India as a civilized nation. The very decision moreover transformed Vivekananda himself into the bold warrior monk confident and competent to win and influence Euro-Americans. Vivekananda's stay in the U.S.A .and his subsequent sojourn in European nations lent imprimatur to his status as the modern incarnation of Adi-Shankaracharya ! One must undertake a succulent review of what did

Vivekananda say about Indian ethos during his foreign sojourn, because it will mirror his vision which got later apt unfoldment in Pandit Deendayal's Integral Humanism.

One may refer at the outset of the review to five essential features of the Vivekananda-sponsored universal religion. (Vivekananda accordingly highlighted peculiarities of the Hindu ethos). First, it must be based on spiritualism and proclaim to the world that every being is inherently divine. Secondly, no single person, nor a single book shapes this religion; whereas certain principles mould the tenets of this religion. Thirdly, it must be rooted in rationality and be prepared on its basis to welcome new ideas and thoughts. Fourthly, it must give priority to the upliftment of the downtrodden through the lever of each being's divinity.; Fifthly, it should not confine itself to any particular sect or creed and treat the entire world as one single family. Elaboration of these features is a must, as it will enable all to highlight Vivekananda's views pertaining to European and Indian ethos. Such an elaboration can also be considered as a condition precedent, to the presentation of Vivekananda as the first sponsor of spiritual humanism.

1) *Everybody is inherently divine*: It was through this feature, that Vivekananda challenged Christian theologians, according to whom every human being is a born sinner, because he is an inheritor of Adam, the violator of Almighty's command. Vivekananda also questioned in the same vein the line of thinking of the protagonists of European renaissance, the line which persuaded people to keep the human being at the centre and forget God, the Almighty. Vivekananda moreover appealed through the same feature to the then emerging Marxists that they should give spiritual basis to the philosophy of socialism. If his interview at Madras in February 1897, granted to 'the Hindu' contained this appeal, his speech titled "My Plan of Campaign" gave the following message, "Before flooding India with socialistic or political ideas, first deluge the land with spiritual Ideas".

   It is obvious that Vivekananda has informed through this feature that Vedas have placed even the ordinary human beings on the praiseworthy pedestal. It was in the paper on Hinduism, presented by Vivekananda at the World's Parliament of Religious that we find a very forceful articulation of the just narrated feature of the universal religion. The extract given below from this paper is self-explanatory,

"You are the children of God, the sharers of immortal bliss, holy and perfect beings. It is a sin to call a man sinner. You are souls, immortal, spirits blest and eternal. You are not goodies. Matter is your servant, not you the servant of matter".[5]

2) *Supremacy of Principles over Persons and Books*: The universal religion from the perspective of Vivekananda is moulded by principles and not by persons and books. This is why it is scientific, and objective. It goes beyond time, place and person. Vivekananda, no doubt does shower full honour on Jesus Christ and appreciates that Jesus has taught us to be genuinely compassionate. Vivekananda in fact took European Christians to task through his admonition "You have become copies of Shylock, you have exploited poor masses for your benefit. You have said good-bye to Jesus Christ''.

He nonetheless refused to consider Jesus-word as final, and decisive because in his opinion neither person, nor book shapes universal religion. Vivekananda also averred that Jesus Christ like any other person had happened to be a bubble on the cosmic ocean[6]. The way Vivekananda counters Christian theologian's argumentation is simply inimitable and therefore unique. His advocacy of the supremacy of principles over that of Jesus informs us of his conviction in the objective test. He, in other words advocated supremacy of principles out of conviction and not in reaction to Christianity. He disagreed similarly with renaissance protagonists over the issue of the divinity of a human being out of conviction-that divinity is immanent.

3) *Rationality of the Universal Religion*: Swami Vivekananda noticed during his sojourn in the Western world that the scientific discoveries had demolished age old biblical myths and made people acquainted with the new truths and convictions. One may, for example refer to some of the new truths: a) The earth is round and not flat, b) The world has not been created by the Almighty-God from outside etc. Vivekananda appreciated these statements as they were based on rationality. He moreover decided to present in one of his papers the theory of the creation of universe based on the Samkhya Philosophy, as he wanted to prove that unlike Christian theology, ancient Indian Vedanta is based on rationality, that our theory regarding the world origin is least afraid of science, that

---

5. *The Complete Works of Swami Vivekananda*, Vol. 1 (Kolkata 2009), p. 11.
6. *The Complete Works Swami Vivekananda*, Vol. VII (Kolkata 2008), p. 8

modern science appears to be an echo of ancient Indian knowledge. The theory presented by him was, of course at variance not only with biblical faith, but also with Darwin's laws. As per biblical faith it was the God-Almighty who created this universe long back at a particular time from outside. Vivekananda questioned this viewpoint, because

"it informs us of an era when the universe was absent. And what did God do then? Was he sleeping?"

Such was the sarcastic doubt expressed by Vivekananda.[7]

Samkhya Philosophy moreover taught Vivekananda that the universe has evolved itself from the subtle to the gross. Vivekananda therefore stated that the evolution of amoeba into the man is quite akin to the evolution of the spider's web. If there is a difference between amoeba and man, it is because of the different manifestation of the soul (The Supreme Intelligence, the God). Man is thus an evolved amoeba, whereas amoeba is an involved man. Vivekananda, in short pointed out that the God resides within and not without. He accordingly gave credit for the evolution of the universe to the inherent divinity, the God, thus challenging Charles Darwin, who underscored the role played by the process of natural selection in the evolution of the universe. When Nicola Tesla the renowned electrical engineer and inventor met Vivekananda and admitted that the Theory of the Evolution of universe based on the Samkhya Philosophy was most rational and that the modern science could rely on this philosophy for resolving cosmological problem, people at large saw the end of the clash between faith and science.

4) *Possibility of the Upliftment of the Downtrodden through Universal Religion*: In the opinion of Vivekananda, belief in the inherent divinity of every human being is the basic feature of a universal religion. Such a belief leads one to consider all human beings as equal. It teaches us to overcome hierarchy and inequality between this one and that one. Honest implementation of equality in practice is, no doubt a must. Logically, 'don't touchism' in India caused great distress to Vivekananda. What is essential is to underscore that from the perspective of Vivekananda, we are expected to take initiative for uplifting our downtrodden brethren. A letter dated 19th November, 1894 written by Swamiji from New York to Alasingha Perumal contains one of the most revealing extracts:

---

7. C.W. Vol. II (Kolkata, 2008), p. 55

"Material Civilization, nay even luxury is necessary to create work for the poor. Bread! Bread! I do not believe in a God, who cannot give me bread here, giving me eternal bliss in heaven! Pooh! India has to be raised, the poor are to be fed, education is to be spread, and the evil of priest craft is to be removed. No priest craft, no social tyranny! More bread, more opportunity for everybody!"

That Vivekananda's guidance is antithetical to Darwin's principle, 'Survival of the fittest' is crystal clear. Such a guidance informs us that in a human society reason prevails and that is why, some thoughtful, well to do elites do rush to uplift destitute members. Such a cooperative spirit shapes human civilization. The story of animal kingdom is different as instinct prevails there, which enables fittest only to survive.

Vivekananda's guidance discards the operation of the Cartesian paradigm as well. Holistic approach on the part of Vivekananda, a legacy of the ancient Indian past is least compatible with the fragmentary approach inherent in Cartesian paradigm. If Vivekananda's guidance inspires us to engage ourselves in the upliftment of downtrodden brethren, the philosophy of Rene Descartes, reflected in Cartesian paradigm guides us to pursue our respective self-interests. Vivekananda's philosophy believes in symbiotic relationship between individual and society, whereas Cartesian paradigm considered each individual as distinct from society. If the former has got faith in the enhancement of public welfare through voluntary individual initiatives the latter believes in automatic, ultimate balancing of multiple individual interests through the operation of market forces. Appearance of grave ill marks like wide inequality and poverty in the nations relying on the operation of Cartesian paradigm informs us of the authenticity of Vivekananda's analysis.

5) *Non-sectarian Nature of the Universal Religion*: Elaboration attempted above of the unique features of Universal religion leads one to comprehend non-sectarian nature of this path. That Vivekananda was the prominent sponsor of this path is evidenced in several happenings like his abstinence from the conversion of a non -Hindu, his advice to a Christian to walk honestly on the track of Jesus Christ, his openness to accept the existence of a gap between the theory and practice of Hindu Society, his readiness to absorb lofty features of all isms of the universe, his guidance to the people at large to render equal honour to all religions in the light of the

vedic maxim- "Ekam Sat, Vipra bahudha vadanti" (Truth is one, sages call it by different names) and so on.

When Mahatma Gandhi stated in one of his essays that the soul of religions is one, but it is encased in a multitude of forms[8], readers must have remembered similar line of thinking advocated by Vivekananda. The accommodative and receptive mindset of this warrior monk has asked us to refrain from relying exclusively on a single instrument as it goes against the great religious orchestras organised by the God. The philosophy of Vedanta teaches us to take cognizance even of an insignificant, evanescent finite, as it holds a portion of the infinite ! No wonder, followers of this philosophy gladly embrace the idea of a cosmo-centric man, as against that of a homo centric or anthropocentric entity propagated by the materialist viewpoint !

Vivekananda in brief advocated the sublime tenets of spiritual humanism, a forerunner of Pandit Deendayal's Integral Humanism !

Vivekananda's views and thoughts on Indian ethos as well as on Western model of development have been elucidated. I therefore find it appropriate now to highlight how such views and thoughts have found unfoldment in Upadyay's Integral Humanism. As Upadhayaya has given in all four lectures at Mumbai in April, 1965 for expounding the philosophy of Integral Humanism, the same has been analysed one after another. One can, of course, afford to club the first two lectures, because the discussion of the Western-*isms* undertaken by Upadhaya in the latter part of the first lecture is continued and enriched further in the second lecture as well. As all Mumbai lectures are separate chapters in the booklet, one can use the word chapter for lecture and vice versa.

The first chapter reveals the scenario that had prevailed in India in the post-independence years preceding 1965. Our rulers were then expected to transform our political freedom into independence. They however failed in this task because of inferiority complex on their part regarding our identity. Upadhayaya blames non Congress leaders also in this connection. His narration suggests that there prevailed then an apathy for things Bharatiya and respect for everything Western[9], contains implicit accusation against the pursuit of pseudo-secularism. Pandit Deendayal moreover invites attention to the following tragedy.

"The neglect of the self in post freedom years caused disorientation and generated opportunist as well as unscrupulous, unprincipled practices in Indian polity". First part of his lecture contains not only

8. *See Young India* September 25, 1924.

9. Deendayal Upadhyaya, *Integral Humanism* (Bombay, 1967), p. 12

diagnosis, but the prescription of remedial measures as well. India cannot afford to opt for the unalloyed backward march, nor can it afford to pursue blind imitation of the Western pattern of development. Such was the line of thought process.

It has already been stated earlier how Swami Vivekananda faced almost similar scenario during the latter half of the 19th century. Indian elites then happened to be not only oblivious but also contemptuous of the Indian ethos. They had moreover developed fascination for the European model of development. Vivekananda's prescription of remedies can similarly be called as forerunner of Pandit Deendayal's recommendation. Both Vivekananda as well as Pandit Deendayal were in favour of ending all outdated customs in our society. Both were equally against the blind pursuit of Euro-American development model.

Juxtaposition of Vivekananda's views about Euro American life pattern with Pandit Deendayal's assessment of the same is indeed immensely revealing. Euro-Americans' remarkable march towards progress through scientific discoveries and agricultural as well as industrial revolutions had undoubtedly impressed Vivekananda.

His view that Indians drowned deeply in poverty should not deny the importance of economic prosperity and his advice to all of us to treat Euro-Americans as our teachers in materialism, of course, in its limited meaning were reflective of his mindset. Vivekananda similarly noticed in Euro-American world an unbridgeable gap between the few handful of wealthy people on the one hand and the large number of unfortunate, destitute citizens. He moreover observed that even the wealthy Euro-Americans suffered equally from discontentment due to widespread hedonistic culture, extreme individualism and artificiality in life. The poetic articulation of his thoughts is evidenced in the extract given below:

> "Social life in the West is like a peal of laughter, but underneath it is a wail. It ends in a sob. The fun and frivolity are all on the surface, really it is full of tragic intensity".[10]

It is necessary to observe Pandit Deendayal's assessment of the post industrial revolution of the Western world. It enables us to hear an echo of Swamiji's findings of the same scenario:

"Industrial revolution had generated faith in the new methods of production. Instead of working within the freedom of home, workers had started working in the factories taking orders from the factory owners. The worker migrated from his home town to dwell in the

10. C.W. Vol-VII (Kolkata, 2008), pp. 261-62

crowded cities. There was no provision of proper housing. There were hardly any rules in the factory to protect the worker. He was not only economically weak but also not organized. He thus became a victim of exploitation, injustice and harassment. Those in whom political power was vested were members of the same group who exploited the workers. Hence there was no hope of redressal from the state.[11] Pandit Deendayal's comment that thoughtless imitation of the West must be scrupulously discarded is also at par with that of Vivekananda!

The analyses by Pandit Deendayal and Vivekananda of the degeneration of the otherwise lofty Western ideas are noteworthy as are similar to each other. Pandit Deendayal draws the graph of the genesis and growth of European Nationalism and points out how this idea generated conflicts between nations and posed a challenge to world unity. He similarly points out that democracy in alliance with capitalism morphed itself into plutocracy causing great distress to common masses. As for the degeneration of the idea of socialism, Integral Humanism refers to the emergence of a leviathan State at the expense of society, making the position of an ordinary person quite pathetic.

Vivekananda's attacks on the British, Dutch and Portuguese imperialists (through his speeches) inform us of his concern over the transformation of European Nationalism into imperialism. He can thus be called a forerunner of thinkers like Andre Gunder Frank, (author of On Capitalist Underdevelopment) Frans Fanon (author of the Wretched of the Earth) and Dr. Rammanohar Lohia (author of Economics after Marx) who considered capitalism as the twin sister of imperialism. One can add the name of Pandit Deendayal in the list of just mentioned legatees of Vivekananda. Vivekananda's observation that capitalism in the Euro-American states had witnessed the growth of giant combinations with crushing power of exploitation is an evidence of his knowledge of the degeneration of democracy. As for the view on degeneration of socialism, one must pay attention to Vivekananda's stand about the process of socio-economic and political transformation. The fact that Swamiji, being a staunch spiritualist had faith in the change in the human mindset needs to be underscored. This very fact informs us, in other words that he had strong reservations about the exclusive reliance on the role of institutional change in the process of socio-economic transformation. One needs little elaboration to prove that the demise of the USSR has confirmed Vivekananda's reservation regarding institutional change. We all know that Marxists-Leninists

---

11. *See* the Note No. 9, p. 14

who launched violent revolution in Russia with a view to grabbing reins of government power and strengthening statism in fact dug their own graveyard.

Pandit Deendayal was confident that the paradigm of development built on the basis of Indian culture would put an end not only to the then prevalent disorientation of Indian polity but also to the just narrated degeneration of Western ideas. We find traces of this confidence in the Vivekananda sponsored Indian culture. As a specimen, one may refer to the claim made in the second lecture on Integral Humanism. As per this claim, the Indian viewpoint that our life is an integrated whole has been endorsed by the interest on the part of the scientists to discover order in the apparent disorder in the universe. Pandit Deendayal has substantiated this claim by attracting attention to the fact that while Chemistry has discovered certain elements which comprise the whole world, Physics has gone a step ahead and proved that very elements consist only of energy.[12]

Here one recollects Vivekananda's assertion that modern science is an echo of ancient Indian Knowledge. This very assertion seemed to have triggered Pandit Deendayal's attacks on Darwinian and Cartesian principles. If Indian Vedanta and modern science believe in basic unity underneath apparent diversity, they logically demonstrate their faith in complementarity. They point out in other words that such complementarity or co-existence between two entities is natural, though clashes and conflicts between them may impress us occasionally. Integral Humanism therefore avers that whereas co-existence or co-operation is a sign of civilization, conflicts and clashes inform us of degradation. We all know that if the instincts such as desire, greed, anger, jealousy sow the seeds of conflicts and clashes in society, sublime tendencies like love, sacrifice, restraint facilitate the growth of corporative spirit. Pandit Deendayal invites our attention in this connection to the fact that animals succumb to lower instincts, human beings can however overcome them. Any human being who loves even his enemy, who sacrifices his claim and who restrains his anger is called civilized and cultured. Animals cannot reach such heights, they give in to the influence of ugly instincts. No wonder, only fit animals survive and that is why, in the opinion of Pandit Deendayal, Darwinian principle is called the law of the jungle.

As ugly instincts dominate animals and reason guides human beings, Darwin's theory fails to take roots in a civilized society. Such a

12. *Ibid.* pp. 24, 25

logic prompted George Orwell to present Soviet Union as Animal Farm. 'Swami Vivekananda, being a committed spiritualist believed in the inherent divinity of a human being and asserted that the spontaneous manifestation of rationality in human society would come in the way of the operation of Darwinian principle.[13] Integral Humanism displays same confidence in human rationality and accordingly gets the honour of being called as the legitimate successor of Vivekananda's spiritual humanism.

Integral Humanism is equality antithetical to the operation of Cartesian principle, as it relies on holistic approach, whereas the latter believes in fragmentary perspective! The former underscores links between man and man, man and nature as well as man and God. The latter however analyses the world into independently existent parts. Actually it goes further and sponsors mind-body dualism in the individual life. Descarte's philosophy informs us, in other words that mind and body in the individual life are distinct from each other. Modern educationists relying on this philosophy ask students to conceive whole surrounding as competitive and acquire a killer's instinct to win the game. Integral Humanism points out however that body, mind, intelligence and the soul-these four make up an individual, they are integrated.[14]

This philosophy naturally offers students an advice totally different from that given by modern educationists. One may thus refer to the speech delivered by Pandit Deendayal while inaugurating Zopadpatti Janata Parishad at Mumbai. This speech contained a valuable extract which can be considered as an advice to the members of young generation.

"Development of the city of Mumbai means development of each area and this is why, priority attention needs to be paid to that part where one comes across wretched slums. Do we not know that it is the weakest link of the rope which deserves to be strengthened on the priority basis?"

Such a speech reminds us of Vivekananda's guidance to the well-do elites to see God in the poor and the lowly and to worship this daridra-narayan wholeheartedly.

Pandit Deendayal's third lecture has been devoted to elaborate relationship between individual and society. One comes across the analyses of the concepts such as class struggle, Dharma, Dharma-Rajya

---

13. C.W. Vol. VII (Kolkata 2008), p. 154
14. *See* the Note no. 9, p. 30

and so on. Throughout these analyses, one hears the echoes of Vivekananda's comments.

Pandit Deendayal's lecture poses in the beginning itself a challenge to the social contract theory. Society, being akin to nation emerges in the organic way thus runs the Indian line of thinking. The model of a club or that of a joint stock company is therefore least applicable to society. Such a viewpoint is in full consonance with Vivekananda's perspective. This is why, it informs us that every society or nation possesses certain inborn qualities and character. And these qualities shape the genesis and growth of conventions and institutions. One may recollect Vivekananda's philosophy which conveys to us that institutions emerge to protect a society and when this necessity for self-preservation disappears, they die a natural death.[15] Such a social fabric shapes links between individual and society. Individual feels attached to society due to this fabric. India has come into existence in the hoary past and therefore we come across several similarities deeply rooted in all provinces and regions of India. Same phenomenon exists astonishingly even in the modern nation of the U.S.A. Louis Michael Seidman, a professor of constitutional law at Georgetown university has written in New York Times (30/12/2012) that social fabric and, most important, the sense that Americans are one nation and not the constitution have preserved America's political stability.

Upadyay's answer to the question what is a nation? reflects Vivekananda's view point, which is mirrored in the following extract,

> "Each nation has a destiny to fulfil. Just as there is an individuality in every man, so there is a national individuality. As one man differs from another in certain particulars, in certain characteristics of his own, so one race differs from another in certain peculiar characteristics, and just as it is the mission of every man to fulfil a certain purpose in the economy of nature, so it is with nation. Each nation has a destiny to fulfil, each nation has a message to deliver, each nation has a mission to accomplish".[16]

Integral Humanism, no doubt inherits Vivekananda's legacy, actually it enriches this legacy while talking about nation. Pandit Deendayal in fact shares Dr. Radhakrishnan's stand and accepts that man in India does not live by bread alone, nor by his work, capital, ambition etc., that he lives by the life of spirit. Self-emancipation (Moksha) is his goal.[17] Pandit Deendayal takes into account that the

15. Quoted in Eknath Ranade, *Rousing Call to Hindu Nation* (Chennai, 2012), p. 35
16. *Ibid.* p. 20
17. Dr. S. Radhakrishnan, *The Hindu View of Life*, p. 58

goal of self-emancipation mentioned here by Dr. Radhakrishnan is naturally the aim to be pursued by the people of India. He acknowledges that this aim is in full consonance with the idea of '*Chiti* '. He however interprets this aim in a new and revealing way. The paragraph below is most relevant in the present context.

> "The right to food is a birth right. The ability to earn is result of education and training. In a society even those who do not earn must have food. The children and the old, the diseased and the invalids, all must be cared for by the society. The social and cultural progress of mankind lies in the readiness to fulfil this responsibility. A man works not merely for bread alone, but also to shoulder this responsibility".

Integral Humanism, in other words points out that the man in India should reach the goal of self-emancipation through taking due care of the children, the old, the diseased and the invalids. The paradigm of development built on the basis of '*Chiti*' of Indian nation is quite remarkable!

Integral Humanism, in line with Vivekananda's philosophy states that the Indic culture which has been shaping our lives, which has been imbibing valuable imprints on our mindsets since pre Islamic centuries is rooted in Hindu mythology and historiography. And as these roots are eclectic and receptive of racial, ethnic and linguistic diversities, the imprints imbibed are fully compatible with our secular constitution. Such a culture guarantees smooth relations between the individual and society. It is heartening that such type of a paradigm of development has received appreciative applause from different corners.[18]

Integral Humanism, again in tune with Vivekananda's philosophy refuses to share Marxian presumption of class struggle, though like Vivekananda's philosophy it shows deep concern about widespread poverty and inequality in the exploitative order of capitalist system. Pandit Deendayal's opposition to the concept of class conflict is rooted in his conviction that neither multifarious dimensions of an individual, nor different institutions of the society clash or conflict with each other. The extract below is the specimen of such conviction:

"If a conflict does exist, it is a sign of decadence, perversion and not of nature or culture. The error in western thinking lies in the fact that some people believe that human progress is a result of this fundamental conflict".[19]

---

18. *See* 1) Rajiv Lall, "The new right" in *The Indian Express* (Mumbai) January 18, 2017
19. p. 13 ii) Also Ramesh Venkataraman, "Hindu way to resist Hindutva" in *The Indian Express*, December 31, 2015, p. 15
19. *See* the Note No. 9, pp. 48-49

It was, in fact the same conviction on the part of Vivekananda which triggered his advice to Swami Akhandananda through the letter dated 21st February, 1900.

"You must take care not to setup class strife between the poor peasants, the labouring people and the wealthy classes".

One cannot of course subject Integral Humanism and Vivekananda's philosophy to subaltern critique as both of them have condemned hierarchical structure of Indian society and exploitative order of capitalism with sharp vehemence. Pandit Deendayal's fourth lecture on Integral Humanism mentions categorically that the principal drawback in capitalist viewpoint lies in its consideration of human labour as a commodity to be purchased with money as well as in displacing and subjecting human being to privations.[20] Pandit Deendayal's agony over alienations and fetishism of capitalist society is evidenced quite vividly in his analysis of capitalism. Pandit Deendayal nonetheless opposes the means of class-struggle, because of his knowledge of what had happened in the Soviet Union, where Marxis-Leninists entrusted the responsibility of the operation of class struggle to the government officials of the state. These officials, according to Pandit Deendayal, did put an end to private property through the elimination of the capitalist class. What hurt Pandit Deendayal most was the emergence of the new class of bureaucrats in the place of old fashioned capitalist exploiters. Here he refers to the book New Class penned by Milovan Djilas and noting the transformation of an ordinary Soviet citizen into an insignificant screw of a huge machine questions the outcome of the bloody Bolshevik Resolution[21]. Pandit Deendayal's attack on statism in the USSR reminds us of Vivekananda's crusade against a Leviathan State. He moreover points out that the Marxian theory of class struggle needs to be criticized for "its automotive and determinist viewpoint as well, because according to Marx, final class struggle is the inevitable, predetermined outcome of the world history. A dynamic, divine human being is thus converted into a tool of history".[22]

Pandit Deendayal has elucidated the concept of 'Dharma' in a very lucid and convincing manner. He has done it with a view to underscoring the significance of 'Dharma' in the Indian life. In his second lecture he offers the following definition of Dharma. All those

---

20. *Ibid.* p. 77
21. *Ibid.* p. 82, 83
22. *Ibid.* p. 28, 24. *Ibid.* p. 53, 25. *Ibid.* p. 58

principles which bring about harmony, peace and progress in the life of mankind are included in the term Dharma.[23]

When nature is channelized according to the principles of 'Dharma' we have culture and civilization. Pandit Deendayal's third lecture informs us that "Dharma sustains society".[24] It gives us to understand later that 'Dharma' connotes norms of human behaviour. Further one comes across, the following:

> "The fundamental law of human nature is the standard for deciding the propriety of behaviour in various situations. We have termed this very law as 'Dharma".[25]

According to Pandit Deendayal, 'Dharma', in short highlights what is appropriate, what is correct and therefore worth pursuit. It is against such background that Pandit Deendayal's apt analysis of 'Dharma-Rajya' gives us a right message. If 'Dharma' sustains our life, if 'Dharma' offers us lofty standards and norms for our behaviour, can we afford to remain deprived ourselves of Dharma? And how can our state say good-bye to Dharma? Pandit Deendayal-sponsored 'Dharma' no doubt, resembles fully with Vivekananda's Humanism. Nobody should indeed consider Dharma-Rajya as equivalent to a theocratic state.

Pandit Deendayal rightly points out that whereas a state in Dharma-Rajya accepts the role of Dharma in society and shoulders responsibilities in the light of Dharma, a theocratic state considers particular sect as supreme and discards all other sects as well as creeds. He further argues that due to a tie up between the state and the specific sect in theocracy the former slips in its duty.[23] Pandit Deendayal refers here to the specimen of Holy Roman Empire, as in his opinion, the idea of secularism had arisen in reaction to such empire. He in short invites our attention to the degeneration of the state as well as to that of Dharma in Holy Roman Empire. He rightly reminds us that the state in India has followed Dharma, that it has refused to confine itself with a specific religion or sect. No wonder, pseudo-secularist-condemnation of Dharma-Rajya is least palatable to Pandit Deendayal.

Pandit Deendayal's analysis brings to our notice that the state came into existence in India as a result of contract, and that is why, the contract theory is applicable to the state, but never to the nation nor to the society. One can substantiate this analysis by referring to the successful public revolt in one of the Indian states, say in the year 511

23. *Ibid.* p. 60
24. *Ibid.* p. 68
25. *Ibid.* p. 88

against Raja Mihirgul, a protagonist of Vedic sect who tortured Buddhists in his state. Pandit Deendayal's enlightening interpretation of one of the quotations of Bhishma Muni is equally worth the attention. This quotation runs as follows:

"Raja Kalasaya Karanam" (King shapes the circumstances).

Pandit Deendayal requests us to keep ourselves away from the widespread but wrong interpretation of this quotation that the king is over and above everything. He informs us that the king in the Indian ethos is akin to the executive in the parliamentary democracy, where it is the legislature which enacts laws and the executive is expected to implement these laws. Deendayal rightly argues here that the persons who are entrusted with the responsibility to implement laws honestly and efficiently must remain extraordinarily attentive even in personal transactions. This is the meaning of Bhishma's statement. It would be a mistake to interpret it as acceptance of approved supremacy of a king[24] Pandit Deendayal thus avers that as per Indian tradition, the king does not enact laws, he merely implements the laws enacted by sages and saints and it is through honest and efficient implementation of the laws, that the king sets an example for the people at large.

Philosophy of Integral Humanism aims at elevating 'nara' to Narayana' or the human to the divine. Sponsor of this philosophy is of course aware of the condition precedent to the achievement of such a sublime aim. This is why there is a mention at the end of the lecture series that each citizen must first be enabled to develop his manifold latent potentialities to the full extent[25]. Pandit Deendayal gives similar message to us through the following,

> "We should have a system which does not overwhelm our human quality, which does not make us slaves of its grinding wheels. **According to our concept, man attains God like perfection as a result of development".**[26]

The underlined portion of this extract is quite significant, as it invites our attention to the necessity of building a new holistic paradigm of development. This necessity was rooted in Pandit Deendayal's awareness of the limitations of one sided, Euro focal, homocentric Western ideologies of capitalism and communism! Pandit Deendayal's line of thinking is, no doubt a replica of Vivekananda's quotation as below:

"Society makes a milieu and opportunity available. Actual benefit

24. *Ibid.* p. 68
25. *Ibid.* p. 88
26. *Ibid.* p. 70

drawn depends on the level of culture absorbed by the individual".[27]

Pandit Deendayal like Vivekananda expects society to provide due surrounding to each member, whereby he or she can attain God-like perfection. Pandit Deendayal, of course, refuses to let market provide essential surrounding, as it enables only fit man to survive. In the same vein he distinguishes between society and state as he is aware of the disastrous consequences of statism. He informs us that as per Integral Humanism several autonomous institutions and organizations carry on the social life. He expects community-clusters, philanthropic organizations, business companies and banks to shape the social life under state guidance. Jaco Cilliers, the country director for the United Nations Development Programming in India substantiates Pandit Deendayal's viewpoint as follows:

> "Investment from the private sector into social development is an important piece for solving the financial puzzle, particularly when it comes to mobilizing capital to maximize development spending in priority areas for the government. India's philanthropic and business sectors can play a critical role in supporting and accelerating ongoing work in these areas. Renewing commitment, coordination and alignment between the government and the philanthropy sector could well bring much needed funds to the table, as well as constitute technical knowledge, skill and energy for development programs".[28]

Pandit Deendayal's reliance on the golden mean between capitalist market and the communist state undoubtedly shows a right direction to the present world, distressed due to Market-Darwinism. I have referred in the beginning of this write up to the healthy role played by community clusters as well as by humanistic, frugal and common sensical practices in India during post-cold war years. Jaco Cilliers adds to the evidence of the golden mean prevalent in India, through the following information:

> "Since 2009, India has added more than 100 million private donors, and they are contributing to a wide array of causes".[29]

Integral Humanism, no doubt opposes statism, It does have strong reservations regarding the role of the state in the development process. It does not, however, mean that this paradigm opts for total boycott of

27. Quated in Santvana Dasgupta, Social Philosophy of Swami Vivekananda (p. 191)
28. Jaco Cilliers, "Lending a Hand, filling a gap" in *The Indian Express* (Mumbai), February 22, 2017. p. 13
29. *Ibid.*

the institution of the state. It is actually quite grateful towards Dr. Ambedkar who had criticized ancient Indian's negligence of the state. Pandit Deendayal's viewpoint that state does play an important role (if not the central role) in the life of a nation seems to be quite relevant in the present context.

The latter half of the Twentieth century and particularly the years from 1947 to 1991 demonstrated ill marks of statism in India, such as widespread lack of work-culture, prevalence of subsidies, indebted state governments and so on. First two decades of the present century have however informed us of the disastrous consequences of the world-wide pursuit of greed on the part of the corporate sector. Oligarchy of large multinationals, property developers, bankers has squeezed the lives of the millions of common people. Such a world scenario has prompted even right wing politicians to favour state intervention in economic activities. A consensus has thus arisen that the state must tame market forces with a view to offering fairer wages, saner prices, affordable houses, and so on. Pandit Deendayal's Integral Humanism being fully aware of the horrible consequences of greedy, callous and self-centered capitalist practices lends credence to state intervention on such occasions.

To conclude, few of the most noteworthy lines that one comes across in Integral Humanism are,

"We want neither capitalism nor socialism. We aim at the progress and happiness of 'Man'- the integral Man. The protagonists of the two systems fight with Man on the stake. Both of them fail to understand man, nor do they care for his interest.

"Man, the highest creation of God is losing his identity. We must re-establish him in his rightful position".[30]

30. *Ibid.* p. 84.

7

Integral Humanism

A Quest for Swaraj in Ideas

The series of four lectures delivered by Pandit Deendayal on Integral Humanism in 1965 informs that Pandit Deendayal was bent on freeing post freedom India from cultural subjugation. The expounder of Integral Humanism was thus interested in carrying forward the legacy of Chandrashekharendra Saraswati, the then Shankaracharya of Kanchi-Kamakoti Peetham, who expected freedom to be converted into independence! Pandit Deendayal was in short, interested in decolonizing Indian Mind. He, of course happened to be affirmative in his approach. That was why, he implemented the views elaborated by Krishna Chandra Bhattacharya through the lecture, titled `Swaraj in Ideas'. Even a cursory glance at Pandit Deendayal's four lectures prompts one to observe that he has succeeded not only in decolonizing Indian mind but also in weaning global think tank away from Euro-centric paradigm. Contemporary global think tank does acknowledge with gratitude the debt, the world owes to Mahatma Gandhi. Such thinkers need to be reminded that Pandit Deendayal, following footsteps of Gandhiji responded in strongly similar idioms in trying to chart an ethical course for a new decolonized India.[1] Pandit Deendayal has, in other words relied heavily on Indian line of thinking not only in diagnosing problems, but also in prescribing remedial measures. And as present thinkers have come close to Indian line of

---

1. *See* Vamsee Juluri, 'Ahimsa has no political hue', in *The Hindu* (Chennai), 2nd October 2015, p. 15. (Vamsee Juluri is a professor at the University of San Francisco and the author of Rearming Hinduism.)

thinking, mirrored spontaneously in the philosophy of Integral Humanism, one can state that the contemporary global distancing from the European paradigm is reflective of the impact of Pandit Deendayal sponsored Integral Humanism.

It is extremely important to elaborate Integral Humanism as a quest for Swaraj in Ideas. First, it is crucial to know why Pandit Deendayal found it essential in 1965 to present the philosophy of Integral Humanism. The fact that almost all disoriented leaders of the early post freedom years of India were fascinated by Euro-centric line of thinking caused an anxiety to Pandit Deendayal. He therefore spent his first lecture for informing us of the disorientation of the then existing Indian leaders and thinkers. He also informed us through the same lecture how Euro-Americans themselves were then groping in dark. His observation that the Indian leaders of immediate post freedom years were aping Euro-Americans made him comment that "a blind is being led by another blind!" (अन्धेननीयमानाः यथान्धा)

Secondly, an attempt would be made to explain how Pandit Deendayal highlights the peculiar tenets of Integral Humanism. Pandit Deendayal thus gives us to understand how the Indian culture moulds our lives with a view to achieving our goal of emancipation set by Dharma. Pandit Deendayal's confidence in our civilization based on holistic foundation, shaped by due concern for the vulnerable sections of society and relying on mutual cooperation is articulated in a very lucid argumentation.

Thirdly, relations between individual and society as well as those between nation and state will be elucidated in the discourse. The elaboration of the concept of Dharma-Rajya in subsequent lines is a very logical unfoldment of this discourse.

Fourth and the final, section of the present paper is devoted to narrate contours of the development-trajectory compatible with our national ethos. Pandit Deendayal reminds that Indian economy is expected to facilitate everybody's march towards reaching divinity, that it is expected to produce and to allocate Indian resources suitable to national goal. The target is to supposedly develop into a cosmo-centric society.

Indian Political Scenario of Immediate Post-freedom Years:

An attempt to grasp the background or the setting against which Pandit Deendayal presented the philosophy of Integral Humanism leads one to study Pandit Deendayal's analysis of the political scenario that prevailed in India in the immediate post freedom years. Pandit

Deendayal points out that this scenario demonstrated certain features such as lack of due direction, absence of affirmative thinking, stark opportunism, fascination for Euro-centric viewpoints, etc. He himself refers to the neglect of 'Self' as the root cause for such perversions. He reminds us that during pre-freedom years, stalwarts like Lokamanya Tilak and Mahatma Gandhi had pondered over national self or national identity and had also thought about the direction towards which our nation should march with a view to accomplishing its mission. The fact that Indian leaders of the immediate post freedom years failed to carry ahead the legacy of such stalwarts caused a disappointment to him. We remember here Krishna Chandra Bhattacharya's historical speech titled 'Swaraj in Ideas' delivered in 1931 at Chandernagore[2], as Pandit Deendayal also expected in post freedom years that India's political Swaraj must be strengthened by Swaraj in Ideas.

It seems that Pandit Deendayal shared the anxiety expressed by Sri Aurobindo in the 1920s that “India's ancient culture, attacked by Western modernism, overpowered in the material field and betrayed by the indifference of her children may perish forever along with the soul of the nation that holds it in its keeping”.[3] It is a fact that all political parties, barring Swatantra Party were fascinated by Marxism. Swatantra Party advocated the cause of capitalism. All of them of course had a commonality, they were indifferent and apathetic about indigenous Indian culture and civilization.

They all actually had strong misgivings about Indian ethos. They, incidentally propagated that some 19th century born Indian stalwarts were advocates of Marxism and Socialism. Quite a few thinkers like Bhupendra Nath Datta, P. Govindan Pillai, K Damodaran went to the extent of calling Vivekananda as the forerunner of socialist thinking in India. In subsequent years one Mr. J. V. Naik rushed to state that “the credit of introducing Marx and his doctrine of class struggle to India for the first time belongs to Bal Gangadhar Tilak”.[4]

It is essential to point out here that the 19th century born Indian stalwarts did have great compassion and empathy for the marginalized and vulnerable members of society. And when they came to know that exploitative transactions of capitalism favoured wealth at the cost of wellbeing of masses, they became harsh critics of capitalism as well. But the source of inspiration in their cases lay in Vedanta sponsored

---

2. Quoted in Rakesh Sinha, *Swaraj in Ideas* (New Delhi, 201), p. 20.
3. Quoted in Anirban Ganguli, *Debating Culture* (New Delhi, 2013), p.132.
4. J. V. Naik, "Lokmanya Tilak on Karl Marx and Class conflict" in *Economic and Political Weekly* (Mumbai, 1 May, 1999), p. 1023

spiritualism and not in Marxism. One may allude to Vishnubawa Brahmachari's essay titled "Sukhadayak Rajyaprakarani" (Beneficent Government) published in 1867 in Mumbai, wherein government was appealed to impose collective ventures in production, consumption, lodging, boarding, etc. One may also refer to Bankim Chandra Chatterjee's write-up titled Samya in 1879. That both of these thinkers became protagonists of equality, equity and collectivity due to the impact of Vedanta-sponsored spiritual humanism is more than obvious. Swami Vivekananda, no doubt, did make a claim that 'I am socialist', but the claim was casual, mirroring his preference to socialism over capitalism. What is essential is to underscore that during the tour from Colombo to Almora, Swamiji pointed out inadequacies in the socialist paradigm and argued that only the foundation of spiritualism would provide solid infrastructure to the building of socialism. Pandit Deendayal's contemporaries in other political parties and organisations ignored all such actualities and took pride in projecting architects of Modern India not as worthy inheritors and apt interpreters of Vedas and Upanishads, but as advocates of socialism. Pandit Deendayal has condemned "such type of a contempt for things Bharatiya and respect for everything western".[5] He made a very notable comment in this context. "We had taken pride in resisting British things while they ruled us, but strangely enough, now that the Britisher's have left us, westernization has become synonymous with progress".[6]

What astonished Pandit Deendayal most was the fact that the Western World, the fountainhead of inspiration for his contemporaries in other political parties no longer had any charisma and glory. He therefore penned a pathetic portrait of the western world before highlighting U.S.Ps of Integral Humanism.

Genesis and Growth of European Doctrines

Pandit Deendayal has stated that three European doctrines such as nationalism, democracy and socialism need to be studied as the genesis and growth of these doctrines in Europe inform us of their peculiar traits. Thus, nationalism in Europe emerged in reaction to the 'holy' Roman Empire. 'New' nations which revolted against hegemonic holy Roman Empire received backing from Protestants from respective new royal families and from mercantile capitalists as well. Such an alliance had to fight against the camp comprising Catholics, old or traditional

5. Deendayal Upadhyay, Integral Humanism (Bombay, 1967), p. 12.
6. *Ibid.*

kings and queens, as well as feudal lords. The new alliance defeated the old camp and as newly emerged nations relied on new royal families, they practically became nation states.

These nation states initially advocated Protestantism; but the resultant theocracy crushed common individuals. No wonder, there emerged democracy, obviously in reaction to theocracy. European democracy took inspiration from the experiments of Greek city states. When democracy upheld the supremacy of individual and that of the Darwinian principle of the survival of the fittest, handful capitalists were bound to be winners. Democracy thus gave birth to plutocracy.

Capitalism naturally took strong roots in Europe. Pandit Deendayal points out here that the concentration of political and economic powers generated unjust and exploitative scenario. The victimized mill-workers were thus eager to seek an alternative path and the doctrine of socialism showed this path. Socialism, like two other doctrines (nationalism, and democracy) emerged in European continent in reaction to preceding order of capitalism.

Pandit Deendayal draws a correct conclusion at the end of this narration that Europe which has witnessed the emergence of reactionary and the state sponsored ideologies one after another cannot be treated as model by India. That the ancient nation such as India must probe into its past and opt for indigenous model of development was also underscored by Pandit Deendayal in the same vein. Pandit Deendayal has further stated that Western ideologies are mutually conflicting. Nationalism thus refuses to walk hand in hand with world peace. Democracy facilitates the rise of plutocracy and socialism gives birth to one party rule endangering individual liberty.

Let Indian Culture Shape our Development Path

Pandit Deendayal's prescription or recommendation to us to take into account the tenets of our culture while shaping our development path is thus logical, in view of his conviction that a disease in a particular place must be cured, though the remedy suitable to that particular place.

Pandit Deendayal-sponsored Integral Humanism is categorically affirmative in the sense that this philosophy is interested in converting India's freedom into independence. Integral Humanism has thus emerged not out of reaction to Western ideologies but due to conviction in Indian ethos.

Pandit Deendayal highlights that whereas Indian ethos believes in holistic or integral approach, the Euro-American paradigm relies on fragmentary or compartmental viewpoint. It is a fact that from the perspective of Indian ethos the divine manifests itself as the cosmos, that the divine is simultaneously transcendent or 'para' (external) as well as immanent or "apara'. So, God is the world; the cosmos. Rajiv Malhotra informs us that whereas Indian religions consider all reality (physical and non-physical) as inseparable from the divine, Abrahamic religions believe in intrinsic split between God and human beings.[7] He therefore points out that from the perspective of Indians, one observes here integral unity, the Euro-Americans, however start with inherently separate entities — 'God and creation, God and humanity, body and mind, spirit and matter, etc. and attempt to unite them. Such attempts on their part prompt us to call them as sponsors of synthetic unity. Thus, faith in the basic unity of all life is the first salient feature of Integral Humanism.

As it is our conviction that one and the same divinity prevails in all beings; in all entities we find that all of them are complementaries to each other. The second tenet of Integral Humanism is in short, an advice to the people at large to support each other and to show compassion and empathy for the vulnerable souls. The issue of National Geographic Magazine published in December 2008 incidentally informed the world that the Darwinian principle of Survival of the fittest need to be discarded because civilizational paradigm of competition is catastrophic. It has in fact recommended that the message given by Alfred Russell Wallace (a contemporary of Charles Darwin) that one should be fit enough to adapt to the environment deserves to be imprinted on our minds.[8] The conclusion drawn by the present world that we exist not to compete but to complete thus mirrors India's' faith in the complementary human transactions.

Third tenet of Integral Humanism that cooperation and not conflict mirrors culture is in tune with ever expanding spiral circles around an individual. These spiral circles inform of individual's symbiotic links with divinity through society and surrounding cosmos. Here Pandit Deendayal's core point is that culture moulds the nature with a view to achieving the social goals. In the same manner, Indian culture accordingly moulds Indian lives with a view to observing certain moral precepts and writs (Patanjali sponsored Yama-Niyams): not causing any

---

7. Rajiv Malhotra, *Being Different* (Noida: U.P, India, 2013), p. 101.
8. Quoted in Barney Wee and Agnes Lou, *Choices of Now* (San Diego, CA, USA, 2014), p. 257.

harm to anybody (Ahimsa), righteousness (Satya) not coveting the property of others (Asteya), complete abstinence (Brahmacharya), non-possession (Aparigraha); etc. Indian culture has also inspired us to be free from the impact of six lower tendencies or instincts such as desire, anger, greed, temptation, insolence and jealousy. Actually, its uniqueness lies in the concept of freedom. If Westerners emphasise "freedom to do what the respective individual wants to do", we Indians are interested in the freedom from above mentioned six lower tendencies. No wonder, we prefer cooperation to conflict; love to confrontation.

Integral Humanism, in short opts for holistic approach in the place of Descartian fragmentary worldview, compassion for the vulnerable souls, in the place of Darwinian Mantra of Survival of the fittest and cooperation in the place of Marx sponsored class-conflict. It does of course sanction Ugra Danda-State (Hard government) in the place of Ksheena Danda-State (Soft government) against unjust exploitative capitalist-kleptocrats.

Fourth tenet of Integral Humanism is the acceptance of the concept of a complete integrated human being as the goal as well as the path. Pandit Deendayal has made the following statement in the course of his lecture series on Integral Humanism: "The fundamental difference between our position and that of the West is that whereas they have regarded body and the satisfaction of its desires as the aim, we regard the body as an instrument for achieving our aim".[9] Pandit Deendayal has elucidated our aim in fourth lecture of the Mumbai-series; where he states that as per Indian ethos, society is supposed to take care of the old, diseased and invalid. And just after this statement he makes the most significant comment mirroring 'our aim'.[10] The comment runs as follows: "Parameter of man's social concern and his culture is his promptness to take care of the downtrodden". The aim, a human being is expected to pursue evidences genuine Swaraj in Ideas.

Fifth tenet of Integral Humanism is the unique idea of the society. Society and nation are synonymous, in the sense that they are self-born; they emerge; they are not created or formed artificially. They are accordingly unlike a club or an organization. A society or a nation is identified by a specific kind of psychological attitude. Badrishah Thulgharia avers that society is a natural, organic, biological creation.

---

9. *See* the Note no. 5, p.33.
10. See *Ekatma Manav Darshan* (New Delhi, 2012), p.65 (A book in Hindi)

.... The features and propensities that are the hallmarks of any biological entity are found also in the communities.[11]

The concept of Nation or Society, from the view-point of Integral Humanism possesses a body in the form of geocultural entity of the land; it also has a mind-the collective urge and the resolve of the society for upliftment and overall progress; its intellect is observable in the formulation of customs and conventions, do's and dont's; and its soul means the conscious identity of the nation, the Chiti.[12]

The Western narration of society is of course different; it informs us that it was the agreement among individuals titled "Social Contract Theory" that has shaped the formation of society. As an individual is given utmost significance in this narration, the most valid question attempted here runs as follows: "As the individuals have created society (through coming together), does an individual enjoy supremacy over society or does society possess veto-power?" Indian ethos considers this question as totally irrelevant because from its viewpoint, society is self-born, it does not come into existence through cohabitation or through contract. I have already stated above that like an individual each society also possesses body, mind, intellect and soul. Integral Humanism asserts that if an individual requires society for his or her development to the full extent, society also finds it indispensable to find and to recognize the worth and specialty of each individual. Thus, there is no conflict or clash between individual and society. K. G. Mashruwala has stated that the relationship of the individual to society is that of a receiver during childhood. In a semi-advanced stage, the relationship grows into one of mutual deal. As development proceeds further, the urge to give and serve the weak becomes intense.[13]

Indian narration about the genesis and growth of social institutions is also quite different from that of Europe. It considers society as a web of relations. An individual who is initially linked with the family, subsequently gets linked with the community, later with society and finally with the cosmos through humanity. All these expanding circles, emanating from the individual are related symbiotically with each other. The European narration based on compartmentalist thinking treats very circles as totally separate from each other. According to Indian ethos, it is gradual development of individual's consciousness that facilitates human journey from self-centred individualism to

---

11. Badrishah Thulgharia, *Daishik Shastra* (Varanasi, 2003), p. 24.
12. Dr. Bapu, Kendurkar, "Ekatma Manava Darshan-Eternal Hindu View of 'Life", in Raveendara Mahajan (ed.) *Ekatma Manava Darshan-Vichar Samgraha* (Ahmedabad, 2014), p. 42.
13. K.G. Mashruwala, *Gandhi & Marx*, pp. 56, 57.

universal citizenship. European ethos however, involves external agency like social contract theory or government to facilitate just mentioned journey. There do emerge several social institutes including the institute of the state though the story of the emergence and rise of the state is unique and therefore it deserves a special treatment.

Sixth tenet: State is one of the institutes of society or Nation. Amongst all social institutes, State is most powerful; this is why it is bound to society through a contract. It cannot afford to ignore societal aspirations. In case, it dares to violate this Laxman-Rekha, society has got right to revolt against state! Demise of the USSR in 1991 is the latest example of this phenomenon; there have emerged fifteen nations at the cost of the USSR. Integral Humanism asks us in the similar vein to take into account the significance of the due role played by state in society. Our Indian nation has not paid due attention to the preservation of state, therefore it had to suffer from subjugation, from external aggressions. Indian ethos, in short offers primacy, if not supremacy to state in the national life. The interpretation offered by Pandit Deendayal to Bhishma-Maharshi's famous quotation deserves to be studied in this context. The quotation runs as follows: राजाकालस्य कारणम् (Raja Kalasya Karanam). Let me now refer to Pandit Deendayal's interpretation: "Bhishma categorically stated that the king shapes his circumstances. Now some persons do interpret this to mean that he considered the king above all. But this is not true. He did not suggest that the king was above Dharma. It is true that the king wielded a great deal of influence and that he was the protector of Dharma in society, but the king could not decide what constitutes Dharma. He only saw to it that people led their lives according to Dharma. In a way he was equivalent to the present-day executive".[14] Pandit Deendayal's interpretation is worth due consideration. In parliamentary democracy, no Prime Minister can ignore parliament's decisions. The Prime Minister is supposed to execute those decisions. Ancient Indian polity thus asked the king to implement the rule of the Law. Pandit Deendayal sponsored Integral Humanism informs us that the English term 'Innate Law' is the nearest equivalent for 'Dharma' This is why, it rejects to call Dharma-Rajya as a theocratic state. 'Dharma' is wider than a religion or a religious place. As it is akin to the Innate Law, manifesting and maintaining or sustaining Chiti or the soul of the nation, state is committed to protect Dharma. Such Dharma-Rajya never discriminates against any religious sect. Nor does it offer secondary citizenship to any person on the basis of his faith.

14. *See* the Note no. 5, pp. 67-68.

Indigenous Development Trajectory

The development-trajectory chalked out by Integral Humanism for India is genuinely indigenous; it mirrors Swaraj in Ideas. Pandit Deendayal reminds us that we Indians do share with Europeans the viewpoint that 'man does not live by bread alone'. He however informs us in the similar vein that 'man lives for shouldering responsibility towards children and the old, the diseased and the invalids'.[15] As per Indian ethos the aim of human life is 'Moksha', or 'Self-emancipation' and each one of us is expected in the light of this aim to work for enhancing the wellbeing of the people.

It has already been stated that during immediate post freedom years of India, our leaders and thinkers suffered not only from self-oblivion, but also from disorientation and confusion. It was against such setting that Integral Humanism conveyed to Indians at large that we-Indians are fundamentally spiritualists, which like all other religions, those emerged in India have also treated downtrodden masses as our Gods to be worshipped and served. Uniqueness of Integral Humanism lies in underscoring the aim of human life while speaking about development trajectory.

Integral Humanism forcefully avers that 'we should have a system which does not overwhelm our humane quality.' It brings to our notice that the very imperative asks us to give priority to the satisfaction of the basic minimum requirements and subsequently to the production of goods and services for greater prosperity and happiness. Pandit Deendayal's philosophy however rushes in this context to warn us against the dangers of consumerism, permissivism and philistinism! It also contains an appeal to us to preserve human values.

That a human being needs to be cosmocentric, in the place of anthropocentric has moreover been emphasized by the paradigm of Integral Humanism. It is essential to remember here that the well-known socialist thinker like Ashok Mehta also articulated his anxiety over the demolition of humane qualities due to the spread of monstrous super-technology of ultra-industrialism. His fear is quotable here: “The march of industrialism loosens some of the organic links between man and nature. He is made rootless and footloose, not in the social dimension, but in his deepest biological foundation”.[16] Pandit Deendayal points out that ultra-industrialism is in-compatible with India's economy, as it causes disharmony between Samashti' and

15. *Ibid.* p. 74.
16. Quoted in Kandarpa Ramachandra Rao, *Integral Humanism* (Hyderabad, 1995), p. 289.

Srishti'. He rightly states that from the angle of Indian economy, our goal as well as our path are worshippers of Integral Humanism.

Man's Place in the Economy

Integral Humanism considers labourer as a very valuable human being. It criticizes the paradigms of capitalism and Marxism on the ground that both 'isms' deprive labourers of surplus values. Both paradigms, moreover sponsor large scale, centralised industrial empires causing alienation and fetishism! No wonder, Integral Humanism favours decentralization with a view to offering opportunity of direct participation to a common worker.

If the demise of the USSR in 1991 brought to notice that entrusting every activity to the state causes catastrophic anarchy; Lehman crisis of 2008 informed us that reliance on self-interest of an individual equally proves catastrophic. The third alternative suggested by Joseph Stiglitz and Thomas Piketty whereby market must be regulated by the state thus deserves our due attention. Integral Humanism reminds us of a very interesting and enlightening shloka from ‘Raghuwansha’ of Kalidas. The shloka runs as follows:

प्रजानांविनयाधानात् रक्षणात् भरणादपि।
सः पितापितरस्तासांकेवलंजन्महेतवः।।

The great Sanskrit poet Kalidas describes here how King Dilip was considered by his subjects as their father! “Being responsible for the maintenance, protection and education, Raja Dilip became the true father for his subjects”- thus runs the Shloka. Pandit Deendayal conveys to us through such description that the government should invite private institutions to come ahead with a view to shouldering responsibilities of providing education and health to the people. Maintenance of law and order as well as guarding of borders of the state are, of course the exclusive domains of the government. But other sectors of economy and society can be entrusted to society at large. The government should however keep a close watch and put its foot down if the wealthy tycoons start exploiting common masses. Here Pandit Deendayal's views seem to be quite resembling with those of Stiglitz and Piketty. In no case there should arise the 'Great Divide' between the 'Haves' and the 'Have Nots'.

Integral Humanism asks the government to provide six public goods to citizens through social institutions. Food, clothing, shelter, education, health and due dignity be provided (of course through public-private participation) by the government. It expects the government to compel the tycoons, kleptocrats and rich 'Shylocks' to do justice to common masses. It suggests in the same vein that the government should honour democratic norms while dealing with 'just' dissenters.

The 'Man' or the 'Woman' from the perspective of Integral Humanism thus occupies a key position in the economy, polity and society at large. The very man as well as woman are of course requested by Integral Humanism to go on widening and broadening their visions, to be compassionate and empathetic regarding marginalized and vulnerable masses.

It was during immediate post freedom years of India that the protagonists of capitalism as well as those of Marxism were busy in making tall claims of the respective paradigms. Simon Kuznets, for example then argued that during post Second World War years, the capitalist societies were bound to witness in subsequent decades withering away of socio-economic inequalities; that they were sure to find wealth and well-being marching together, hand in hand. Protagonists of the USSR were equally enthusiastic in advocating the cause of Marxism. Pandit Deendayal's Integral Humanism however challenged all such claims during 1960s. One comes across a very categorical critical analyses of both 'isms' in Integral Humanism. Read the following statements: "Both 'isms' result in dehumanization of man". "We want neither capitalism, nor socialism". We aim at the progress and happiness of "Man", "the Integrated Man".

Pandit Deendayal's prescription of remedial measures which asks us to implement `Swadeshi' in everything, from thinking, management, capital, methods of production, technology etc, to the standards and forms of consumption is really a reflection of Swaraj in Ideas. It is a conviction on the part of Integral Humanism that only the Swaraj in Ideas would enable us to free ourselves from cultural subjugation, from colonisation.

8

Gita-Rahasya

A Fountainhead of Integral Humanism

It was in April 1965 that Pandit Deendayal spoke about expounding the philosophy of Integral Humanism in all four lectures delivered in Mumbai. Pandit Deendayal seemed immensely perturbed over the then prevailing serious disorientation in the Indian polity. He vented his perturbation through the following content of the first lecture:

> "Having attained independence the question naturally ought to have occurred to us: "Now that we are independent what shall be the direction of our progress?" However, serious thought has not been given to this question and today even after seventeen years of independence we cannot say that a definite direction has been decided upon".[1]

Pandit Deendayal found that post-independence Indian leaders lacked in clarity about the direction of the trajectory of India's development and hence, they were interested in finding out short term solutions of the then existing problems. Pandit Deendayal noted that whereas pre-independence Indian leaders like Gandhi and Tilak were determined in shaping India in the mould suitable to the Indian ethos, post-independence Indian leaders suffered from disorientation. He therefore stated at the outset of the first lecture that Gandhi and Tilak pondered over the face of the new Bharat after independence and also

1. *Ekatma Manav Darshan* (New Delhi, 2012), p. 2

over the direction Bharat would opt for in its march on the development -path. He pointed out in other words that Gandhi and Tilak were exceptional leaders, that they pursued long term vision of India and accordingly refused to confine themselves exclusively to anti-British activities. The fact that Tilak's 'Gita-Rahasya' had acquired a special space in the heart of Pandit Deendayal, is mirrored in the following lines of the first lecture on Integral Humanism:

> "Lokamanya Tilak discussed the philosophical basis of the rejuvenation of Bharat in his book "Gita-Rahasya." He gave a comparative exposition of various schools of thought all over the world at that time".[2]

Pandit Deendayal referred to Tilak again during the course of the third lecture where he highlighted the fact that the undaunted pursuit of 'Dharma' enabled Tilak to be a unique architect of Modern India.

> "No wonder, his pledge that "Swaraj is my birth right and I shall have it" became the articulation of the people's voice".[3]

It is a fact that Tilak practiced what he preached, that he led his life in the light of the esoteric import of Gita. This reality explains to us why he became Lokamanya, acceptable to people at large. And Pandit Deendayal was impressed by this very reality. A succinct review of the essays written by Pandit Deendayal on the life and mission of Tilak informs us very vividly of Pandit Deendayal's devotion for Tilak.

Survey of Pandit Deendayal's Essays on Tilak

Pandit Deendayal's first write up on Tilak titled 'Lokamanya's Political Astuteness' saw the light of the day in the issue of ' Panchajaynna' dated 29th July 1948. Pandit Deendayal was perhaps the only non-Marathi leader who considered the first post-independence birthday of Tilak as the right occasion for underscoring how Tilak's legacy needed to be carried forward in the post-independence years in India. Pandit Deendayal's observation articulated in this write-up that Tilak's political astuteness was shaped by his vision pertaining to national reconstruction. This was remarkable as Pandit Deendayal himself considered Jana Sangha, the political formation nursed by him with utmost concern as an instrument of national reconstruction. His statement quoted below is thus autobiographical:

2. *Ibid.* p. 1
3. *Ibid.* p. 55

> "Lokamanya's conviction led him to believe that national reconstruction is impossible without imbibing individuals with national spirit and such sort of imbibing or instilling is impossible without awakening national soul. That is why, Lokamanya gave priority to the awakening of national soul over all other activities".[4]

Pandit Deendayal substantiates his view point by alluding to Tilok's unique innovations such as launching of newspapers like *'Kesari'* and *'Marhatta'*, initiative in organising *Ganeshotsava* and *Shivajayantyutsava*. Efforts were taken to involve the common masses in constructive as well as agitational activities, etc. According to Pandit Deendayal, it was a conviction on the part of Tilak that political agitations in India succeed only if innate national spirit of Indians is awakened through spiritual tune. As Tilak shared this vision with Vivekananda and Dayananda, India underwent a historical civilizational and cultural upsurge under the leadership of these visionaries.

After the death of Vivekananda and Dayananda, Tilak walked hand in hand with Lala Lajpat Rai and Bipin Chandra Pal. Indian polity thus marched ahead under the captainship of the trinity of Lal, Bal and Pal.

From Pandit Deendayal's perspective, Tilak succeeded through the above mentioned unique innovations in generating historical bonhomie and togetherness among people at large. It was again through such innovations that Tilak made people aware not only of their cultural identity, but also of the necessity to be prepared to face ordeals for preserving this identity. As Tilak volunteered to confront all ordeals including imprisonments, he became Lokamanya, acceptable to masses. Pandit Deendayal points out in this context that whereas moderate congress leaders were hungry for being 'rajamanya' to get accepted by the government, Tilak was least interested in getting recognized or honoured by anybody in any respect. Pandit Deendayal's write up reminds us of Sri Aurobindo's appreciation of Tilak through the following words:

> "The Congress-movement was for a long time purely occidental in its mind, character and methods, confined to the English educated few, founded on the political rights and interests of the people read in the light of English history and European ideals, but with no roots either in the past of the country or in the inner spirit of the nation. Mr. Tilak was the first political leader to break through the

---

4. *See* 'Lokamanyaki Rajniti' in *Deendayal: Sampoorna Vangmaya*: Vol.1 (New Delhi, 2016), p. 210

routine of its somewhat academical methods, to bridge the gulf between the present and the past and to restore continuity to the political life of the nation. He developed a language and a spirit and he used methods which Indianized the movement and brought into it the masses".[5]

The paragraph titled 'Gita Dharma' in Pandit Deendayal's first write-up on Tilak's life and mission mirrors his ability to grasp the crux of his life. Pandit Deendayal informs us through this paragraph that according to Tilak, religious spirit is a 'sine qua non' in our national life in the sense that without generating this spirit our nation can never progress. From Tilak's viewpoint, our nation's religious spirit, that is, our 'Rashtra-Dharma' is equivalent to 'Gita-Dharma'. It seems that Pandit Deendayal was quite fascinated by Tilak's elaboration of 'Gita-Dharma', attempted in the concluding section of the magnum opus Gita -Rahasya. He therefore quotes the following extract verbatim from the concluding section of *Gita-Rahasya.*

> "The religion of the Gita which is a combination of Spiritual Knowledge, Devotion and Action, which is in all respects undauntable and comprehensive, and is further equable, that is, which does not maintain any distinction between classes, castes, countries or any other distinction, but gives release to everyone in the same measure, and at the same time shows proper forbearance towards other religions, is thus seen to be the sweetest and immortal fruit of the tree of the Vedic Religion".[6]

Just after quoting this extract, Pandit Deendayal reminds one that Tilak implemented Gita-Dharma through uninterrupted active life both personal and social. Later it was on 1st August 1955 that Pandit Deendayal penned another write up on Lokamanya Tilak in the issue of *Panchajanya.* This write up contained very notable points which give us to understand the lessons drawn by Pandit Deendayal from the dedicated life of Tilak. They are as follows:

1) Lokamanya was the first national leader who rid freedom struggle of the hackneyed and stereotype conferences, speeches and also of armed chair deliberations.
2) From the perspective of Tilak, Indians would obtain freedom through self-reliance and not through the mercy of the Britishers.

5. "An Appreciation by Babu Aurobind Ghose", a Preface to Bal Gangadhar Tilak: His writings and speeches (Madras), p. XV
6. B.G. Tialk, *Gita-Rahasya* (Pune, 2012), p. 712 (English version)

3) Indians have seen in Tilak a self-confident sage fully competent to dive in the ocean of knowledge with a view to presenting to the world the supremacy of Hindu philosophy.

Such a survey of Pandit Deendayal's essays on Tilak will remain incomplete if we ignore his write-up titled 'India from the vision of Lokamanya' published in the issue of 'Panchajanya' dated 24th August 1959. Most remarkable content from the write-up runs as follows:

> "Tilak's *Karma Yoga Shastra* (the Science of Right Action) and Badri Shah Tooldharia's *Deshik Shastra* are complementary to each other. A study of both of these books is a 'must' for the fellow engaged in the task of national reconstruction".

Tilak's Exposition of Gita-Dharma

As stated above that the equivalence between *Gita Dharma* and *Rashtra-Dharma* as advocated by Tilak received hearty welcome from Pandit Deendayal. From the perspective of Pandit Deendayal, Tilak's advocacy of Gita-Dharma on the basis of the convincing interpretation of Gita, caters to the needs of contemporary India as well. This is why, Pandit Deendayal felt deeply fascinated by the peculiarities of the exposition of Gita-Dharma in Tilak's magnum opus. As these shaped Pandit Deendayal's unique view-point, elaboration of such peculiarities is essential here. One must, however first note the unique viewpoint articulated by Pandit Deendayal through the following content:

> "We must absorb the knowledge and gains of the entire humanity so far eternal principles and truths are concerned. Of these the ones that have originated in our midst must be adapted to changed times, and those that we take from other societies have to be adapted to our conditions".[7]

As for the unique peculiarities of the Gita-Rahasya, one can list them as follows:

1) Tilak succeeded in scattering the fog of misunderstanding regarding the import of Gita. He has thus proved that the principal subject-matter of the Gita is neither renunciation, nor devotion but unattached action.
2) Tilak accepts that the Bhagavad Gita does show interest in exposing the path of obtaining release through the acquisition of knowledge of the pure form of the *Parameshwara*. He has in fact stated quite categorically that acquisition of this knowledge

7. *See* the Note no. 1, p. 16

is the primary duty of every human being because such an acquisition enables all to purify reason as far as possible. Tilak has in fact stated that according to Gita, one must pursue Karma Yoga, in the sense that one should engage himself in the worship of God through desireless action based on knowledge. ज्ञानमूलक and भक्तिप्रधान action is the genuine कर्मयोग. Interpretation of Gita thus amounts in other words to convince reconciliation of renunciation, devotion and action.

3) Tilak has proved that various theses pertaining to *Karma Yoga* put forth by ancient Indian sages continue to be relevant in the modern times. He has actually stated that the Western thinkers have now found it essential to go beyond material knowledge for grasping ethics and the science of release. That Western metaphysics merely echoes the doctrines of Gita was also pointed out rationally by Tilak. For instance, Tilak admits that in Christian and Jewish religious texts, one comes across the most golden metaphysical commandment:
"Thou shalt love thy neighbour as thy self".
This commandment thus articulates the principle of self-identification (आत्मौपम्य). Tilak however reminds that it was not Jesus Christ who initiated this principle as traces are found in the writings of Greek philosopher Aristotle as well as in Chinese philosopher Confucius who were predecessors of Jesus. He points out in the same vein that the very principle of self-identification was pronounced quite clearly, long before Confucius in the *Upanishads*. This peculiarity of Tilak's *Gita Rahasya* in short lies, in its assertive presentation that Upanishads and Gita deserve to be honoured as first treatise on the discrimination between Right and Wrong Action (कार्याकार्यविवेक) or (नीतिशास्त्र).

4) Gita has demonstrated that the materialistic philosophers' perception of the conflict between concepts such as Release (मो क्ष), Devotion (भक्ती) and Ethics (नीतिशास्त्र) is groundless. It has actually proved that there is no conflict between knowledge (ब्रह्मज्ञान) and action (कर्म) and accordingly declared the viewpoint of the protagonists of the School of Renunciation (संन्यासमार्ग) as baseless. Tilak in fact points out that according to Gita, ethics is based on the fundamental principles of Knowledge (ब्रह्मज्ञान) and Devotion (भक्ती) . Gita is thus unique as it goes a step ahead and asks every one of us to consider

unattached or desireless action based on knowledge as the worship of God. Tilak's comment states:

> "The Gita is thus essentially a treatise on Right or Proper Action (कर्मयोग) , and that is why, it has been given a position of supreme importance in all Vedic treatise, which refer to it as ब्रहमविद्यान्तर्गत कर्मयोगशास्त्र (the Science of Right Action included in the Science of the Brahamna)".[8]

Tilak's Disquisition and its Impact on Pandit Deendayal

It is a fact that Tilak's disquisition of the esoteric import of Gita left indelible imprints on Pandit Deendayal. That certain salient features of Tilak's disquisition endeared themselves to Pandit Deendayal is crystal clear! One may thus refer to them as commencement as well as the end of disquisition, uninterrupted pursuit of the mission, logical rebuttal of sectarian interpretations, systematic substantiation of the thesis through solid evidences, dexterity in weaving several thought currents with a view to arriving at the truth, and so on.

Commencement as well as the End of Disquisition

Pandit Deendayal felt that in the opinion of Tilak, Indians are basically religious minded and therefore awakening of the religious spirit is a 'must' in the task of national reconstruction in India. And as the Gita contains very clear and succinct elaboration of the principles of Hindu Dharma, Tilak decided to highlight the esoteric import of Gita through his magnum opus. The preface of Gita-Rahasya vividly suggests Tilak's motive behind commencing his disquisition. The content most relevant in this connection runs as follows :

> "In Gita lies the entire essence of Right and Wrong Action and the Blessed Lord Himself has confidently given us the assurance that the observance of this Religion, even to a small extent delivers a person from great difficulties. What more can anybody want? Keep in mind the universal rule that 'Nothing happens unless something is done', and devote yourselves to Desireless Action, that is all".[9]

If Tilak's disquisition commences with an appeal to the Indian youth to pursue *Karma-Yoga*, it culminates in the end in inculcating in the Indian youth the imprint that *Gita-Dharma* is the *Rashtra-Dharma.* As Pandit Deendayal epitomised unattached life he was quite impressed

8. *See* the Note no. 6, p. xxv
9. "Author's Preface to *Gita-Rahasya*", *Ibid.* p. xxxi

by Tilak's unswerving emphasis on unattached action during the discourse of disquisition from commencement to the end.

Uninterrupted Pursuit of the Mission

As earlier stated, according to Sri Aurobindo, it was Tilak (before Gandhi) who brought common masses into India's freedom movement. It was in fact a mission on the part of Tilak to activate common people to fight against British rule in India. That is why, the energetic interpretation of Gita gripped his mind. Once he grasped that Gita considers judicious combination of jnana and karma as the best path, the propagation of this path became a life mission for him. Tilak has succeeded in demonstrating that as per Gita, unattached social involvement before as well as after self-realization is preferable to the path of renunciation. He has quoted the eleventh stanza of *Ishavasya Upanishad* as follows:

विद्या चाऽविद्यांच यस्तद्वेदोभयं सह। अविद्यया मृत्युं तीर्त्वा विद्ययाऽमृतमश्नुते।।

(That man who understands both vidya (Jnana) and *avidya (Karma)* at the same time goes through the affairs of the *mrityu* that is, of the perishable illusory world, by means of *avidya (Karma),* and attains immortality by means of *vidya.* (the realisation of the Brahman)

Tilak has accordingly substantiated his advocacy of the simultaneous possession of Jnana and Karma through this quotation. He has later offered the unique definition of Lokasamgraha (लोकसंग्रह) with a view to pleading that even the attainment of मोक्ष, that is, emancipation depends on social involvement. This definition is as follows:

> "carrying on properly the affairs of the mortal world is called Lokasamgraha in the Gita. The commentary of Tilak in this connection is worth mentioning".

"It is true that obtaining Release (मोक्ष) is the duty of every man, yet, as it is also essential that he should simultaneously bring about universal welfare (लोकसंग्रह) that the Gita has laid down the doctrine that the Jnanin should not give up this *Karma*, which is productive of universal welfare, and the same doctrine has been propounded in the line, "अविद्यया मृत्युं तीर्त्वा विद्ययाऽमृतमश्नुते।" mentioned above, with only a verbal difference".[10]

Pandit Deendayal's similar statement that even the, attainment of release or मोक्ष depends on one's social involvement is indeed in full consonance with Tilak's argumentation. One comes across Pandit

10. *See* the Note no. 6, p. 502

Deendayal's statement in one of his essays published in the issue of *Rashtra-Dharma* dated September 5, 1956. Pandit Deendayal has actually interpreted the following सुभाषितम् in a unique manner: "यतो धर्मस्ततो जयः ।" (Victory follows the pursuit of Dharma.)

According to Pandit Deendayal, *Dharma* means समूहधर्म (the Dharma of collectivity). He reminds all in this context that Pandavas won in the war against Kauravas because whereas they followed समूहधर्म , the latter ran after respective individual's name and fame.[11]

Such elaboration thus provides evidence to the claim that *Gita-Rahasya* is a fountain head of Pandit Deendayal's Integral Humanism!

What must have impressed Pandit Deendayal most is the fact that during the course of disquisition, Tilak never deviates even by an inch from the pursuit of his mission of activating people to engage themselves in desireless actions. One may refer to the last chapter - "Conclusion" of the *Gita-Rahasya*. Tilak provides at the outset of this chapter the following line from the Gita and literally rushes to offer a comment over this line through the footnote on one and the same page. The line from the Gita is as follows:

"तस्मात् सर्वेषु कालेषु मामनुस्मर युद्धयच च ।।"

(Therefore at all times remember me and fight.)

The comment at the footnote, interestingly, runs as follows:

"The word 'fight' has been used in regard to the occasion, but it does not mean only fight, but must be considered to'perform all Actions pertaining to life'.[12]

Tilak has in short utilized *Bhagwan Shri Krishna's* guidance to *Arjuna* as an effective means for generating apt activism among Indian masses. He has thus accomplished his life-mission even while undergoing six years of his confinement or punishment in the jail at Mandaley. And from the perspective of Pandit Deendayal he has adapted our ancient philosophy to the modern circumstance.

Logical Rebuttal of Sectarian Interpretations:

Tilak's rationale in rebutting sectarian interpretations of *Gita* seems to have impacted Pandit Deendayal. Thus the 17th verse of the third chapter of *Gita* prompted the protagonists of the path of renunciation to claim that according to Bhagawan Shri Krishna, for the fellow who is merged only in the *Atman*, no work is there to do. Swami Vivekananda

---

11. *See* 'मम मम मम' in Rashtra-Dharma, 5 September 1956
12. *See* the Note no. 6, p. 664: footnote

also shares the view that apparent interpretation of this verse does run on these lines. He says, the verse यत् स्वात्मरनिरेवस्यादात्मतृप्तश्च मानवः आत्मन्येवच संतुष्टस् तस्य कार्यम् न विद्यते। can be translated in the following wording:

> "He whose devotion is to the *Atman*, he who does not want anything beyond *Atman*, he who has become satisfied in the *Atman*, what work is there for him to do?"[13]

From the perspective of Swamiji, such an apparent interpretation, however, does not do genuine justice to the purport of Gita. The phrase 'तस्य कार्यं न विद्यते।' - actually means, "for the knower, nothing (as of his own) remains in balance".

The knower in other words is not supposed to engage himself or herself in any selfish activity. If Tilak substantiates his rationale by referring to Vasishtha Muni's advice to Shri Ram, Swamiji alludes to Shri Ramakrishna Paramhamsa's catechism. Swami Vivekananda has stated his views in the following way:

> "After realization, what is ordinarily called work does not persist. It changes the character. The work which the Jnani (knower) does only conduces to the well-being of the world. Whatever a man of realisation says or does contributes to the welfare of all. We have observed Shri Ramakrishna - he was as it were देहस्थोऽपि न देहस्थ : "in the body, but not out of it".[14]

Tilak's style of rebuttal of sectarian interpretations of Gita nowhere mirrors an iota of dogmatism. He in fact showers appreciation on the life of a real Jnanin through the following content:

> "If a Jnanin is filled with a sincere disgust for worldly life and renounces the world...there is no sense in finding fault with him".[15]

Tilak's accommodative approach similarly favours the path of devotion as 'it is easy for everybody to follow this path'.[16]

Systematic Substantiation of the Thesis

Tilak's painstaking marshalling of facts, examples and quotations - for strengthening his argumentation, is equally impressive. Thus in 'the Introductory' of *Gita–Rahasya*, a reader comes across the energistic

13. *See* selections from Swami Vivekananda, (Culcutta, 1981), p. 221
14. *Ibid.* p. 442
15. *See* the Note no. 6, p. 659
16. *Ibid.* p. 613

purport of Gita. Tilak informs the reader at the end of the Introductory that if the Non-Dualistic philosopher Paramahamsa Shri Krishnananda Swami (a resident of Kashi) underscored the viewpoint that *Gita* is the philosophy of Duty, the German philosopher Prof. Daussen as well as several Eastern and Western critics of the *Gita* have endorsed the same comment. Entire *Gita-Rahasya* is indeed full of supportive specimens! Pandit Deendayal must have felt fascinated by the missionary zeal on the part of Tilak.

Dexterity in Weaving Several Thought Currents

It was a conviction on the part of Tilak that unattached action is superior to renunciation. The eleventh chapter of *Gita-Rahasya* has therefore been devoted to substantiate this conviction. Thus when the Blessed Lord himself performs several actions for the maintenance of the world, there is no sense in saying that the performance of actions after the acquisition of knowledge is useless. Great personalities like Adi Shankaracharya and Samartha Ramadas Swami also remained busy throughout their lives with a view to enhancing public welfare. Tilak thus weaves various specimens and underscores the point that desireless actions need to be pursued by all of us.

Elaboration of Tilak's Skill in Weaving Arguments

It seems that Tilak's dexterity or skill in superb weaving of several thought-currents must have impacted Pandit Deendayal, as it mirrors wide reach, rationality as well as selection of apt terms and phrases. As for wide reach, one must read *Gita-Rahasya's* chapter titled 'Renunciation and Karma-Yoga'.

Tilak underscores here the statement in the *Gita:*

"कर्म ज्यायो ह्यकर्मण:" (Action is superior to Non-Action) by referring to the comment made by Augustus Comte, a well-known French philosopher. As per this comment, no philosopher is supposed to abandon the activity of public welfare. Tilak endorses in this vein the just mentioned *Gita* statement by alluding to a very harsh remark passed by one of the modern philosophers 'Nietzsche'. The remark is as follows:

One cannot refer to the supporters of renunciation by any milder terms than 'fools of fools'. Tilak's wide plunge is observable equally at the end of the subsequent chapter titled 'State of Siddha and worldly affairs'. Tilak in fact ends this chapter by proving the superiority of

Indian philosophy over the philosophy of utilitarianism advocated by Mill and others. Indian philosophy, for instance teaches me to rely on equability through realising that "the other man is the same as myself".

Our philosophy thus asks me to enquire whether the motive of the doer is pure. The philosophy of utilitarianism on the other hand asks people at large to pay attention to the external results of action and to judge if the greatest good of the greatest number is served. Tilak concludes that ethics is superior to far-sightedness. His rationality or logical argumentation acquires very bold profile in his commentary on the 17th, 18th and 19th verses of the third chapter of *Gita.* The quotation given below is inimitable indeed.

". . . Seeing that the third chapter of *Gita* contains an exposition of the Karma-Yoga, no sane person will bring forward a totally out-of-place proposition like 'Renunciation of Action is the best' in the middle of the exposition of the Yoga of Action. Then how could the Blessed Lord have done such a foolish thing?"[17]

The concern shown by Tilak in using apt English words for translating original Sanskrit terms must have impressed Pandit Deendayal. In one of the footnotes in the Eleventh chapter of the *Gita,* Tilak invites our attention to the writing of Sully (a Western philosopher) wherein one comes across the English words 'Optimism' and 'Pessimism' respectively for 'Karma-Yoga' and 'Karma-Tyaga'. Tilak not only disagrees with this translation, but offers better alternatives. He accordingly suggests that Karma-Yoga deserves to be translated as 'Energism' and Karma-Tyaga be translated as 'Quietism'. Tilak in short aptly honours those who opt for Karma-Tyaga on the ground that such persons who give up such life, treating it as transient are joyful. Tilak, an advocate of Karma-Yoga (the path of unattached Action) thus refuses to call genuine followers of Karma-Tyaga as pessimists. He is indeed least dogmatic!

Tilak's Legacy and Integral Humanism

Pandit Deendayal's first lecture on Integral Humanism informs us of his faith in the pursuit of development – trajectory in the light of our national identity. It also conveys to us that according to Pandit Deendayal, our leaders in the immediate post-independence years, however disregarded our national identity and that was why we faced several problems. Pandit Deendayal naturally relied on Indian ethos while elucidating the tenets of Integral Humanism. He must have found

17. *Ibid.* p.925

solid source of inspiration in *Gita-Rahasya*. Tilak has stated in *Gita-Rahasya's* second chapter, titled 'Karma-Jijnasa' (The desire to know the Right Action) that *Gita* does provide due guidance to the great and responsible fellows who in their social lives want to undertake righteous and moral duties! He has in fact proved quite logically that Indian ethos is full of aphorisms apt enough to show us the right directions in our worldly activities. From his perspective the claim made by Mahabharata through the following statement is quite legitimate:

"यदिहास्ति तदन्यत्र, यन्नेहास्ति न तत् क्वचित्!"

("What is to be found here, is to be found everywhere, and what cannot be found here can be found nowhere else".)

Such confidence on the part of Tilak in the potentiality of Indian philosophy must have prompted Pandit Deendayal to shape 'Integral Humanism' in consonance with our national identity.

As per Integral Humanism, the relationship between individual and society is harmonious because same spirit or Chaitanya pervades everything. Pleasantly enough, Tilak also articulated the same viewpoint in the speech delivered at Benaras on 3rd January 1906. One can therefore infer that Tilak's Benaras speech provided inspiration to Pandit Deendayal in this connection.

As Tilak and Pandit Deendayal well believed in the spiritual tune of Indian nation, both of them took deep interest in infusing Indian politics with Indian religious fervour and spirituality. Both of them moreover took pride in the fact that the principle of self-identification (that is, आत्मौपम्यबुद्धि) has been a genuine contribution of Indian philosophy to the world. Both also offer similar interpretation of the spiritual tune of India. If the spiritual tune of our nation lies at the root of the principle of self-identification, faith in the same tune makes our Indian thinkers underscore the significance of psychological transformation in the process of broad socio-economic and political change! The following conclusion drawn by Tilak in the last chapter of *Gita-Rahasya* is quotable here:

> "The true test of Righteous Action is knowledge-full and unlimited Pure Reason, or rectitude, and it is more to the point, more comprehensive, more correct, and more faultless than the western Intuitionist or Materialistic doctrines".[18]

18. *Ibid.* p. 679

It is obvious that Tilak has informed through this quotation how pure Reason or Motive of the doer is crucial in the transformation process. He has, in other words asked to pay priority attention to the psychological or consciousness transformation.

Pandit Deendayal must have taken clue from such statements of *Gita-Rahasya* and expressed his determination in the following resolve in the concluding part of his lecture-series on Integral Humanism:

> "We shall be required to produce such institution as will kindle the spirit of action in us, which will replace the self-centeredness and selfishness by a desire to serve the Nation, which will produce not only sympathy towards our brethren, but a sense of affection and oneness with them. Such institutions can truly reflect our *Chiti*".[19]

Both Tilak as well as Pandit Deendayal were aware of the wrong interpretation or perception of the spiritual tune of Indian nation. And both of them took pains for offering correct interpretation of spirituality. Tilak has thus noted that the spiritual tune of our philosophy enjoins upon us to try our level best to realize the *Atman*, because the resultant reason born happiness or Metaphysical beatitude (आध्यात्मिक आनंद) is the most superior happiness. He has stated in the same vein that our philosophy does not deny the due significance of material objects which are necessary for the protection of the body along with Peace. The evidence supplied by Tilak in this context is quite solid.

> "In the phrases used for blessing, one does not say simply: "शान्तिरस्तु" (May there be Peace) but say *"shantih, pushtih, tushtih, chastu"*, that is, may there be *pushti* (material happiness) and *tushti* (contentedness) along with *shanti* (peace)".[20]

It is interesting to juxtapose Pandit Deendayal's argumentation side by side with that of Tilak. Pandit Deendayal's second lecture on Integral Humanism contains a special section, under the heading: 'Bharatiya Approach to Life'. We come across here the following statements:

> "Often it has been propagated that Bharatiya culture thinks of salvation of the soul, that it does not bother about the rest. This is wrong. We do think of the soul, but it is not true that we ignore body, mind and intellect"... We do not neglect the body.

19. *See* the Note no. 1, pp. 77-78
20. *See* the Note no. 6, p. 159

Upanishads declare in unambiguous words. "नायमात्मा बलहीनेन लभ्यः ।" ("weakling cannot realize the Self.")[21]

Pandit Deendayal's Integral Humanism, in tune with Tilak's *Gita-Rahasya* asks one in short to maintain a balance between material prosperity and metaphysical beatitude! We should not run after accomplishing more and more wants nor should we renounce or give up the worldly life!

Certain viewpoints articulated by Tilak must have pleased and endeared Pandit Deendayal.

1. Saints like Ramdas and Tukaram awakened common masses with a view to making them broad- minded and kind-hearted. They have asked us to renounce not the worldly activities, but the six animal instincts such as anger, desire, greed, temptation, insolence and jealousy"
   {*See*: "Shri Ramdas: Energysim and Quietism" in Essays of Lokamanya Tilak (a book in Marathi) Edited by Ram Shevalkar, New Delhi, 1997, pp. 278 to 291}
2. "Social reforms don't mean mere change in customs and conventions. They aim basically at generating devotion and affection for specific nationalism and in India nationalism is equivalent to Hindutva". (Ibid. Hindutva and Reforms, p. 124)
3. "The person who treats the entire world as his family or nation will fail in achieving anything in the practical life. Similarly, if he confines himself to his selfish interests, to the periphery of selfhood only, he will also suffer from a big failure! He must therefore narrow down his horizon from the whole world and simultaneously broaden his vision from selfhood. Such an exercise will bring him on the periphery of nation. He will realize that it is the union of the hearts of the people that determines the periphery of the nation". (Ibid. "Concept of Nationalism," p. 200)
4. "That man whose 'Reason' has become equable towards all, is the highest of men, whether he is a carpenter, or a merchant, or a butcher by profession. It is clear that, according to the Blessed Lord, the spiritual worth of a man does not depend on the profession followed by him, or on the caste to which he belongs, but entirely on the purity of his conscience".[22]

21. *See* the Note no. 1, pp. 25, 26
22. *See* the Note no. 6, p. 615

From the perspective of Tilak, our mother-land will reach the zenith in her career when all of us will be genuinely noble and pure through implementing *Gita* Religion in our practice. One comes across this perspective in the concluding paragraph of the last chapter of *Gita-Rahasya.*

Tilak writes: "I now pray to the Parameshwara, at the end of this book that there should come to birth again in this country such noble and pure men who will worship the parameshwara according to this equable and brilliant religion of the *Gita,* which harmonizes Devotion, Spiritual Knowledge and Energism!"

As each and every action on the part of Tilak mirrored his surrender at the feet of Bharat-Mata, his magnum-opus articulated such prayer in the concluding section. Pandit Deendayal rightly considered Tilak as the absolute epitome of a patriot, and *Gita-Rahasya* as the sacred guide. He therefore wound up his lecture series on Integral Humanism through his earnest urge.

> "With the support of universal knowledge and our heritage, we shall create a Bharat which will excel all its past glories, and will enable every citizen in its fold to develop his manifold latent potentialities and to achieve, through a sense of unity with the entire creation, a state even higher than that of a complete human being. It is a state in which Nara (Man) becomes Narayan (God). This is the eternal and continuous divine form of our culture. This is our message to humanity at the crossroads. May god give us the strength to succeed in this task".
>
> Bharat Mata Ki Jai!

PART - III

9

Integral Humanism and Marxism

Commonalities and Contrasts

Whoever presents a paper on the topic chosen by him is expected to elaborate relevance of the discussion on this topic. Thus it is required on the priority basis to highlight how and why the discussion in connection with the comparison between Integral Humanism and Marxism is quite relevant in the present decade of the 21st Century?

It is well-known that within twenty five years after the presentation by Deendayalji of the views on Integral Humanism, the Soviet Union began to wither away itself. The year 1991 finally witnessed the tragic demise of the Soviet Union. It is needless to point out that the Soviet Union was the first incarnation of the implementation of Marxism in the world and that was why, the tragedy of the USSR caused a great shock to the devotees of Marxism and the very scenario proved the prediction made by Pandit Deendayal Upadhyay in his lecture series in Mumbai in 1965. In the opinion of Deendayalji, 'The Nations whose life centred in the state were found to be finished with the end of the state'.[1] Deendayalji's viewpoint that the school of thought which offers supremacy to the state over society is bound to face serious fatal tragedies was forcefully substantiated later by Lech Valesa, the renowned Polish dissident. Valesa thus stated in 1989 that he and his colleagues were determined to enrich the legacy of Copernicus who made the sun stand still and the earth move around. Valesa articulation

1. Pt. Deendayal Upadhyay, There is an Alternative: Integral Humanism (Mumbai, 1965), p. 29.

is worth quotation here. "We want to make the Polish society stand still and the single party state move around". Gorbachevian campaign titled as "Glassnost and Perestroika" also aimed at curbing the supremacy of the state in the then existing Soviet Union.

If Deendayalji's prediction about the repercussions of the exclusive reliance on state proved true in the years preceding to the demise of the USSR, his criticism of the Western theory and practice of Nationalism, Democracy etc. proved its authenticity in the post-Soviet years in the Eurasian land space. One may here refer to happenings like 2008-bloody confrontation between Russia and Georgia, recent Russian annexation of Crimea at the cost of Ukraine, strains and tensions caused to all non-Russian nations due to notable presence of Russian citizens in their respective territorial area, etc. Has not Deendayal Upadhyay rightly stated in the above mentioned Mumbai- lecture series that in the West world unity and nationalism do conflict with each other?[2] Deendayalji's views about Integral Humanism and Marxism undoubtedly deserve to be discussed today for two reasons, first, they enable us to highlight the fatal consequences of the naked pursuit of statism and secondly, they offer penetrating analysis of the West sponsored concepts like nationalism, democracy etc.

Background

Having explained the present day relevance of the discussion on the topic chosen, it is necessary to elaborate the background as well as the sources of inspirations in connection not only with Integral Humanism but also with Marxism. This section of the paper, of course deals with the background of the both schools of thought.

As for the background of the Integral Humanism, one should initially take into account the life pattern of Pandit Deendayal Upadhyay, the sponsor of this paradigm as the seeds of Integral Humanism are traceable in his life pattern. Upadhyayji, born in 1916, opted for being a whole time worker, the Pracharak of the Rashtriya Swayamsevak Sangha, the organisation founded by the Dr. K. B Hedgewar in 1925. His peculiar qualities left deep impression on Shri Guruji, the second Chief of the R.S.S. Deendayalji thus had a very high I.Q. (Intellectual Quotient) as well as E.Q. (Emotional Quotient). Equipped with positive and constructive viewpoint, his approach was also pragmatic. He had unique skill and ability to explain sublime thoughts in simple, lucid language, and always had very compassionate

---

2. *Ibid*, p. 11

attitude towards others. When Shri Guruji and his colleagues decided to render whole hearted cooperation to Dr. Shyama Prasad Mukherjee in his mission to launch a new political party under the title Bhartiya Jana Sangha they requested Pandit Upadhyay to be the right hand of Dr. Mukherjee with a view to strengthening the new political party and to disseminating the message of the Indian political thought throughout India.

The fact that Panditji was known for high I.Q. and E.Q. got reflected itself through his quick grasp of the historical role which R.S.S had decided to play. Deendayalji thus rightly comprehended that the root cause of the problems faced by India from centuries together was the lack of organisation of Hindu Society. That was why he opted for keeping aside all sorts of personal ambitions and for dedicating his life for organising Hindu Samaj. It was his deep emotional attachment for the entire Hindu society which strengthened his resolve.

Deendayalji being basically positive and constructive correctly shared the view of Dr. Hedgewar that priority needed to be given to the generation of social consciousness in every Hindu citizen. Deendayalji rightly felt that as the members of Hindu society became parochial and began to take pride in narrow identities based on caste, creed and language, foreign invaders succeeded in subjugating India. Deendayalji pursued his lofty life mission with utmost dedication. He was at the same time fully aware of the limitations of the common man. Least wonder his approach was down to earth pragmatic. It was naturally just possible for him to establish and develop a cordial rapport with thousands of Indians. And his ability to articulate solid, sublime thoughts in lucid language carved out a unique place for him in the RSS History. One may here refer to his lucid interpretation of the famous Sanskrit Subhashita" "शरीरमाद्यं खलु धर्मसाधनम्।" In the opinion of Deendayal, human body is an instrument in the pursuit of Dharma. One should therefore take due care of his body. One should neither pamper, nor neglect such an instrument. The very command on lucid language enabled Panditji to articulate his concern for slum dwellers in the following words. "Each municipality must pay priority attention to enhancing the well-being of slum dwellers as strengthening of each weak link adds to the total strength of the entire rope". It was through the transparent compassion for the downtrodden that Deendayal Upadhyay did full justice to his name. The pen portrait of Adi Shankaracharya drawn by Upadhyay in the novel on the pioneer Hindu Seer was reflective of the compassionate nature of the writer himself.

Deendayal Upadhyay thus informs readers of his compassionate nature through Shankaracharya's quotable quote – "One who fails to feel the pulse of the hungry and thirsty will surely be deprived of the divine blessings".[3] Deendayalji's compassion for the downtrodden victims of capitalism got an expression in one of his speeches delivered in the capacity of one of the most prominent RSS activists of Uttar Pradesh during the latter half of 1940s. The rhetorical question raised by him through this lecture was quite typical. It ran as follows: "Does the daily drill on the part of thousands of Swayamsevaks all over India aim at creating an army of volunteers for spreading the message of cruel capitalism?". He categorically pointed out the allegation that the RSS favours capitalism and landlordism is totally baseless and mischievous. Nobody from among the lakhs of educated young RSS activitists wants to strengthen handful landlords and capitalists".[4]

If the study of the life pattern of Deendayal Upadhyay, or to be more precise, if the analysis of the years spent by Deendayalji as a full time worker of RSS in U.P in the period from 1942 to 1951 has enabled us to find the early symptoms of Integral Humanism, similar attempt to study the life pattern of Karl Marx is bound to help us in tracing the seeds of the philosophy of Marxism.

Karl Marx, born in 1818 acquired world fame at the age of 30 in 1848 through the publication of Communist Manifesto which assured workers of the world that the golden future was awaiting them. World at large noticed several peculiar traits of his nature during these three decades. Marx had sharp intelligence along with appetite as well as energy essential for acquiring knowledge. Marx moreover had genuine compassion for the vulnerable and miserable sections of the society. Capitalism which emerged in Europe due to historical industrial revolution widened the gap between "Haves" and "Have-Nots". And the compassion for the "Have-Nots" prompted Marx to set the goal for the life to emancipate these "Have-Nots" from the inhuman exploitation of capitalism. Once the goal was set, Marx dedicated his intelligence, energy, in fact entire life to accomplish this goal. Hiren Mukherjee has aptly described the life pattern of Marx. "Active in the most gruelling sense and with utterest dedication and self-abnegation, Marx lived in extreme poverty, oblivious of everything except the great task. He had strong conviction about the rightness of the goal and also about that of the means which led Marx to challenge Prussian ruler and to revolt

3. *See* Dr. Mahesh Chandra Sharma, *Deendayal Upadhyay: Kartritva Evam Vichar* (New Delhi, 1994), p. 24.
4. *Ibid.* p.259

against them".[5] Prussian rulers therefore compelled him to seek shelter in France, Marx, however continued to defy. No wonder French rulers also served a notice to Marx who finally opted for residing in Britain Till the end of his life Marx refused to succumb to all adversities and preferred to walk on the thorny path. Marx indeed paid a very heavy price through the implementation in his personal life of the following content of his Communist Manifesto. "The communists disdain to conceal their views and aims. They openly declare that their ends can be achieved by the forceful overthrow of all existing social condition. Let the ruling class tremble at a communist revolution".

All the above illustrated sublime characteristics of Marx such as sharp intelligence, inexhaustible energy, full dedication for the cause of the mission, self-abnegation etc. are appreciable pluses. They are however overawed by certain minuses such as adamant or dogmatic attitude, recklessness about sex as well as spending money and inability to make proper predictions.

That Marx was dogmatic or adamant about the views expressed in Communist Manifesto became visible in his life pattern. This "Magnum Opus" thus expected leftist revolutionaries to hate pro-establishment activists and all rightists. It demanded from revolutionaries, hundred percent participation in organised violence with a view to destroying total social order. Marx never tolerated slightest possible deviation from the Communist Manifesto. He was equally adamant about dialectical materialism, class conflict and the final victory of the working class. If Bakunin one time admirer of Marx pointed out that Karl Marx expected from his colleagues and followers unalloyed worship, Fritz J Raddoats, one of the biographers of Marx offered following criticism "Marx's career is strewn with the debris of broken or abandoned relationships – with his corevolutionaries, co-émigrés or co-communists, hardly any one of them remained".[6] According to P Parameswaran, the "First International", founded by Marx on 28 September 1864 could not survive beyond eight years because Marx was totally intolerant of persons of different perspectives.[7]

The fact that Marx was reckless has been evidenced in his extra marital affairs with Helen Demuth, his maid servant, the affairs which resulted in the birth of a son named as Frederick Demuth. If these affairs mirrored Marx's marital infidelity, they also informed the world

5. Hiren Mukherjee, Marx Great October, India and Future. p. 14.
6. Fritz Raddoats, *Karl Marx a Political Biography*. p. 63.
7. P. Parameshwaran, Marx and Vivekananda (Madras, 2007). p. 95.

of his irresponsible and care-two-pence attitude. Marx thus disowned Fredrick Demuth and indulged in humiliating him as well. Marx in fact went to the extent of calling this son an illegitimate child of Engels.[8]

Marx's opposition to the love affair of his daughter with one Paul Lafarge was equally shameful. Marx forgot quite conveniently that he also had his love affairs first with Jenny who subsequently became his legitimate wife and later with above mentioned Helen Demuth, his housekeeper. Marx nonetheless applied another yardstick to his daughter's love affairs and thus prompted his critics to state that this is the case or the application of the double standard! Marx's opposition to his daughter's love affair with Paul Lafarge on the ground of the Negroid origin of the latter was obviously still more reprehensible. Critics rightly pointed out that Marx failed to live up to the ideal of equality which he sponsored time and again throughout his life. Third minus point on the part of Marx is widely known to all, namely Marxian predictions proved fake and fictitious. As per Marxian prediction, for example, the era of capitalism was expected to be over in the due course of history. Astonishingly enough, in the aftermath of the publication of *Das Capital*, capitalism has acquired new strengths and abilities thanks to its survival instinct. Secondly, socialism was expected to emerge in a well industrialised nation. In actuality, the so called socialism unfolded itself in Russia and China when both of them happened to be agricultural nations. Thirdly, class consciousness was supposed to envelope workers throughout the world. We have observed that it is colour consciousness or creed consciousness or status consciousness rather than class consciousness which impressed the workers. Furthermore, the institution of the state is supposed to wither away itself during the communist stage of the world history. Lenin and his colleagues who were the architects of the Bolshevik Revolution in Russia proclaimed that the Soviet Union that emerged in 1922 would march first towards socialism and subsequently towards communism. What shocked the world most was the fact that within seven decades of its existence, the Soviet Union itself began to wither away and ultimately disappeared from the globe. Thus Marx and Lenin proved bankrupt!

Circumstances that Shaped Integral Humanism

In this section, we intend to elaborate objective factors in the form of circumstances which must have impacted these philosophies. As for

8. *See* W.O Henderson, *The life of Frederick Engels*. p. 203.

the philosophy of Integral Humanism, it is crucial to pay attention to the events which culminated in the partition of India. Taking into account policies and practices chalked out by the Indian Government in the first two post-freedom decades is a must. Similarly total thought pattern that prevailed among elites in pre-freedom decades also deserves due elaboration! It is, of course, essential to point out here that the just mentioned thought pattern did not disappear in the post-freedom years in India. The so called progressives continued to assert that India was "A nation in making" during British Raj, that it was freedom on August 15, 1947 that facilitated the completion of the nation making process. India according to this thinking in short became a nation in 1947 only. One may list certain features of the ostrich like thought pattern that took roots in Indian elites particularly since the emergence of the Khilafat agitation:

i) Refusal to accept that India had been a nation in the pre-Islamic centuries.
ii) Advice to Hindus to keep aside their past and to ignore extra-territorial tendencies and bargaining mentality on the part of Muslims.
iii) Conviction that common Muslims would never endorse the partition of India.
iv) Acknowledgement of the superiority of the Euro American model in nation building process.
v) Attraction for the Soviet model of development.
vi) Diffidence about the Indian ethos etc.

As this thought pattern dominated the minds of India elites particularly since 1920 and as one and the same thought pattern continued to prevail even after freedom, we can afford to concentrate our attention on the events and policies mirrored in the years from 1947 to 1965. Elaboration of such events and policies will enable us to locate circumstances of the years immediately preceding the presentation of the philosophy of Integral Humanism.

Common Indian masses expected Indian government to facilitate the articulation of Indian ethos in the immediate aftermath of freedom. Shri Chandrashekharendra Saraswati, the Shankaracharya of the Kanchi Kamakoti Peetham, gave legitimate expression to the popular expectation through the following statement. "Let the freedom be transformed into independence".[9] Several members of the Constituent

9. *See* S. Gurumurthy, *Eternal India and the Constitution* (New Delhi), p. 46.

Assembly ventilated same expectations while expressing their views on the draft of the Indian Constitution. Thus, they stated that the draft hardly bothered to incorporate Gandhiji's views published in "Hind Swaraj", some members of the assembly went to the extent of saying that those who drafted our constitution were least concerned with trying to adapt ancient Indian principles to modern era. It was the pressure from these members that the final draft of our constitution saw the inclusion of directive principles pertaining to significant issues like common civil code, ban on cow slaughter, functioning of Gram Panchayats etc. One may also refer here to two very important events such as the reconstruction of the Somnath temple and the placement of the idols of Rama-Sita at the birth place of God Ram at Ayodhya. These two events which received grand public welcome unfortunately caused a division among all India leaders. The lobby under the command of Pandit Jawaharlal Nehru opposed the moves of the reconstruction of Somnath temple and the placement of the Rama Sita idols at Ayodhya on the ground that a secular state should keep itself away from a religious activity. Soon, it became obvious that from the perspective of this lobby secularism in India meant sponsoring of anti-Hindu policies.

The very Nehru lobby, which differed in pre-freedom years with Gandhian convictions regarding ancient India, pleaded for implementing Euro-American model in polity and Soviet model of development in economy. As this lobby occupied government posts in free India, the goal of carving out socialist system of society obtained official sanction and the programme of creating cooperative farming societies also became a government programme. Tragically however neither socialism took roots in India nor cooperative farming saw the light of the day. The Nehru lobby thus informed world of its ignorance not only of Indian moorings but also of Soviet happenings like Khruschevian campaign of de Stalinization, Soviet dissidence movement, unpopularity of cooperative and collective farms in the Soviet land, etc. A thought about the circumstances which shaped the philosophy of Integral Humanism leads one to refer to the ideological chaos in Indian policy in the decade of 1950s as well as in early 1960s. If most of political leaders were fascinated by the Soviet experiment, some leaders developed attraction for capitalism. All of them were, however, sceptical of the spiritual path. Diffidence about indigenous path was a striking commonality between pro-socialists and pro-capitalists.

The years preceding to Deendayalji's presentation of Integral Humanism also witnessed the emergence of a strong coterie of intellectuals busy in lecturing as well as in pen pushing activities with a view to condemning the pursuit of indigenous path in India. These intellectuals took pride in projecting Hindutva-protagonists as parochial reactionaries as opponents of liberalism, pluralism, democracy and as eager to crush minorities as anti-poor, anti-slum dwellers etc. They also elaborated that the economic thinking on the part of the protagonists of Hindutva was akin to the camouflaged advocacy of capitalism. As these intellectuals were known for their distrust in private enterprise and complacency in public sector, any viewpoint different from such conviction was criticised harshly by self-proclaimed opinion makers. A very simplistic or crude equation dominated the minds of these professional pen pushers. Thus they thought that the followers of Marxism were inclusive, liberal, broad minded and progressive souls, whereas opponents of Marxism were exclusive, illiberal, narrow-minded and regressive communalists. "These left intellectuals" according to Prof. Shiv Viswanathan, moreover, behaved as a club snobbish about secularism treating religion not as a way of life but as a superstition.[10] They of course distinguished between majoritarian religion and that pursued by minorities as the latter was condonable from the perspective of the very snobbish club. Shiv Viswanathan's comment is quite apt and therefore quotable here. "The secularism preached by these intellectuals has become an Orwellian club where some prejudices were more equal than others".[11]

Discussion of circumstances which shaped the background of Integral Humanism will remain incomplete if a reference to Sonia Gandhi's speech delivered at New Delhi on 27th May 2014 is omitted. Mrs. Soniaji delivered this speech on the occasion of the Nehru- death anniversary. "There she recalled what Rajiv Gandhi said three decade ago that over time the socialist model as practised in India developed many flaws".[12] Two comments can be made in this connection. First, if Rajiv Gandhi pointed out flaws in socialism in 1984 Pandit Deendayal Upadhyay had attacked these flaws in 1960s only. Secondly, sycophants of the Nehruvian dynasty have proved their bankruptcy through their head-in-the-sand approach.

---

10. Shiv Viswanathan "How Modi defeated liberals like me" in *The Hindu* (Chennai) 22 May 2014, p. 10.
11. *Ibid.*
12. *See The Hindu* (Chennai), 28 May 2014, p. 13.

Circumstances Shaping Marxism

It was in 1848, that is in the midst of the 19th century that Communist Manifesto, one of the most significant historical documents, co-authored by Marx with Engels saw the light of the day. We must, therefore, take into account certain relevant happenings which marked one hundred years preceding to the publication of the Communist Manifesto with a view to knowing circumstances which shaped Marxism. P. Parameswaran has underscored in this connection four strands such as capitalism, scientific and technological advancement, industrialisation and imperialism. He has further mentioned that it was the combination of accumulated capital and scientific as well as technological advancement that gave birth to the industrial revolution with an ever-growing supply of goods which needed both raw materials and markets. And the search for these two paved the way for imperialist expansion and colonisation[13]. It was the cumulative effect of all these strands that caused the great earth-shaking force affecting the entire world.

The industrial revolution which introduced steam engine and latest techniques in the field of manufacturing literally generated miracles in the economy of Great Britain in the period from 1760 to 1830. Thus it facilitated the production of several goods and services on the massive scale. It also expedited the process of production. The big capitalist tycoons who could afford to use latest techniques accordingly succeeded in reaching the commanding heights of the economy causing immiserisation to other competitors in the due course of time. The industrial revolution also facilitated the emergence of big metropolitan cities in the place of small villages and shanty townships. In the new circumstances, if old feudal lords were replaced by big industrial capitalists, the surfs and handicraftsmen were ousted by poor proletariats. One of the most notable consequences of the industrial revolution was the encouragement given to the minutest division of labour among many workers as a result of which the worker who used to produce previously the entire article later began to produce a part of the article. Once the world realised that such a division of labour boosted the supply of product more speedily and more cheaply, it endorsed the further reduction of labour to a very simple mechanical operation. No wonder, the economy of each industrialised country witnessed the domination of steam power, machinery and the factory

13. P. Parameshwaran, *Marx and Vivekananda: A comparative Study*. (Chennai, 2007), p. 6.

system over all branches of industry. This very phenomenon strengthened the position of big capitalists and simultaneously deprived the workers of the last shred of independence. The big capitalists who ousted feudal landlords and converted handicraftsmen into poor proletariats similarly made successful inroads in the polity of each industrialised country. They not only ended the supremacy of hereditary monarchs, kings and queens but also transformed democracy into plutocracy.

One comes across very impressive delineation of the effects of capitalism in the Communists Manifesto. The following paragraphs are vivid evidences.

A) "The bourgeoisie (the capitalist class) during its rule of scarcely one hundred years has created more massive and more colossal productive forces than have all preceding generations together. Subjection of nature's forces to man, machinery, application of chemistry to industry and agriculture, steam navigation, railways electric telegraphs, clearing of whole continents for cultivation, canalisation of rivers whole populations conjured out of the ground- what earlier century had even a presentiment that such productive forces slumbered in the lap of social labour"?[14]

B) "The bourgeoisie wherever it has got the upper hand has put an end to all feudal patriarchal, idyllic relations. It has pitilessly torn asunder the motley feudal ties that bound man to his natural superior, and has left remaining no other nexus between man and man than naked self-interest than callous cash payment. It has drowned the most heavenly ecstasies of religious fervour of chivalrous enthusiasm of philistine sentimentalism in the icy water of egotistical calculation. In one word, for exploitation veiled by religious and political illusions it has substituted naked, shameless, direct, brutal exploitation".[15]

C) "-----The bourgeoisie has at last, since the establishment of Modern Industry of the world market, conquered for itself in the modern representative state, exclusive political sway".[16]

14. *See Karl Marx and Fredrick Engels, Selected Works* Vol. One (Moscow, 1969). p. 113.
15. *Ibid.* p. 111.
16. *Ibid.* p.110.

We must not of course ignore that in the age of capitalism wealth increased at the cost of wellbeing due to the uneven spreading of the fruits of technical achievement. This age thus witnessed smiling faces of few as against innumerable suffering faces. The contrast between the apparent fulfilment on the one hand and the great and growing emptiness on the other was the most notable sign of the age of capitalism.

Marxian delineation of the pathetic position of proletariat is also worth quotation here: "Owing to the extensive use of machinery and to division of labour the work of the proletarians has lost all individual character and consequently all charm for the workman. He becomes an appendage of the machine and it is only the most simple, most monotonous and most easily acquired knack that is required of him".[17]

Such a typical Marxian delineation of various aspects of capitalism reminds us of the indelible imprints of several events and thought currents on Marx's mind since his childhood. One may thus refer to the fact that his father, a born Jew had to embrace Christianity through baptism as otherwise he would have suffered unjust discriminatory treatment at the hands of non-Jews. One may also refer to anti-rational, anti-science, dogmatic and cruel transactions on the part of Christian missionaries. These happenings made Marx anti-religion. The thought current of Hegelian dialectics provided him moral and psychological reassurance and prompted him to conclude that the conflict between the thesis of capitalist exploitation of proletariats and the anti-thesis of workers' unity would result in the synthesis of socialism which would expedite the world march toward communism. The impact of the philosophy of Ludwig Feverbach rid him of the influence of Hegelian idealism. The acquaintance with Smithian and Ricardian economic thinking led Marx to underscore the importance of economic forces in general and the significance of the labour theory of value in particular. Friendship with Frederic Engels of course played a crucial role in Marx's life as it shaped uncompromisingly materialistic framework of his mind.

Commonalities between Integral Humanism and Marxism

As for the commonalities one may state that Integral Humanism as well as Marxism share five points with each other. Thus

i. Both philosophies aim at making a human being happy.

17. *Ibid.* p. 114.

ii. Both intend to transform social-economic and political order.
iii. Pioneers of both philosophies were determined to stake their lives on implementing respective philosophies.
iv. Both philosophies have criticised the perverted genesis and the growth of nationalism as well as democracy in West Europe.
v. Both of them have articulated their resentment against alienation, fetishism etc. caused to the common human being.

It is essential to add a precautionary note in advance before elaborating all the above mentioned commonalities or similarities. Thus for example Deendayal Upadhyay did share with Marx the aim of making a human being happy though his concept of human happiness was different from the Marxian one. Similarly, both of them no doubt, broadly agree with each other in their assessment of the repercussions of the occidental concepts such as nationalism, democracy etc. though the analysis in depth enables us to come across certain nuances and niceties in their assessments. As for their views on world transformation, it is tempting to refer to the quotation from the writing of Dr. S. Radhakrishnan.

> "In its concern for the poor and the lowly, in its demand for a more equitable distribution of wealth and opportunity, in its insistence on rational equality, Marxism gives us a social message with which all idealists are in agreement. But our sympathy for the social programme does not necessarily commit us to the Marxian philosophy of life, authentic conception of ultimate reality, its naturalistic view of man and its disregard of the sacredness of personality".[18]

The fact that both philosophies aim at making the human being happy can be substantiated by referring respectively to Deendayalji's Mumbai lecture series and to Communist Manifesto as well. The Mumbai lecture series delivered by Deendayal Upadhyay in 1965 informs us of the aim of Integral Humanism through the following words. "We aim at the progress and happiness of Man, the Integral Man. Man, the highest creation of God is losing his identity. We must re-establish him in his rightful position, bring him the realisation of his greatness, reawaken his abilities and encourage him to exert for attaining divine heights of his latent personality. This is possible only through a decentralised economy".[19]

---

18. Dr. S. Radhkrishnan, *Religion and Society* (London,1959), p. 25
19. Deendayal Upadhyay, *Integral Humanism* (Bombay,1967), p. 84

The communist Manifesto articulated the aim of Marxism through the following statement. "The communist fight for the attainment of the immediate aims, for the enforcement of the momentary interests of the working class, but in the movements of the present they also represent and take care of the future of that movement". "......... They never cease for a single instant to instil into the working class the clearest possible recognition of the hostile antagonism between bourgeoisie and proletariat". "...The communist in short support everywhere every revolutionary movement against the existing social and political order of things".[20]

The just mentioned extracts inform us that the commonalities contain distinct nuances and niceties. Thus Integral Humanism though aims at enhancing human happiness pursues this aim in the holistic manner, and to that extent differs with Marxism as the latter believes in homocentric humanism. The Integral Humanism indeed happens to be broad, as it accommodates due concern for the entire universe, whereas Marx-sponsored homocentric humanism is lopsided and anti-God, as it considers man as the centre of all things. Integral humanism is moreover deep as it pays attention not only to physical, but also to mental, intellectual and spiritual happiness as well. Thirdly, its reach is quite long in the sense that it aims at emancipation of labour not only from the grip of bourgeois exploitation of capitalism but also from the bureaucratic trap of socialist statism.

One can locate similar nuances in connection with the aim of the transformation of socio economic and political order. Integral Humanism, no doubt aspires to change the present order. Deendayalji's speech delivered at Calicut (Kerala) in the capacity of the President of Bhartiya Jana Sangh proved to be quite historical in this context. That speech conveyed to the delegates assembled there for the All India Session of Jana Sangh that the pioneer of Integral Humanism was "in favour of mass agitation for changing the present order as in his opinion such an agitation mirrors social awakening". He appealed to party workers "to be on the alert as pro-establishment elements are bent on crushing every agitation on the ground that it is backed by the communists". Deendayalji stated further "We must in fact take initiative and lead the mass agitation and keep ourselves away from status-quoists, who being frightened try to stop inevitable march of the time".[21]

20. *See* footnote no.14, pp. 136-137.
21. *See* footnote no.3, pp. 105-106.

Deendayalji was indeed least status-quoist. He himself stated in the above mentioned Calicut speech that he refused to be a prisoner of the past, that he was unwilling to be tied to the present and that he had his dreams for the future. He similarly mentioned there that he was the last person to remain in the dream world. He, in other words, opted for fighting against unjust, exploitative socio-political, economical order. It was however a conviction on his part that fighting or antagonistic spirit was a means to be opted for occasionally and not a goal to be pursued permanently. How beautifully he vented his conviction, "Anger etc. are natural to man and beasts. For that reason if we make anger a standard in our life and arrange our efforts accordingly then the result will be a lack of harmony in our life".[22] He articulated one and the same conviction in the following way. "The concept of a complete human being, an integrated individual is both our goal as well as our path".[23] Upadhyayji in short advised Indians to pursue the goal of Integral Humanism as according to him, the pursuit of this goal would make workers in particular and common people in general march towards happiness. Marx's viewpoint was different. Martin Malia has argued that "from the view point of Marx the goal of communism needs to be pursued not because it takes workers toward happy future but because it enables them to take revenge against capitalism".[24]

The aim of Integral Humanism is thus positive and constructive, whereas that of Marxism is negative and destructive.

The fact that both pioneers devoted their lives for accomplishing their mission is acceptable to all. Pandit Deendayal Upadhyay thus spelt his life mission in his letter addressed to his maternal uncle on July 21, 1942. Deendayalji conveyed his determination to the uncle in the following way:

> "I have decided to be a full timer of R.S.S. I will accordingly sacrifice everything for the sake of the nation, which had invited Bhagwan Ram to opt for a long stay in forest, which had called Bhagwan Shri Krishna to shoulder herculean responsibilities, which inspired Rana Pratap, Chhatrapati Shivaji and Guru Govind Singh to stake their lives".[25]

---

22. *See* footnote no. 19, p. 28.
23. *Ibid.* p. 36
24. Quoted by Govind Talwalkar, Soviet Samrajyacha Uday Aani Asta, a book in Marathi. (Mumbai 2001), pp. 204-251.
25. *See* footnote no. 3, pp. 11, 12, 13.

We all know that Deendayalji did not deviate from this pledge even for a second in his life. Marx was also a full timer, he staked his life for changing the world and accordingly concretised in his personal life his expectation: "Philosopher should change the world"! It was for the cause of human wellbeing that Marx dedicated his life and therefore Lala Hardayal penned the biography of Marx under the caption: "Karl Marx– A Modern Rishi".

The fact that both Deendayalji as well as Marx attacked Western or occidental concepts of nationalism and democracy, is also a notable commonality between the two pioneers of two philosophies. Deendayal Upadhyay thus pointed out that the growth of a nation in the West endangered world peace as with the strength nations there aspired to have empires in Asia, Africa and Latin America.[26] Karl Marx stated that Germany and Britain took pride in subduing other nations.[27] Both of them launched similar attack on democracy in the west, they felt that plutocracy knocked down democracy. Thus Deendayal Upadhyay has made the following comments. "Democracy grants individual liberty but the same is used by capitalistic system for exploitation and monopoly"[28] Marx's comment is equally notable: "The bourgeoisie has at last since the establishment of modern industry and of the world market, conquered for itself, in the modern representative state, exclusive political sway".[29]

The contrast behind this commonality needs to be underscored in this context. Thus Deendayalji's attack is not confined to occidental nationalism and democracy only as it does not spare socialism. In his opinion all the three concepts have emerged in reaction to something else. They have moreover proved to be incomplete and mutually opposing. Deendayalji did not criticise these concepts per se. He pointed out that integral perspective toward these concepts would enhance human wellbeing. I am tempted to quote Deendayal Upadhyay. "All these are good ideas. They reflect the higher aspiration of mankind. By itself however each stands opposed to the rest in practice".[30] Marx does not look at them in the integral perspective. And as for socialism he refuses to believe in the minuses of statism.

As both philosophies aim at making the human being happy, they resent the system which caused unhappiness to a human being. Least

26. *See* footnote no. 19, p. 23.
27. *See* footnote no. 14, p. 364 and p. 498.
28. *See* footnote no. 19. p. 23.
29. *See* footnote no. 14. p. 110.
30. *See* footnote no. 19. p. 15.

wonder, they are quite resentful about capitalism- which treats human being as a means of production. Deendayal Upadhyay and Marx are extremely perturbed over dehumanisation or alienation, the product of capitalism. In capitalism one comes across fetishism as well.

Thus the machine which came into existence with a view to facilitating the production process soon became the master giving employment to the labourer. Deendayalji has criticised this phenomenon as it cannot distinguish between the object and the instrument.[31] Marx also attacked it as the product starts governing the producers.[32] Deendayal Upadhyay was of course a spiritualist to the core, he therefore considered every human being essentially as soul, endowed with a bodymind complex suffers from alienation. Marx was on the other hand a believer in materialism. He therefore paid exclusive attention to the material and social aspect of alienation. Of course Deendayalji was also deeply concerned with the material aspect of alienation. One may conclude that Integral Humanism aims at ending both types of alienation; Marxism however confines itself to ending the material aspect of alienation. Marxism is moreover convinced that the root cause of alienation lies in private property and that is why it has asserted that the dawn of socialism will witness the end of alienation as well as that of fetishism.

Contrasts between Integral Humanism and Marxism

Having analysed in the lines above the commonalities between Integral Humanism and Marxism, it is legitimate to elaborate in the present final section of this essay the contrasts between the two philosophies. The final section aims at analyzing explicit contrasts and the elaboration of contrasts begins with the discussion on the concept of Man, as the Integral Humanism considers Man as a physical - mental – intellectual – spiritual being, whereas Marxism treats Man as a mere material being.

This contrast is basic because one who grasps this contrast, easily comprehends how both philosophies differ from each other in their conclusions about other concepts such as human happiness, alienation, fetishism etc. P. Parameswaran has explained very lucidly the concept of Man from the perspective of Integral Humanism. He writes:

> "Man is a multidimensional entity with the Soul (Atma) as the core. Atma is an abstract entity which is encased within five different

31. *Ibid*, p. 78.
32. *See* footnote no. 14, p. 138.

sheaths or Koshas. In the Hindu terminology they are Annamaya, Pranamaya, Manomaya, Vijnanamaya and Anandamaya (the physical, vital, mental, intellectual and blissful). Though termed differently and though each has its own specific characteristics, they are not entirely disconnected, but are so intimately interrelated that all these together constitute one integral whole".[33]

Deendayal Upadhyay has rightly stated that Integral Humanism aspires to enhance human happiness holistically in the sense that though it considers the soul as the core it does not neglect the body. Body is the primary instrument to discharge the responsibilities which Dharma enjoins. He has further commented. "The fundamental difference between our position and that of the West is that whereas they have regarded body and satisfaction of its desires as the aim, we regard the body as an instrument for achieving sublime aims".[34]

Integral Humanism similarly aspires to coordinate materialistic values of life with non-materialistic ones. It pays attention to artha and kama as they articulate materialistic values, but blending of them in the nice way with Dharma and moksha is underscored in the emphatic manner.

Integral Humanism accordingly provides material gains and enjoyment as incentives for achieving artha and kama. Simultaneously it offers social status and recognition as incentives for achieving Dharma and moksha. Then Thengadiji adds a very significant footnote here. "Everyone is free to follow either of the two with the proviso that the sphere of enjoyment and that of social status would invariably be in inverse ratio".[35] Thus the fellow who is accorded highest social status, is offered a relatively narrow sphere of enjoyment and the person who enjoys wide field of enjoyment is denied the status enjoyed by Rishis and Munis. Integral Humanism indeed emphasises the parameters of Purushartha Chatustayam whereas Marxism pays exclusive attention to artha and kama.

As Integral Humanism considers man as divine as a microcosmic manifestation of the Supreme Self, it begs to differ with the viewpoint that man is merely a biological organism. This philosophy believes in the ability of man to be God. This is why human subservience to artha and kama to matter is "alienation" in real sense. This philosophy nonetheless shares with Marxism the agony over meaninglessness of

33. P. Parameswaran, Integral Humanism Revised (Unpublished paper), p. 6.
34. *See* footnote no. 19, p. 33.
35. D. B, Thengadi, Third Way (New Delhi, 1995), p. 15.

human life in capitalism. Deendayalji's agony is vividly evidenced in the following words: "The principal drawback of the capitalist viewpoint lies in the fact that by making the machine a competitor of human labour and thereby displacing and subjecting human being to privations, the very purpose of creating machine has been defied".[36]

Deendayalji's comment that the very purpose of creating machine has been defied, moreover, informs us of his agreement with the Marxist concept of fetishism, as according to him capitalism converts machines from the means to the end! The fact that each victim of deprivation in the capitalist set up used to elicit deep compassion from Deendayal Upadhyay was mirrored in his advice to party workers to fight for the happiness of jobless youth, shopless hawker, landless farmer and homeless slum dweller! The origin of such transparent compassion of course lay in spiritualism. And whoever studies Marx's writings on alienation and fetishism invariably concludes that Marxian approach is more moral and ethical- if not spiritual than merely materialistic.

The discussion logically leads us to face the question: How far are economic phenomena important in public and individual life? The concern shown by Deendayal Upadhyay for destitutes like jobless youth, homeless slum dwellers, landless farmers, etc. does inform us of his acknowledgement of the significance of materialistic or economic phenomena. Integral Humanism thus shares the viewpoint of Dr. S. Radhakrishnan. "The emphasis on the importance of economic conditions is correct; the suggestion that they are exclusively determinant of history is totally incorrect".[37]

Integral Humanism, no doubt accepts that minimum of economic needs must be satisfied. It has got however reservation about multiplication of wants. This philosophy gives us to understand that whereas desires increase in geometrical progression, the power to satisfy these desires increases in arithmetical progression and therefore one who runs after satisfying more and more wants always remains unhappy. No wonder, Integral Humanism which supports agitations for enhancing the well-being of vulnerable and marginalized sections of society advises affluent members to show restraint in consumption.

Through Integral Humanism supports agitations for ending exploitative unjust social order, it refuses to offer key role to clashes and conflicts. This philosophy accordingly differs with Marxism which believes in the key role of clashes and conflicts. All of us know that

36. *See* footnote no. 19, p. 77.
37. *See* footnote no. 18, p. 26- 35.

dialectical materialism was an article of faith for Marx. The philosophy of Integral Humanism neither accepts materialism nor honours dialectism. It has already been explained how Integral Humanism does acknowledge some significance of materialism in the life of Daridranarain. The fact that occasionally dialectism or antagonism also acquires some significance is equally acceptable from the viewpoint of Deendayalji's philosophy. Marxism however asserts quite dogmatically that the history of all hitherto existing society is the history of class struggle. Integral Humanism agrees on the other hand with Sorokin who has endorsed the role played by cooperation and solidarity in the history of the world.[38] Marxian glorification of class conflict, antagonism and hatred thus places Marx and Deendayal on two opposite poles.

Curiously enough, Marx points out emphatically that once capitalism is replaced by socialism, neither class conflict, nor antagonism not hatred plays any role. All such Marxian assertions have proved historically false and logically untenable! Marx in fact believed in the Darwinian principle. "Survival of the fittest" and goaded proletariats to create unity among themselves through the dissemination of revenge and hatred against capitalists with a view to acquiring strength for defeating capitalist set up. That the heaven of socialism will emerge on its own out of the hell of hatred and revenge is beyond our comprehension. Deendayalji's sublime comment is worth quotation here:

"We have recognized desire, anger, etc. among the six lower tendencies of human nature but we did not use them as the foundation or the basis of civilized life or culture".[39] "Survival of the fittest" is the law of the jungle and the set up that will be built on the foundation of such a law can hardly be called as the civilized set up.

Another arena of contrast between Integral Humanism and Marxism is that of perception about the genesis and the growth of the institution of state. Integral Humanism is convinced that the state came into existence for curbing the operation of the above mentioned law of jungle. Marxism, on the other hand, avers that the state emerged for facilitating the operation of this law. The fact that during capitalism, the wealthy tycoons grabbed the state with a view to guarding their interests prompted Marx to build the theory of the state in the typical manner. Deendayal Upadhyay was also aware of the plutocratic grab of the democratic state. Marx and Deendayalji thus shared the same knowledge. The conclusions reached by them were, however different

38. Sorokin Pitrim, *Contemporary Sociological Theories*. (New Delhi, 1978), pp. 541-542.
39. *See* footnote no. 19, p. 26.

from each other. According to Marx in every social set up whichever class is dominant becomes supreme in every respect. Logically if feudalism witnesses the emergence of feudal lords as kings and queens, capitalism blesses the rise of capitalists as rulers. State is thus subservient to the dominant class as per Marxism. Hence the Marxian advice to proletariats to be dominant and to acquire supreme political power! Deendayalji reached another and valid conclusion on the basis of his knowledge of plutocracy. He stated that in every social set up it is the nation which shapes circumstances and carves out the state conducive to carry forward its mission and as such a mission is sublime, the state is the last entity to endorse the principle of survival of the fittest- thus seems to be the viewpoint of Integral Humanism.

If Marxism considers state as supreme, Integral Humanism just refuses to share this viewpoint as according to the latter it is the nation which is superior to state. Integral Humanism does of course recognize due importance of the state. Indian nation has for instance remained alive despite foreign invaders captured the state. It has similarly remained weak because we neglected the throne of Delhi. One should, in short, refrain either from overestimating or from underestimating the institution of the state. The Hindu concept of state without statism has been elucidated quite beautifully by DattopantThengadi through the extract given below : "In India during ancient years the state, sovereign or supreme political authority was an instrument of co-ordination and of a general control and efficiency and exercised a supreme but not an absolute authority for in all its rights and powers it was limited by the law and by the will of the people and in all its internal functions only a co-partner with the other members of the socio-political body".[40]

Marxism, with its faith in statism entrusts entire responsibility of total socio-economic and political transformation to the state in socialism and pleads for dictatorship of the proletariat. Same philosophy moreover expresses its confidence that the socialist state will accomplish its mission and realizing the futility of its existence will opt for withering away itself. Integral Humanism neither believes in statism not endorses the viewpoint that the socialist state will opt for withering away itself. Tragedy of the demise of Soviet Union informs us of the superiority of Integral Humanism over Marxism.

Discussion of the contrasts between these two philosophies will remain incomplete if we omit elaboration of the distinct convictions on the part of these philosophies. Integral Humanism indeed believes in

---

40. *See* footnote no. 35, p. 45.

changing the mindset of a human being, whereas Marxism has deep faith in the transformation of institutions. It was indeed the solid conviction on the part of Marx that the institution of private property caused unbridgeable gap between haves and havenots in capitalism. Marx similarly believed that if the socialist state under the command of the former "have-nots" abolishes private property the world will enjoy genuine happiness of the El Dorado. History of the then existing Soviet Union informs us of the diametrically opposite scenario. Bureaucratic philistinism and permissivism which took roots there subsequently acquired horrible dimensions and caused the death of the first experiment of Marxism.

Deendayalji's view point that institutional transformation without psychological change does not deliver the goods obtained support from Dr. Ram Manohar Lohia who made a noteworthy prediction in 1952 through the following extract:

"As long as the emotional lure of private property exists, Marxism or any similar social doctrine will be continually at war with its own handiwork. Private property may be abolished in a major way but the desire for unequal comfort or show will continually make erosions on the social order".[41] Integral Humanism has, no doubt, proved its worth!

41. Dr. Rammanohar Lohia: *Marx, Gandhi and Socialism*. (Hyderbad, 1963), p. 117.

10

Integral Humanism and Sustainable Development Goals

Sustainable Development Goals adopted by the United Nations in 2015 have generated legitimate worldwide debate. They are ambitious and bold as compared to Millennium. Development Goals endorsed before the beginning of the present millennium India seems to have welcomed these goals as they have a strong Indian foot print.[1]

Our Prime Minister Narendra Modi has stated that these goals are closely aligned with India's vision for sustainable development and our flagship programmes also strive for the same.[2]

According to Ashok Kumar Mukherji, these goals provide a holistic approach and India also needs to have similar perspectives.[3] Mukherji was the former Indian diplomat and Permanent Representative of India to the United Nations. His viewpoint carries significant weight. The comment made by Arvind Panagariya, the former vice-chairman of NITI Aayog is equally quotable here. It runs as follows: "Improving the lives of 1.4 billion Indians would make a major dent in the goal of improving the lives of all humanity".[4]

Sustainable Development Goals (SDGs) have, no doubt, elicited a very positive response from India. And this fact prompts one to

1. Kumkum Das Gupta, "Big, Bold and ambitious", in *Hindustan Times* (Mumbai), September 25, 2015.
2. *Ibid.*
3. *Ibid.*
4. *Ibid*.

elaborate how Integral Humanism, expounded by Pandit Deendayal, contains notable similarities with the paradigm of development mirrored in the SDGs. It was on September 25, 2015 that the United Nations adopted the comprehensive SDGs. This day happened to be the 99th birthday of Pandit Deendayal. The year 2015 reminded us moreover of the completion of fifty years of Pandit Deendayal‘s presentation of the philosophy of Integral Humanism through a lecture series in Mumbai.

The Proud Inheritor of Indian Thinkers

Pandit Deendayal was a proud inheritor of the 19th century born Indian stalwarts such as Vivekananda, Aurobindo, Tilak, Gandhi, Savarkar and Ambedkar. Least wonder, he used to quote from the writings and speeches of all such architects of modern India with a view to substantiating his arguments. Even a cursory glance at any of recently published volumes pertaining to Pandit Deendayal's life and philosophy endorses his pride in the above mentioned inheritance. This is why, the present section seems to be eclectic, in the sense that it relies on several sources such as shlokas from ancient scriptures as well as statements from the above mentioned architects of modern India. Secondly, references to flagship programmes launched by present rulers of India are also indispensable in this essay because these programmes contain foot prints of Pandit Deendayal's Integral Humanism.

Aim of Integral Humanism

What strikes one the most is the fact that the aim of Integral Humanism as well as that of the development paradigm adopted by the United Nations is quite akin to each other. Amongst four Mumbai-lectures of Pandit Deendayal, delivered for elucidating the philosophy of Integral Humanism, the fourth one contains the aim of this philosophy. As for the aim placed by the United Nations, one can refer to the first chapter of the Human Development Report 2016. 'Overview' attempted in the pages preceding the first chapter is also quite relevant for grasping the aim of the U.N. sponsored development paradigm.

The following extract from the fourth lecture on Integral Humanism spells out the aim of this philosophy:

> "We must have such an economic system which helps in the development of our humane qualities, or civilisation and enables us to attain a still higher level of all round perfection. We should

have a system which does not overwhelm our human quality, which does not make us slaves of its own grinding wheels. According to our concept man attains God like perfection as a result of development".[5]

The extract informs us that Integral Humanism aims at all round perfection or development of a human being, whereby a man reaches the highest point in the divine trajectory. It also contains implicit criticism of the Euro-American scenario which unfolded itself in the aftermath of the industrial revolution when capitalists engaged themselves in the inhuman exploitation of downtrodden labourers. The very extract contains equally harsh attack on socialist order which enabled statism to transform a divine human being into a slave! Last sentence of this extract reminds us of the impact of Indian ethos as it underscores that a man is supposed to attain God like perfection as a result of development.

UN Development Paradigm

The extract in the first chapter of the Human Development Report 2016, invites our attention to the aim of U.N. sponsored development paradigm:

> "Human development is development of the people through the building of human resources, for the people through the translation of development benefits in their lives and by the people through active participation in the processes that influence and shape their lives. Income is a means to human development but not an end in itself ".[6]

This extract which emphasises that the development paradigm sponsored by the U.N. is relying on the people centred approach, gives us in the same vein as the most relevant message that income is a means to human development but not an end in itself. This message builds a bridge between U.N. sponsored development paradigm and Pandit Deendayal enunciated Integral Humanism. The infographic titled "The World We Want" strengthens this bridge.

Here in this infographic, one comes across five dimensions of the aim which the U.N. wants us to pursue. First we must end poverty as well as hunger and ensure dignity and equality. Secondly we must ensure prosperity and fulfil lives in harmony with nature. Thirdly, we

5. Deendayal Upadhyaya, Integral Humanism (Bombay, 1967), pp. 69-70
6. *Human Development Report* 2016 (New York, 2016), p. 25

must protect our planet's natural resources and climate for future generations. Fourthly, we must foster peaceful, just and inclusive societies and finally, we must implement the agenda through a solid global partnership.

Holistic thrust is clearly observable through all these dimensions. We are thus asked to bother for everybody's dignity while ending his or her poverty. The human society as a whole is further advised to weave harmonious relationship with nature. Present generation is expected to use natural resources in such a way that future generations are also benefited. All sects, creeds and religious groups are supposed to consolidate peaceful relations with each other and nations are requested to cement global partnership. The overview in the beginning of the Human Development Report 2016 brings to our notice certain notable shifts undergone by development discourse. Thus initially the Western development discourse was wealth oriented. Enhancement of wealth at the cost of human welfare during the aftermath of the industrial revaluation in Great Britain however compelled one to pay priority attention to human welfare.

So the first shift was that from wealth orientation to welfare inclination. In subsequent years, when we began to pay excessive attention to the rise in the level of monetary income of an individual, realisation dawned on us that a human being needs along with income a long, healthy and knowledgeable life as well. World therefore witnessed second shift from maximizing income to expanding capabilities. Still later we came to know that a hike in income or that in capabilities facilitates growth which is distinct from development. Logically therefore, the shift (the third in order) from growth to development became inevitable. Ultimately development has become equivalent to enlargement of human freedoms. A consensus has indeed arisen that every human being must be free to achieve his wellbeing and also to achieve the goals of his choice. And in order to do full justice to the concept of human freedom world has decided to overcome lingering challenges like deprivations, deepening challenges such as inequalities and emerging challenges in the form of violent extremism.

The Indians feel quite delighted to see the whole course of development–discourse as it began with the acceptance of the equation between development and acquisition of wealth though finally at the end it has sanctioned that development means enlargement of freedoms for each human being. The United Nation's expectation from the world community, in line with the culmination of the development discourse, is also quite enlightening. We are thus expected to put an end to all deprivations, inequalities and terrorist activities with a view to assuring genuine freedom to each human being. This expectation is in full consonance with the deep attachment of the Upanishads to the idea of freedom. We can't forget that the very attachment prompted Upanishads to articulate sublime wishes:

सर्वे भवन्तु सुखिनः, सर्वे सन्तु निरामया। सर्वे भद्राणि पश्यन्तु, मा कश्चित् दुःखभाग् भवेत्।।

("May all be happy. May all enjoy health. May all come by prosperity. Let none have misfortune for his lot".)

Integral Humanism, being the apt 20th Century articulation of the Upanishadic vision places before us the same type of lofty dream: "We aim at the progress and happiness of 'Man', the Integral Man".[7]

It seems that Pandit Deendayal's insistence on the happiness of the 'Integral Man' is also acceptable to U.N. development paradigm. Pandit Deendayal has shown deep concern over the damage caused to ecology due to the greed on the part of the homocentric or anthropocentric modern man.[8] He has underscored that an individual is integrated not only with society, but also with surrounding ecology, not only with his nation but with the global community at large.

The 'Integral Man' from this angle is therefore Cosmo centric, showing interest in the entire cosmos. The following view point is naturally quite logical. "The economic system from the perspective of Integral Humanism will be constructive rather than destructive. It will not thrive on the exploitation of nature but will sustain nature and will in turn itself be nourished. **Milking rather than exploitation should be our aim.** The system should be such that overflow from nature is used to sustain our lives".[9]

The underlined portion of this extract is relevant as it demonstrates how the future generations are integrated with us and that is why we all are expected to show parsimony and not profligacy while dealing with nature.

Pandit Deendayal's concept of 'Integral Man' is thus closely aligned with the man projected by the U.N. sponsored development paradigm. Such a man does not cause any damage to environment, thinks about the wellbeing of future generations, opts for holistic thinking and assures sustainable development of everybody. It is

---

7. *See* the Note no. 5, p. 84
8. *Ibid.* p. 72
9. *Ibid.* p. 73

interesting to study how the U.N. sponsored development paradigm shares Pandit Deendayal's views![10]

Poverty-Environment Nexus

Amongst 17 SDGs endorsed by the United Nations, three goals (no.13, no.14 & no.15) are closely linked to environmental issues. The goal no.15 needs to be taken into account here. It is as follows: "Protect, restore and promote sustainable use of terrestrial ecosystems, sustainably manage forests, combat desertification and halt and reverse land degradation and halt biodiversity loss".

Human Development Report 2016 underscores this goal in the following manner:

"There needs to be a balance between people and the planet".[11]

Uniqueness of the latest development discourse, however lies in its focus on the poverty-environment nexus. World think tank has realised that the environment damage due to air and water pollution and also because of drought and desertification affects marginalised people the most. It is in the vicinity of such places like dirty factories, busy roads, waste dumps and ecologically fragile lands that unfortunate souls live. No wonder, they suffer from the environmental damage for which they are least responsible. If the resource degradation caused by our rich forebears has deepened the poverty of above mentioned unfortunate souls, the depletion of resources caused by the latter has added to the environmental damage. It is obvious that the few rich people belonging to the present generation or to the previous ones have forced poor people to deplete resources. Poverty environment nexus needs to be broken on a war footing as it has posed serious challenges to biodiversity. The solution of 'climate-smart agriculture' suggested by the United Nations Development Programme for breaking this nexus reminds us of Pandit Deendayal-mentioned concept – '*Adeva Matrika Krishi.*'

Pandit Deendayal reminds us of the fact that our ancient Indian kings used to dig and conserve wells and canals, tanks and ponds with a view of keeping our *'Krishi'* or agriculture '*Adeva Matrika'*, least dependent on the ups and downs in the natural rainfall. *Valmiki Ramayana* indeed informs us of the dialogue between *Bhagwan Ram* and his brother Bharat wherein the former enquires weather our *Kaushal Raj* retains its peculiarities such as well irrigated agriculture,

10. *See* the Note no. 6, p. 46
11. *Ibid.* p. 169

beautiful scenery, and habitations free from the damage of wild beast". The relevant Sanskrit line runs as follows:

"अदेवमातृकोरम्यः श्वापदैः परिवर्जितः ।"

'Climate–smart agriculture' enables farmers not only to raise productivity but also to improve their capacity to withstand shock of climate change. According to U.N. Development Programme climate-smart agriculture (that is, *Adevamatrikakrishi*) makes farms as well as forests absorb and store carbon and creates carbon sinks as well as reduces overall emissions.[12]

The UNDP has suggested, besides climate smart agriculture, two additional policy measure like carbon pricing mechanism and the initiative to increase energy efficiency and the use of renewable energy. Paris agreement on climate change endorsed by 195 member states in 2015 must be noted as a significant watershed because it evidenced unprecedented attention to environment sustainability and climate change.

Caring for Future Generations

Dr. T. V. Muralivallabhan (former Principal of NSS College and Academic Coordinator of Sri Ramakrishna Math, Pala, Kerala) has invited our attention in this context to the report of the World Conference on Environment and Development (WCED) published in 1987 as it suggested that sustainable development is the best alternative to the present mechanistic models of development.[13]

Muralivallabham points out that "this report envisages the development that meets the needs of the present without compromising the ability of future generations to meet their own needs".[14]

The 2016 Human Development Report is also deeply concerned with the wellbeing of future generations. Following two specimens mirror this concern.

i) Closing the human development gaps is critical, but so is ensuring that future generations have the same or even better opportunities".[15]

ii) Sustainable development is an issue of social justice. It relates to intergenerational equity - the freedoms of future generations and those of today".[16]

12. *Ibid.* p. 128
13. T.V. Muralivallabhan, "Integral Approach to Sustainable Development" in *Organiser* (New Delhi), December 6, 2015, p. 11
14. *Ibid.*
15. *See* the Note no. 6, p.4
16. *Ibid.* p. 9

Deliberations over the topic of sustainable development involve long term and multidimensional considerations. They mirror broader and deeper visions pertaining to development. They become more and more holistic and inclusive. Shifts in development-discourse traced above confirm these transitions. They moreover lend credence to the fact that succeeding generations are born beneficiaries of all transitions which become reference points to the successors. Replacement of the initial exclusive emphasis on wealth during (Adam) Smithian era by that on freedom and justice at present, has no doubt enriched more and more lives for more than 200 years thus endorsing intergenerational equity claim made in the lines above. Categorical imperative on the part of the present development-discourse to overcome on war footing all lingering, deepening and emerging challenges is indeed a very healthy shift in the discourse on development.

It we succeed in overcoming all such challenges our future generations will get benefited. S. Gurumurthy expects all of us to broaden our vision through serving social causes, through reducing conspicuous consumption and through considerations for future![17]

The 2016 Human Development Report also endorses the view point that interventions to overcome deprivations must be viewed as opportunities among future generations.[18]

The world has undoubtedly realised that human society should bother to preserve its environment. Nonetheless it has not yet fully grasped the content of integral or holistic approach, though simultaneously, it has given us some indications of growing closeness with Integral Humanism.

The U.N. sponsored development paradigm keeps the individual at the centre and draws around him concentric circles one after another such as family, village, nation, nature and universe. These circles are discrete or separate from each other. The development model sponsored by Integral Humanism also draws around individual, circles one after another such as family, village, nation, nature and universe. These circles are however spiral in the sense that one single thread encircles each of these components and enables the unfoldment of a seamless cosmic structure. Such structure is called in Sanskrit '*Akhand MandalakarRachana*' resembling with a spider's web. As Integral Humanism believes in the integrity between individual and society, it informs us through spiral circles that the individual who occupies the

17. S. Gurumurthy, India's Time has come (Chennai, 2008), p. 65
18. *See* the Note no. 6, p. 73

centre is integrated symbiotically with the constituents represented by outer circles in succession.

The 2016 Human Development Report, however, still continues to believe in the duality between individual and society. This is why, it depicts around individual such concentric circles which are separate from each other. Same belief in the duality has prompted this report to articulate its concern regarding a balance between the protection and the empowerment of the individual on the one hand and the survival as well as the wellness of the family, village, nation, (The constituents represented by outer circles) on the other. The solution suggested by this report for achieving the balance is also rooted in its belief in the duality. The extract given below is revealing in this connection.

> "The government's role is to ensure a balance between the protection and the empowerment of the individual and the concentric circles of security providers which are either extensions of the individual or, if they are malfunctioning, the threat to the individual".[19]

The 2016 Report, in short, expects the government to facilitate cordial healthy relations between the individual and the constituents of outer circles.

The solution suggested by Integral Humanism is in consonance with Indian Culture. It expects the individual, the constituent of the innermost circle and the constituents of outer circles as well to broaden their respective visions with a view to achieving the above mentioned balance. From the perspective of Indian Culture if the perceptions and actions of an individual influence his or her family, society and surrounding nature as well, the feelings and reactions on the part of the constituents of outer circles impact similarly members of the inner circles in succession, one after another. Integral Humanism expects an individual to take initiative and to coordinate proactively with the members of his family. Similarly it expects other members of the family as well to reciprocate favourably to the individual initiatives. Each constituent of the universe is in short expected by Integral Humanism to show concern for the interests of other members, to be complementary to each other in nutshell.

The comment that the philosophy of Integral Humanism has carried forward the legacy of Indian Culture can be substantiated by referring to certain hymns of Isha Vasyopanishad. We can begin with:

'सर्वं खल्विदंब्रह्म' ।

(Entire universe is indwelt enveloped and covered by the Supreme Being.)

19. *Ibid.* p. 128

Then there is another hymn: *'तेनत्यक्तेनभुंजीथा:'* (Everyone should enjoy happiness with minimum consumption and maximum sacrifices for wellness of all other living beings.) Another equally valuable hymn runs as follows:

'मा गृधः कस्यस्विद्धनम् ।।' (One should not covet or grab unjustly, the wealth of any other creature in existence in the world).

Integral Humanism, in line with Indian Culture in short intends to rectify any imbalance in universe through cooperation among constituent units of the whole cosmos. The U.N. sponsored development-paradigm relies on the other hand on the external agency of the government for rectifying imbalance between individual and other constituents of the universe. One should not however rush to conclude that Integral Humanism and the 2016 Development Report occupy two poles extremely opposite to each other. There are certain signs in the latter model of development which bring it closer to Pandit Deendayal indicated development–paradigm. The extract quoted above from the 2016 Report thus points out to us that "concentric circles of security providers (such as family, village, nation, etc.) generally happen to be extensions of the individual and occasionally become threats to the individual".[20]

Relationship between HDR and Integral Humanism

Thus the 2016 Report calls constituents of outer circles such as family, village, nations etc. as extensions of the individual and providers of security to the constituents of inner circles. Same report moreover informs us that the goal of universal human development still continues to face barriers through deprivations among groups like women, ethnic minorities, indigenous peoples, persons with disabilities, migrants etc. And the solutions suggested by the 2016 Report in this connection consolidate closeness between this report and Integral Humanism. Read the solutions in the lines below: "Overcoming of these barriers will require putting empathy, tolerance and moral commitments to global justice and sustainability at the centre of individual and collective choices. People should consider themselves part of a cohesive global whole rather than a fragmented terrain of rival groups and interests".[21]

This extract plainly vents not only clear recognition of holistic approach but also categorical rejection of fragmentary methodology.

21. *See* the Note no. 6, p. 6
20. *Ibid.* p. 128

Once we recognize that all of us are members of the cohesive global whole, cooperation and coordination become sacred 'mantras' of our lives. Pandit Deendayal being a pragmatic thinker accepts that in the world along with cooperation, conflicts and competitions do prevail but civilized life is shaped through cooperation and never through conflict. This very conviction on the part of Pandit Deendayal finds due expression in the following paragraph in one of the lectures on Integral Humanism: "Cooperation also obtains in abundance just as conflict and competition in this world. Vegetation and animal life keep each other alive. We get our oxygen supply with the help of vegetation whereas we provide carbon dioxide so essential for the growth of vegetable life. Thus mutual cooperation sustains life on this earth. The recognition of this element of mutual sustenance among different forms of life and taking that as basis of an effort to make human life mutually sustaining is the primary characteristic of civilisation".[22]

Prof. Bhagawati Prakash Sharma laments over the fact that although Pandit Deendayal prescribed remedial measures based on cooperation during mid 1960s, ceaseless conflicts inter-se constituents of the universe continue to prevail at present.[23] He would be pleased to note that the latest development-discourse shares Pandit Deendayal sponsored cooperative spirit as an antidote to the tatters of present day disarray and violence. The emphasis in the 2016 Report on the necessity to inculcate sublime tendencies like empathy, tolerance, moral commitments to global justice etc. in society at large needs to be focussed. Latest development discourse thus shares another commonality with Integral Humanism when it underscores the priority to be given to psychological change over institutional transformation in the march towards sustainable Development Goals. Integral Humanism has plainly pointed out that whereas tendencies like love, compassion, sacrifice are signs[24] of civilized life, the tendencies such as greed, anger, jealousy, etc. are mere animal instincts. As animals cannot overcome such instincts, only the fittest beasts survive in the jungle! Integral Humanism as well as the latest development-discourse ask us rightly to overcome all such animal instincts and pursue sublime human tendencies. This is why, we comment that both paradigms reject the operation of Darwin's Law. Both of them, moreover opt for holistic approach. We therefore, observe that from the perspectives of both

22. *See* the Note no. 5, p. 26
23. Bhagawati Prakash Sharma, "Key to Holistic Well-being in the Globalised World," in *Organiser* (New Delhi) September 27, 2015, p. 16
24. *See* the Note no. 5, p. 28

models of developments, the operation of fragmentary approach sponsored by Descartes' philosophy is equally rejectable!

One comes across very thought-provoking analyses about complex development challenges in the 2016 Human Development Report. Such deliberations are quite logical and legitimate in this report as it is devoted to the theme of human development for everyone. The concern shown by Pandit Deendayal in this connection is equally legitimate as the humanism worshipped by him is integral. No wonder, The 2016 Report as well as Integral Humanism share equal eagerness to put an end to deprivations caused to human beings on account of gender, caste, colour and creed or religion. The following lines in third chapter of the 2016 Report can comfortably fit in the elucidation of Integral Humanism.

> "Many anachronistic and sometimes perverse social norms persist for generations. Traditions including dowry from the families of brides and child marriage are maintained by households under social pressure".[25]

It is needless to state that both paradigms are desperately eager to end all such outdated and inhuman customs. Both development models acknowledge that the factor of caste in Indian society is a hurdle in the path of liberty and equality as it prohibits its members from pursuing multiple identities.

They therefore, recommend that India's affirmative action programme articulated through reservation policy deserves world applause. The 2016 Report, of course does express its worry or anxiety over the fact that certain sub-castes among reserved categories manipulate to grab all opportunities and keep other sub castes deprived of due benefits.[26]

The U.N. Development Report calls challenges linked with deprivation as lingering because they have been frightening us since years together. Same report calls challenges pertaining to inequalities as deepening, because during post-cold war years, they have become catastrophic. Neoliberalism that has taken solid roots during the last two and half decades has fostered corporate interests at the cost of millions of poor souls.

The 2016 Human Development Report informs us that at present global wealth has become far more concentrated. The wealthiest one per cent of the population had 32 per cent of global wealth around 2000

25. *See* the Note no. 6, p. 92
26. *See* the Note no. 6, pp. 76 and 93

and 46 per cent around 2010.[27] Deprivations deepen inequalities. Systemic deprivations of women have naturally elicited several pages in the 2016 report, as they pose challenges to fifty per cent portion of the world population. The report rightly states that

> "Gender based discrimination starts before school, even before birth. The preference for a son can lead to sex-selective abortions and missing women particularly in some South Asian countries".[28]

It favours legislation for promoting gender equality. Integral Humanism also favours governmental intervention in such cases, though as a general principle it does not entertain any external intervention for redressing imbalance between two constituents of the universe! Pandit Deendayalviews the state as a guardian of society, in the sense that it prefers social institutions to provide basic necessities to individuals. Also in case, any social institution fails in its duties, the Indian government is supposed to rely on legislation suitable to the occasion. Integral Humanism rightly refers to one of the most relevant *shlokas* in '*Raghuvansha,*' the epic of Kalidas. This *shloka* is full of praise for king Dilip – who was responsible for the maintenance, protection and education of his subjects and was therefore called as the true father of the latter.[29] Integral Humanism would endorse in the same vein the Joseph Stiglitz sponsored idea of managed markets.[30] Pandit Deendayal, being a vehement critic of the exploitative disorder of capitalism would have definitely opposed unjust market fundamentalism – of the post cold war years and endorsed the idea of managed markets!

The 2016 Report speaks at length about the genesis and growth of the lingering as well as deepening challenges. It does not do however full justice to the emerging challenges of violent extremism. Bloody terrorist attack on the New York twin towers on Nine-Eleven of 2001 has inaugurated present century and this is why, somebody has rightly stated that the 21st Century is born in fire and baptized in blood. Naturally therefore, the so called emerging challenges of the present century pose an existential threat to the world. Astonishingly enough, however, the 2016 Report refers to Islamic Militancy only at one place on page no. 45. We cannot forget that the survival of the world is at

27. *See* the Note no. 6, p. 31
28. *See* the Note no. 6, p. 58
29. *See* the Note no. 5, p. 74
30. Joseph Stiglitz, "Let bygones be bygones,". in *Hindustan Times*, July 7, 2016, p. 12

stake due to worldwide violent extremist activities of the Islamic State of Iraq and Syria.

Indian Initiatives

Finally, certain innovative Indian initiatives launched in post-cold war years for facilitating the process of development will be discussed. If some of these initiatives resemble with U.N. sponsored development programmes, some others do justice to the U.N. pleaded ideas. Incidentally, all of them coincide or correspond with Pandit Deendayal favoured search for the golden mean between free market operations and government sector transactions.

All the developing countries find it immensely difficult to mobilise capital to maximise development spending in priority areas. India's philanthropic and business sectors have however played a crucial role in supporting and accelerating ongoing works in these areas. As per the India Philanthropy Report 2015, India has added since 2009 more than 100 million private donors and they are contributing to a wide array of social causes.[31] One may also refer in this context to the Indian initiative of Corporate Social Responsibility Act, passed in 2013. This Act underscores the significance of three 'P's -... profit, people and planet and obliges companies as well as corporations to go beyond the pursuit of profit with a view to bothering for the interests of people and planet. Vikram Mehta, Chairman of Brookings India has made a quotable comment in this connection:

> "Helping hand of collaborative partnerships between the social enterprises and the community is no doubt superior to the invisible hand of the market".[32]

Jaco Cilliers the country director for the United Nation Development Programme in India has rightly pointed out that the financial model, blended by India through the above mentioned partnerships is in tune with the SDG Philanthropy Platform launched jointly by the Rockefeller Philanthropy Advisors, the Foundation Centre and the UNDP.[33]

---

31. Quoted in Jaco Cilliers, "Lending a hand, filling a gap" in *The Indian Express* (Mumbai) February 22, 2017, p. 13
32. Vikram Mehta, "C.S.R. Corporate should reach out" in *The Indian Express* (Mumbai) August 4, 2015, p. 13
33. Jaco Cilliers, *See* the Note no. 31, p. 13

The C.S.R. Act, 2013 mirrors not only India's initiative of state-philanthropy partnership but also Indian cosmo-centric approach based on holistic paradigm. Closeness between the 2016 Human Development Report and the philosophy of Integral Humanism is thus more than obvious. Commonality between UNDP and Indian ethos evidenced through philanthropy is also simply remarkable. India's reliance during post-cold war years not only on philanthropic organisations, corporations, companies and banks but also on community clusters as well as family based initiatives has proved the mettle of the golden mean between Market Darwinism and Marx-sponsored statism!

Appreciative references made in the fourth chapter of the 2016 Human Development Report to two notable Indian initiatives deserve special mention in this write–up as they inform us of the world applause of India's interest in reaching SDGs. The UN Development Programme favours social protection for those left out, as it wants to make vulnerable people resilient, capable of withstanding shocks due to climate change, environmental degradation, and so on. The 2016 Report appreciates Mahatma Gandhi National Rural Employment Programme of India in this context because such a programme has combined social protection with appropriate employment–strategy.[34] Incidentally, it was in the year 2016 only that the Modi-government of India decided to spend nearly Rs.60 thousand crore on this flagship rural job programme, the highest amount in the history of this scheme! As per one estimate, one and the same year (2016) saw the highest turnaround of 138.32 crore person-days of employment generated so far, as against 116.06 core during the same period of 2015-16. Under the present government of India, the quality of the spending over this programme equally got improved. Thus 94 per cent of around 11 crore active workers employed under this flagship programme were the recipients of Direct Benefit Transfer (DBT) Initiative! They must have, moreover got their wages through Aadhar Payment Bridge (APB) System. The creation of assets on ground like roads, bridges, ponds through the allocations over this programme also reflects quality improvement of the programme spending.

Government of India's reservation policy in favour of scheduled castes and scheduled tribes which has subsequently benefited other Backward classes as well is equally a subject of appreciation from the perspective of UNDP. And even in this case as well Narendra Modi Government has made its own distinct contribution through the setting

34. *See* the Note no. 6, p. 123

up of a venture capital fund for giving loans to first generation entrepreneurs belonging to SCs & STs. The Prime Minister's speech at the conference of Dalit entrepreneurs organised by the Dalit Indian Chamber of Commerce and Industry at New Delhi, in December 2015, gave revealing information to the audience. As per this information 80 lakh Dalit industrialists have been granted loans worth Rs.50,000 crores without any collateral under the MUDRA scheme. MUDRA is the acronym or Micro Units Development and Refinance Agency. Job seekers have thus become job givers.[35]

As stated earlier the UNDP sponsored Climate Smart Agriculture which aims at breaking poverty environment nexus is quite akin to Pandit Deendayal favoured '*Adeva Matrika Krishi*'. Through the provision of Rs.12,517 crore over such schemes such as Accelerated Irrigation Benefit Programme (AIBP) the Modi Government has given strong boost to '*Adeva Matrika Krishi.*' A specific extract in the 2015 Report on Human Development pertaining to 'green' activities is quite interesting as it reminds reader of one of the unique initiatives on the part of the 2016 budget of the Modi-Government. The extract is as follows:

> "Replacing of traditional biomass burning, cook stoves with solar cookers is green activity and it can have greater meaning for human development if it frees women and girls from having to collect firewood and enables them instead to take part in economic activities or going to schools".[36]

As for the similar initiative mirrored in the 2016 budget presented by Arun Jaitley to the Indian Parliament one can allude to the assurance "that the B.P.L. (Below Poverty Line) families are provided with a cooking gas connection, supported by a Government subsidy".

As this budget proposal gives a great relief to the females of B.P.L. families suffering adversely from the ill effects of chullah-cooking, all commentators have admired the Finance Minister of India. Swaminatham S. Anklesaria has for instanced extended a hearty welcome to subsidies for rural gas, as they would rid poor family women of respiratory diseases, caused by *chullah* cooking assignments.[37]

35. Harish Damodaran, Work and welfare: MGNREGA 2.0 in *The Indian Express* (Mumbai) October 20, 2016. p. 16
36. *Human Development Report 2015* (New York, 2015), p. 136
37. Swaminathan S. Anklesaria Aiyar, 'The key Budget proposal that you probably missed' in *Sunday Times of India* (Mumbai), March 13, 2016, p. 16

The 2016 budget of the Modi-Government informs us that the Indian leadership has decided to implement a broad and compassionate development agenda. Such a decision is in line with the course of thinking pursued by the United Nations during the period of twenty five years since 1990 when the first Human Development Report (HDR) saw the light of the day. First chapter of the 2016-HDR reviews this course in an apt perspective. It highlights, for example how the HDRs went on extending the frontier of thought leadership, public policy advocacy and influence on development agenda.[38] During these twenty five years, HDRs deliberated deeply over several themes such as human security, human poverty, cultural diversity, climate change, sustainability, equity and so on. It seems that the world think tank has drawn proper lessons from all these reports and set before us Sustainable Development Goals to be achieved by 2030.

The 2016 HDR which is subtitled as 'Human Development for Everyone' rightly recommends the use of disaggregated measures for monitoring progress in human development.[39] Our march towards SDGs depends badly on the detailed identification of deprived individuals. We are therefore required to rely on the analyses duly disaggregated by age, gender, sub national units, ethnicity and other parameters. Melinda Gates, Co-chair of the Bill and Melinda Gates Foundation has provided the following rationale for the use of disaggregated measures:

> "Getting a clearer picture of poverty and deprivation is a fundamental first step towards designing and implementing more effective policies and interventions as well as better targeting scarce resources where they will have the greatest impact".[40]

First step of identifying marginalised and deprived persons must of course be followed by other steps such as pressurising policy makers to draft suitable policies, enabling practitioners to implement these policies and seeing over the provision of benefits to genuinely needy people. Only motivated social workers can take such steps, as they are interested in furthering the wellbeing of marginalised citizens. The 2016 HDR calls such people as agents and links their activities to the development paradigm. It argues that development is considered at present as equivalent to enlargement of freedoms and therefore each one should be free not only to be happy and healthy but also to

38. *See* the Note no. 6, p. 25
39. *See* the Note no. 6, p. 52
40. Quoted in Note no. 6, p. 57

volunteer for social causes. This Report contains a special contribution of Olafur Eliason, artist and founder of Little Sun. Last paragraph of this contribution is highly relevant, as it brings to our notice how culture can motivate people to serve the social cause. This paragraph is as follows:

> "Culture can inspire people to move from thinking to doing, and it holds the potential to inspire great social change. It is only by connecting the head and the heart that we will succeed in building a future for the planet shaped by positive, powerful climate action".[41]

The UN Development Programme and the Integral Humanism based on Indian ethos thus admire in the same tune the role of psychological change in the process of development-oriented socio-economic and political transformation. The 2016 HDR in fact contains certain information-pieces which inform us of the fulfilment to some extent at least of Pandit Deendayal's dream of a healthy society. The following specimen exemplifies this view point:

> "Inspired by a particular cause and by the desire to give back to society, numerous successful young commercial entrepreneurs around the world are transitioning from for profit ventures to engage in social change".[42]

Now let us take into account the dream of a healthy society articulated by Pandit Deendayal in Integral Humanism:

"In a society even those who don't earn require food to eat. There are, for example children and the old, diseased and the invalids. Society is supposed to take care of such human beings. Parameter of man's social concern and his culture is his promptness to take care of the downtrodden".[43]

Juxtaposition of these two extracts side by side at the end generates a hope that U.N. aspiration of 'Human Development for Everyone' will be accomplished in future in the light of Indian ethos!

---

41. Quoted in Note no. 6, p. 44
42. Quoted in Note no. 6, p. 115
43. Quoted in Ashok Modak, *Uniquences of Integral Humanism* (Nashik, 2016), p. 37.

PART - IV

11

Uniqueness of Integral Humanism

It is simply appropriate to ponder over the philosophy of Integral Humanism in 2016, as the year happens to be the birth centenary year of Pandit Deendayal Upadhyay, the exponent of this philosophy. This very year moreover informs of the completion of the period of tumultuous Twenty Five years; the period which at the outset witnessed the collapse of the U.S.S.R. and subsequently the unfoldment of the subprime and Lehman crises. If the breakdown of the U.S.S.R. marked the end of the first experiment in the world of the implementation of Marxism, the unfoldment of the Lehman crisis mirrored the failure of capitalism. That both 'isms' failed in making a human being happy is a matter of consensus. S. Gurumurthy, a leading Indian thinker and astute political strategist has rightly remarked that if socialism or Marxism survived for seven decades in the then existing Soviet Union, global capitalism which proclaimed in the post-Soviet World its triumphant and cheerful predominance, in fact began to fold up within a decade and finally vanished like ripples on the face of waters"[1]. S. Gurumurthy has further pointed out that due to Lehman Crisis, not only Washington's dream of a quick move to global financial liberalization got shattered, but American arrogance reflected in forcing developing countries to obey the I.M.F. also got exposed. Astonishingly enough, India implemented the strategy in consonance with its ethos and remained alive and kicking. Least wonder, several dignitaries have

1. S. Gurumurthy, India's Time has come (Chennai, 2008), p. 116

showered appreciation on the performance of Indian economy. Paul Krugman has, for instance, cited Indian economy as the model for the world.[2] And Christine Lagarde, the I.M.F. managing director has called India as a bright spot on a cloudy horizon".[3] A miracle has indeed happened in India because a foreign dependent mind-set of the years preceding to 1991 has given way to an India-centric approach. It was Pandit Deendayal Upadhyay who recognised the potential of the India-centric approach and articulated it very cogently in his lecture series in 1965 in Mumbai. We must, therefore, take into account the uniqueness of the philosophy of Integral Humanism expounded by Pandit Deendayal Upadhyayji through his Mumbai lectures in 1965. That our economy has opted for India-Centric approach since 1991 can be substantiated by referring to certain phenomena such as preservation of the institution of family, renewal of community-oriented industrial clusters, retention of relation based social environment, good-bye to the excessive reliance on public sector, sanction to the nuclear explosion, etc. Pursuit of L.P.G. trends in general and the long rope given to entrepreneurs in particular facilitated the operation of all these phenomena.

One can elaborate the uniqueness of Deendayalji's Integral Humanism by referring to certain salient features such as (i) apt Twentieth Century articulation of the Indian ethos, (ii) positive or constructive outlook, (iii) spiritual tune, (iv) integral approach, (v) holistic paradigm, (vi) emphasis on psychological transformation , and (vii) reliance on 'as well as 'ism' in the place of either or 'ism'.

i) Apt Twentieth Century articulation of the Indian ethos. Vamsee Juluri's comment about the booklet Integral Humanism" deserves to be discussed at the outset of the delineation of the first feature of this philosophy as it argues that this booklet shares with Gandhiji's 'Hind Swaraj' the deep affection for India's civilization which aims at elevating 'Nara' to Narayan' or the human to the divine.[4] Such a comment of Juluri, a professor of media studies at the University of San Francisco reminds us of the view point that Gandhiji wanted to sponsor an alternative to the centralized, consumerist and ecologically destructive communist and capitalist techno-states.[5] The same viewpoint was also articulated by James Petras, a co-author of Dynamix of Social Change' in Latin America. Deendayalji as well as Gandhiji

2. *Ibid*, p. 117
3. Christine Lagarde, quoted in *Times of India* (Mumbai), 18 March 2015, p. 16
4. Vamsee Juluri, 'Ahimsa has no political hue,' in *The Hindu* (Chennai, 2 October,2015), p. 15
5. James Petras, 'The Third Way: Myth and Reality', in *Monthly Review* March, 2000.

were devotees of India-Centric Approach and that was why, they were the legitimate inheritors of the galaxy of great Indian thinkers like Vivekananda and Lokmanya Tilak, worthy specimens of the builders of modern India. And, as these specimens took legitimate pride in the Indian ethos, one can say quite logically that Integral Humanism was the apt Twentieth Century articulation of the Indian ethos.

If Integral Humanism disagrees with the viewpoint that 'we must go back to the position when we lost our independence and proceed from there', it opposes with equal force the opinion that western life and thoughts are the last word in progress and all of them should be imported here if we are to develop.'[6] This philosophy reminds us of the fact that during the past one thousand years, we have attempted to reshape our life as required to face the new situations. [7] It also informs us that western ideologies are not necessarily universal, that they cannot be free from the limitations of the particular people and their culture which gave birth to these 'isms'. Do the Indians remember the right perspective on the part of Vivekananda as well as that sponsored by Tilak? Have they not advised us to seek the right balance between contemplative nature of the East and the active life pattern of the West? Is it not a fact that both of these nation builders facilitated with their attitude the process of reshaping of Indian life? If the philosophy of Swami Vivekananda preached us to bridge the gulf between action and contemplation, work and worship; the secular and the sacred, as well as that between the past and the future, that of Lokmanya Tilak preached us a dynamic social ethic, a doctrine of social activism, where action for human good without personal attachment is recommended as the first imperative.[8] It is known that Swamiji as well as Tilakji revived the tradition of reconciliation initiated by Vedas and Upanishads and reshaped Indian ethos. That Pandit Deendayal Upadhyay carried forward the same legacy has been underscored by Gautam Sen in his inimitable style. The following extract mirrors this fact only.

"In engaging with contemporary Western ideas and socialist alternatives for society and questioning their validity, Pandit Deendayal Upadhyay does not espouse, in their place, the idea of an inviolable Indic tradition that would restore some mythical golden age. Indeed, he explicitly rejected such a possibility on the ground that adaptation to changed circumstances was both a necessity and acknowledged

6. Deendayal Upadhyay, *Integral Humanism* (Bombay, 1967), p. 20.
7. *Ibid.*
8. K.Ramachandra Rao, *Integral Humanism* (Hyderabad,1995), p. 74 and 67.

foundation of Sanatan Dharma. This is the great strength of the living tradition of Sanatan Dharma that inspired Pandit Deendayal Upadhyay".[9] From the view point of Shri K. R. Rao, Deendayalji's Integral Humanism was a crystal clear and a relevant synthesis of the thought currents of the period and a worthy attempt to re-state and re-shape all the thought currents to respond to the call of the Time-sprit.[10]

Positive or Constructive Outlook

Pandit Deendayal Upadhyay was, no doubt, a very unique leader. He had the ability to go beyond the then existing time and to articulate solid thoughts containing eternal values in a lucid language. No wonder, the individual, the society and the nature were viewed by him as one great whole and the individuals were treated by him as representatives of human society in mutual and perpetual interaction with each other and with nature. It was again this viewpoint which led Deendayalji not only to emphasise the unbroken wholeness underlying the relationship between the man and the ecosystem but also to offer human personality the central position without resorting to homocentricism. It was Deendayalji's inquisitiveness to seek eternal principles and truths that has found reflection in the oft-quoted paragraph of the philosophy of Integral Humanism. And as this paragraph informs us of the positive content of integral humanism, it deserves to be quoted here as well:

> "We must absorb the knowledge and gains of the entire humanity so far as eternal principles and truths are concerned. Of these the ones that originated in our midst have to be clarified and adapted to changed times and those that we take from other societies have to be adapted to our conditions."[11]

Positive or constructive outlook of Integral Humanism is vividly reflected in the concept of '*Chiti*' (the soul of a nation) which is the most remarkable, in fact original contribution of Pandit Deendayal Upadhyay. We cannot of course ignore that Western thinkers like Mazzini and Ernest Renan have also underscored the view that each nation possesses its own soul. They have thus pointed out that every people has its special mission which will cooperate towards the fulfilment of the general mission of humanity. One may also refer to the

9. Gautam Sen, 'Integral Humanism of Deendayal Upadhyay' http://indiafacts.co.in/integral_humanism_of_deendayal_upadhyaya
10. *See* the Note no. 8, p. 97.
11. *See* the Note no. 6, p. 22.

rediscovery and reassertion of the pre-Islamic traditions in the post-Soviet Central Asian nations such as Kazakhstan, Kyrgyzstan, Tajikistan, Turkmenistan and Uzbekistan, as the following lines from the Uzbek poet-Abdu, Razzaq Adbuvashidaw's ballad – 'Dear Soul' are resonating in that region -

"Every Nation has its own desire
Its own song, its own epic
It has its own place - its own garden
So far preserved thousands of years".[12]

The concept of '*Chiti*' is accepted as the original contribution of Pandit Deendayal Upadhyay because he applies it while elaborating the process of development. Deendayalji, for instance, states that an Indian should try to attain (in the light of Chiti) God like perfection as a result of development and accordingly, the children and the old, the diseased and the invalids must be cared for by our society. "Pandit Deendayal Upadhyay further mentions that Economics as a Science does not account for this responsibility"[13]. The protagonist of Integral Humanism indeed makes a unique contribution to the deliberations over development.

One should not rush to state that the recent genesis and growth of nativism in Europe as well as proclamation of American affiliation to the so called W.A.S.P. (White Anglo Saxon Protestantism) are quite akin to Deendayalji's advocacy of '*Chiti*'. If the Euro-Americans' attachment to 'nativism' is a reaction to the global spread of violent activities sponsored by Islamic State of Iraq and Syria, Deendayalji's advocacy of '*Chiti*' was an articulation of the conviction on his part in the positive or constructive content of each nation. Secondly, if the recent revival of the 'nativism' in the Western world informs us of the likelihood of the emergence of the faith-driven polity in each nation there, Upadhyay-sponsored 'Chiti' assures us of the strengthening of the faith-neutral polity. Euro-Americans' nativism, for instance underscores the superiority of the respective faiths pursued by natives over all other faiths pursued by aliens in those nations Deendayalji's integral humanism on the other hand proclaims that in India everybody is free to follow his or her path in the light of the respective faith. The following extract from the speech delivered by Pandit Deendayal

12. Quoted in Anita Sengupta " The Performative State" in P. L. Dash (ed.) *India and Central Asia: Two Decades of Transition* (New Delhi,2012), pp. 175, 176
13. *See* the Note no. 6, pages 70, 74

Upadhyay on 27 June 1962 deserves quotation here:

> "So long as Hinduism is alive there is no danger to Islam. A Hindu does not differentiate between Ram and Allah. He recites Vishnu Sahasranam in the daily schedule, he will be too happy to add one or two names to the thousand terms attributed to God Vishnu! The concept of Hindu Nation is neither negative, nor reactionary, nor territorial, it is a cultural and civilizational concept connoting positive direction".[14]

Spiritual Tune

Third feature of Integral Humanism is spiritual tune. It reminds us of the Vivekananda-sponsored definition of Indian Nation which runs as follows:

> "India is the union of those whose hearts beat to the same spiritual tune". One comes across this definition of our nation in the speech delivered by Vivekananda in November 1897 at Lahore. But, in various speeches delivered at different places in India on preceding dates, Swamiji pointed out forcefully that our nation has been preaching spiritual oneness of the whole universe. And at Kumbakonam in February 1897, Vivekananda highlighted the implication of the mission of our nation: "The infinite oneness of the Soul is the eternal sanction of all morality, that you and I are not only brothers- every literature voicing man's struggles towards freedom has preached that for you, but that you and I are really one".[15]

That Vivekananda here refers to the superiority of selfhood over brotherhood is quite obvious. It is indeed the feeling of selfhood rather than that of brotherhood which generates in me the unattached concern for the other and it is the very feeling which also motivates me to concretise this concern in a befitting action. Vivekananda, of course used one and the same Kumbakonam speech for articulating his anguish over the fact that our aristocratic ancestors just forgot to apply in practice the ideal of the oneness of things. The relevant extract is quite revealing.[16]

---

14. Quoted in Mahesh Chandra Sharma, *Deendayal Upadhyaya : Kartrtva evam Vichar* (New Delhi, 1994), p. 369
15. *See* the Note no. 6, p. 52
16. Quoted in P. Parameswaran, *Marx and Vivekananda : A Comparative Study* (Madras, 2007), p. 132

"Our aristocratic ancestors went on treading the common masses of our country underfoot till they became helpless, till under this torment the poor, poor people nearly forgot that they were human beings. They have been compelled to be merely hewers of wood and drawers of water for centuries, so much so, that they are made to believe that they are born as slaves......." Pandit Deendayal Upadhyay shares Vivekananda's anguish and brings to our notice that from the perspective of the Indian ethos, the state is expected to produce and maintain conditions in which the ideals of the nation can be translated into reality.[15] The spiritual tune of Deendayalji's Integral Humanism in short does not ignore the role of the state, actually it invites the state to bring the 'Haves' on the track with a view to getting the ideals of the nation implemented in due proportion.

As per the spiritual tune of the philosophy of Integral Humanism, both the individual as well as the society are the articulations of the basic reality and therefore this philosophy recommends due reconciliation between the individual interest and the interest of the society. This philosophy asks us, in other words to bother for the interests of individuals as well as for those of the society. Sri Aurobindo has rightly stated that a spiritualized society makes it possible for the individual as well as the society to find their balance and harmony.[16] As the worship of materialism or the oblivious attitude about spiritualism is the commonality between Marxism and Capitalism, both paradigms failed in achieving a balance or harmony between individual and society. If Marxism strengthened state at the cost of individual, capitalism consolidated plutocracy at the expense of democracy! Resultant dehumanisation of man needs to be ended on the war footing. And here, Integral Humanism is the right antidote, because it considers Man as the highest creation of God and encourages him to exert for attaining divine heights of his latent personality. Deendayalji has noted that the concept of economic man and the principle of individual liberty sponsored in capitalism have resulted in the growth of middle class Parliamentarism, whereas the concept of abstract man and the principle of social equality sanctioned by Marxism have sparked cruel statism. He has accordingly invited our attention to the missing link of fraternity in the above mentioned paradigms. The concept of divine man and the principle of selfhood inherent in the philosophy of Integral Humanism do take care of genuine and transparent fraternity and provide due relief to the world !

---

15. *See* the Note no. 6, p. 52
16. Quoted in P. Parameswaran, *Marx and Vivekananda : A Comparative Study* (Madras,2007), p. 132

Integral Approach

Just elucidated spiritual tune of Integral Humanism reminds us of the following memorable statement of Nikolai Berdyaev, a Russian Philosopher: "If the concept of divinity is human, that of humanity is divine!" And once we accept that everything in universe including humanity is divine we emphasise quite logically that there is mutual interdependence and harmony between a) man and nature, b) individual and society, c) agriculture and industry, d) labour and capital and so on. Integral approach is indeed a right derivative of the spiritual tune of Deendayalji's philosophy Dr. M. Mohandas points out that it is the very derivative that spars Integral Humanism to make very valuable prescriptions in the field of economy, some of which run as follows:

1) We must resolve conflicting interests between labour and capital through appropriate sharing and participative systems such as ownership sharing, capital participation and sharing of rightful entitlements,
2) We must secondly, treat labour as a partner in production and not as a factor of production as in Western System,
3) Thirdly, we should apt for a broad based and widely dispersed production- system with partnership between small and big units and strategic cooperation for enhancing production distribution with a view to minimizing unwanted cut throat competition between different scales of producing units and wastage of scarce resources,
4) We must also implement Gandhiji's recommendation in favour of production by masses and avoid mass production of the West.[17]

Unlike the Western paradigm which has favoured humanism in reaction to unjust socio-political regulations and constraints, the humanism sponsored by Pandit Deendayal Upadhyay is an articulation of conviction in immanent divinity. That is why, whereas Western isms underscore that relations between individuals and society are full of clashes, conflicts and confrontations, Integral Humanism believes in mutual co-operation and co-ordination between individuals and society. Incidentally, it is interesting to recollect that during 1960s when Pandit Deendayal Upadhyay elaborated the relevance of co-operation and co-ordination between individuals and society through his Mumbai lectures on integral humanism, the world witnessed historical

17. Dr. M. Mohandas, Ekatma Manav Darshan and Economic Development, unpublished paper.

convergence between Marxism and capitalism. Government of the U.S.S.R. then found it indispensable to sanction through reforms the concept of private entrepreneurship and the principle of profit. Governments of capitalist countries found it desirable almost simultaneously to bless government interventions in their economies. Inevitable retreat on the part of the Western paradigms from the initial positions, which was rationalised and legitimised as a specimen of convergence actually disproved the thesis of confrontation and substantiated the Indian conviction in cooperation between individuals and society.

The Marxists' emphasis on statism ultimately culminated in the collapse of the U.S.S.R. Similarly it was the opposite emphasis on the individual initiative proclaimed with pride in the capitalist world that resulted in a chaos in the form of Lehman crisis in 2008.That is why, leading economists like Joseph Stiglitz have advanced a thesis in the recent past that 'market fundamentalism' needs to be replaced by 'managed markets' in the sense that the few fortunate who have become tycoons at the cost of millions of unfortunate destitute should keep aside extreme pursuit of self-interest and bother for the wellbeing of masses and the state should also take some steps for enhancing public welfare. The world has thus endorsed Deendayalji's viewpoint that interconnection between individuals and society is the antidote to be implemented on the war footing for overcoming the chaos and catastrophe.

Deendayalji's philosophy emphasises in a similar vein that proper development of each personality depends on the nursing of interconnection between the body and the soul and for that purpose one must pay due attention to the full development of each dimension of every being. P.Parameswaran, a renowned commentator on Integral Humanism has very cogently elaborated that the fullest development of each of the five dimensions of a human being shapes the integrated or developed personality and it is essential to note that all these dimensions are interconnected or interlinked with each other. His elaboration runs as follows:

> "Man is a multidimensional entity with the soul (Atma) as the core. Atma is an abstract entity which is encased within five different sheaths (koshas). In the Hindu terminology they are Annamaya (physical), Pranamaya (vital), Manomaya (mental), Vijnanamaya (intellectual) and Anandamaya (blissful)......All these dimensions

are interconnected and all these together constitute one integrated whole. It is thus integrated individual that is called PurnaManav".[18]

Holistic Paradigm

Deendayalji's criticism against capitalism as well as that against Marxism bring to our notice that both of these 'isms' look at a human being from very partial and parochial perspectives! Deendayalji Upadhyay has thus stated that if from the perspective of capitalism every man is an economic man, from that of Marxism, everybody is an abstract entity. He has further argued that if the 'economic man' of capitalism runs exclusively for pocketing personal profit in each walk of life, the 'abstract man' of Marxism finds himself totally helpless , unable to exercise his individuality, his tastes and preferences. Capitalism converts democracy into plutocracy. Marxism generates rigid and inert bureaucracy. Both 'isms', Deendayalji avers, refuse to grasp man holistically and facilitate dehumanisation of human being. As 'Man" the highest creation of God is losing his own identity due to both isms, the philosophy of Integral Humanism is interested in re-establishing 'Man' in his rightful position, in bringing him to the realisation of his greatness, in encouraging him to exert for attaining divine heights of his latent personality. Integral Humanism is confident of achieving its aim because of holistic paradigm as well as Cosmo-centric approach unlike ego-centric or homocentric approach blessed by capitalism and Marxism. Both these isms share belief in the Cartesian paradigm of rationality and mechanistic world view. They thus believe that all the complex phenomena can be understood first by reducing them to their constituent parts and later by reassembling them! Such a fragmentary approach has led Westerners to sanction the principle: 'Survival of the fittest'. Rich persons are thus allowed to exploit poor and the human society is prompted to exploit nature. World has, of course, come to realise that various dichotomies as well as the viewpoint that only the fit should survive and the unfit should wither away itself are rooted in the fragmentary approach and this very realisation has led it to opt for holistic approach. Integral Humanism does indeed provide the best alternative, as from its perspective man is a whole and so all his activities have an overarching unity.' We may divide human life into different compartments for the sake of analysis and study. Real life however does not entertain an artificial individual as it knows that a split personality and an unbalanced social group

18. P. Parameswaran, "Integral Humanism Revisited" in Raveendra Mahajan (ed.) *Ekatma Manav Darshan-Vichar Samgraha* (Ahmedabad, 2014), pp. 19, 20.

cause tragic catastrophes. Holistic paradigm of integral humanism not only considers 'man' as a whole, but also emphasises inseparability between man and society and indivisibility between society and nature. The very paradigm moreover underscores that cosmic influences interpenetrate our human world. This is why, it is mentioned above that whereas integral humanism blesses Cosmo-centric approach, capitalism as well as Marxism opt for egocentric or homocentric approach. It is the Cosmocentric approach on the part of Pandit Deendayal Upadhyay which had generated agony in his mind that 'Western societies encourage people to increase desires and needs and to destroy nature with a view to accomplishing ever increasing demands and needs.' Deendayalji's agony or distress over the fact that Western societies have not only become consumption oriented but are also bent on destroying nature led him to make the following comment:

'Supposing that we need not worry about the limited supply of natural resources, there is yet the question of balance in nature. There is a cyclic relationship in different parts of Nature. If from the three sticks standing with mutual support, one is removed, the other two will automatically fall. The present economic system and the system of production are fast disturbing this equilibrium of nature. As a result, on the one hand new products are manufactured for satisfying ever increasing desires, on the other hand new problems arise everyday, threatening the very existence of entire humanity and civilization.'[19]

Incidentally, recent Indian ratification of the Paris climate deal and its commitment to following the low carbon path to progress has informed the world of our faith in holistic paradigm only. The new companies Act 2013 which has imposed corporate social responsibility obligations on Indian corporations and companies is also a right step toward implementing holistic approach, as it has underscored the significance of three 'P's... profit, people and planet. Mr.Vikram Mehta, Chairman of Brookings India has made a very notable comment in this connection. The comment runs as follows: "Helping Hand of collaborative partnerships between the social enterprises and the community is, no doubt, superior to the invisible hand of the market".[20]

World-acceptance of holistic paradigm in the place of fragmentary approach is bound to replace competition and confrontation by cooperation and co-ordination and such a side effect is definitely a boon for the entire globe.

19. *See* the Note no.6, PP.71-72
20. Vikram Mehta, "C.S.R.: Corporates should reach out" in *The Indian Express* (Mumbai), 4 August 2015, p. 13

That the pursuit of holistic paradigm makes one happy and successful in all respects is a fact and it can be substantiated with certain instances and examples.

Mr. V.P. Malik, our former military chief is thus reported to have stated that one must look at security issues from the holistic angle.[21] And the success achieved by our military soldiers in the early morning of 29 September 2016 this year not only in demolishing the seven camps established by the government of Pakistan in the Pak occupied Kashmir for training terrorists there but also in killing around 40 terrorists and in arriving safely back in the Indian territory has mirrored the implementation of the holistic paradigm only. Least wonder, India could deliver a historical shock to Pakistan in terms of scale, dimension and impact.

It is similarly the holistic paradigm which informs that each individual plays multiple roles in his life. Pandit Deendayal Upadhyay has for example stated that each individual in India happens to be a member of his family, a constituent part of his caste, a worker in a firm or a businessman engaged in different activities, a member of a specific group, a resident of a particular locality, a citizen of the state, an inheritor of the nation and so on. Deendayalji has also stated that each one is connected with the entire cosmos. Thus there is a linkage between the man as the centre as a miniature cosmos on the one hand and the universe as a whole as an infinite magnification of man, on the other.[22] Deendayalji's comment in this connection is a quotable quote here: "Man lives a variety of lives. The most important aspect is that despite this multiple personality, he can and should behave in a way which does not bring different aspects of his life into mutual conflict but which is mutually sustaining, complementary and unifying., This quality is inherent in man".[23]

Pleasantly enough, the Upadhyaya-sponsored Cosmocentric approach based on holistic paradigm is quite close to the viewpoint of Ms Jill Stein, Green Party candidate for the U.S. presidency; whose manifesto informs us of the following lofty, sublime goal: "We need to put people, planet and peace over profit for facilitating transformational change so that we can survive into the next century".[24] It is obvious that as per the prescription of the Green Party; each one of us should give priority to *Samashti* (People), *Srushti* (Planet) and *Parameshti* (Peace)

21. *See* the interview of V. P. Malik, Times of India (Mumbai) 26 September, 2016, p. 16
22. *See* the Note no. 6, pp. 47-48
23. *Ibid.* p. 48
24. *See* Vijay Prashad, The power to create a new world is in our hands', in *Frontline* (Chennai), 15 April 2016, p. 64

over *Vyashti* (Profit). That the viewpoint of the Green Party in the U.S.A. is quite close to the holistic paradigm of Integral Humanism is quite obvious.

Emphasis on Psychological Transformation

Integral Humanism being basically based on spiritualism emphasises that broad socio-economic and political transformation depends mainly on the change in consciousness or psychological change. Philosophies based on stark materialism obviously refuse to share such an emphasis on psychological change; as they believe in systemic or institutional change. Capitalists thus thought it essential during and after industrial revolution in Great Britain to grab the state machinery with a view to replacing feudalism by capitalism. And they did succeed in their venture, although the resultant socio-economic and political transformation facilitated concentration of power in the few hands of tycoons through the endorsement of the principle of survival of the fittest, widened the gap between the 'Haves' and the 'Have Nots' and caused incalculable miseries to millions of destitute. That was why, Swami Vivekananda took the tycoons to task by abusing them as 'Shylocks'. If the institutional transformation blessed by capitalism proved disastrous, inhuman and unjust, that which was implemented later by Marxists-Leninists in U.S.S.R. strengthened statist domination over society and proved literally disastrous, as it caused the demise of the Soviet Union. World has indeed witnessed the eternal validity of the spiritualists' thesis that it is the change in consciousness or in mind-set rather than that in institutions which gives desirable; sustainable results.

It is essential to point out here that Herbert Spencer challenged the Marxian faith in institutional or systemic transformation in 1881 when he underscored the necessity to give priority to psychological change or to change in consciousness. Spencer's comment is quit penetrating: "The machinery of communism, like existing social machinery has to be framed out of existing human nature, and the defects of existing nature will generate one and the same evils as in the other.'[25] Spencer in fact raised the question whether well working institutes would ever succeed in transforming ill working humanity.[26] Still later, during the catastrophic months of Bolshevik Revolution Maxim Gorky raised the same question while interacting with Lenin.[27] Pandit Deendayal

25. Herbert Spencer, *The Man Versus the state* (London, 1881), pp. 40-43
26. *Ibid.*
27. Maxim Gorky, *Untimely Thoughts* (NewYork,1968), pp. 229-233

Upadhyay was equally sceptical about desirable socio-political transformation exclusively through institutional change. He thus referred to Milovan Djilas during his lecture series on integral humanism and informed his audience that in the Soviet Union, the institution of private property was abolished, the class of old fashioned exploiters was eliminated but the newly emerged bureaucratic class of exploiters carried forward the legacy of old exploiters thus putting an end to the aim of desirable socio-economic and political transformation.[28] Pandit Deendayal Upadhyay, being an inheritor of Indian philosophy believes in the divinity of a human being. He therefore launched a severe attack on the determinist dialectical materialism sponsored by Marx, as according to him, such a view destroys the urge for reform and dynamism in man. Man, from the perspective of Marx is no longer the creator of a new order; he is merely incidental to a predetermined historic process. His task is only to accelerate the process. Therefore, even as he tries to organise workers he cares little for their welfare, but uses them as mere tools for the revolution.[29] History has, no doubt endorsed Deendayalji's viewpoint that any ideology which relies exclusively on system and institution, on legislation and administration and takes deep interest in developing in place of a living people, a mechanical state is bound to result in dehumanisation of man. What is basic or fundamental is to change the mind-set of a man. Lokmanya Tilak has rightly stated in Gita-Rahasya that the guidance given by Mother Kunti to her sons after the end of the Mahabharat war "to broaden your minds" possesses eternal worth.[30] And the very emphasis on the transformation of the mind prompted Dr. Ram Manohar Lohia to challenge Soviet leaders through the following question: 'How can the world filled with the spirit of greed achieve the aim of a classless society ?'[31] Tragic demise of the U.S.S.R. in 1991 has undoubtedly proved that the reliance on institutional change without changing human mind-set causes historical catastrophe!

Integral Humanism of course does not ignore the role played by the institutional or systemic change in the broad socio-economic and political transformation. It merely underscores the significance of the change in the human consciousness. Pandit Deendayal Upadhyay, like Swami Vivekananda asks leadership to facilitate broad socio-political

---

28. *See* the Note no. 6, pp. 82, 83
29. *Ibid.*
30. Lokmanya Tilak, *Gita-Rahasya* (Pune, 1950), p. 460
31. Dr. Rammanohar Lohia, *Marx, Gandhi and Socialism* (Hyderabad, 1963), p. 117.

transformation through resort to the four-fold strategy comprising *Sama* (conciliation) *Dama* (incentive), *Bheda* (Sowing the seeds of division) and *Danda* (State machinery). He thus integrates subjective and objective realities, in the sense that after underscoring the crucial role of subjective change, he also refers to the objective reality and prescribes that institutional change must also be implemented. Shri Kandarpa Ramachandra Rao, whose commentary on Integral Humanism is considered as a set worthy of explanatory notes quite in line with the Hindu scholastic pursuit has summed up very aptly Deendayalji's views regarding the process of socio-economic and political transformation. The extract given below therefore deserves to be reproduced here:

> "Forms must not be changed before the indwelling life has altered. The social mind is all important. But many political revolutionaries believe that one must first change the political and economic structure radically, and then, as a second and almost necessary step, the human mind will also change, that the new society once established will quasi automatically produce the new human being. They do not see that the new elite, being motivated by the same character as the old one, will tend to recreate the conditions of the old society in the new socio-political institutions the revolution has created; that the victory of the revolution will be its defeat as a revolution".[32]

Reliance on 'As Well As Ism' in the Place of 'Either Or Ism'

It has been stated above that integral humanism is a very apt Twentieth Century articulation of the Indian ethos.

Such an articulation is therefore bound to be open minded and receptive of all the thought currents, ancient as well as modern, western as well as Eastern, Monist as well as Dualist, etc. What is essential of course is to adapt each thought current to our land and to our times! Integral Humanism is thus least dogmatic. Deendayalji thus shares with Marx the empathy for the victims of the capitalist exploitative order through his statement that the capitalist viewpoint makes the machine a competitor of human labour. He is also in agreement with Marx when he analyses the phenomenon of fetishism. One can quote his statement: "Machines cannot be blamed, if the labours are displaced and subjected to privations. It is the fault of the economic and social system which cannot distinguish between the object and the instrument.'[33]

32. *See* the Note no. 8, p. 56
33. *See* the Note no. 6, p. 78

Deendayalji's diagnosis of capitalism is quite apt, and it is in tune with that attempted by Marx, though his remedial measures are quite different.

Pandit Deendayal Upadhyay also shares with Joseph Stiglitz, a recipient of the Nobel Prize in Economics and one-time chairman of Bill Clinton's Economic Advisory Council the most convincing comprehensive definition of Development which runs as follows:

"It is an enhancement of the totality of a nation's four fold capital-stocks: the capital of material goods, natural capital such as soil, water, forest and fish, human capital including health, education and employment, and social capital comprising mutual trust and social harmony".[34]

The vision of development on the part of Pandit Deendayal Upadhyay is also in tune with that sponsored by Bhutan, a tiny country located in the Himalayan ranges. All of us know that if from the world perspective it is the GNP criterion which is adopted for measuring development, the government of Bhutan has on the other hand adopted the GNH (Gross National Happiness) Criterion for doing the same. And Deendayal-sponsored Integral Humanism can very well accommodate this criterion!

Integral Humanism similarly supports the concept of a 'welfare state', which provides the minimum necessities, ensures free education and medical care as a right, and so on. In the ideal scenario, sponsored by Pandit Deendayal Upadhyay the state is of course supposed to be a guardian invoking 'well to do' people to take care of children, the old, the diseased and the invalids. Deendayalji states that the right to food is a birth right. The ability to earn is a result of education and training. In a society even those who do not earn must have food. And every society generally fulfils this responsibility.[35]

Least dogmatism or 'as well as ism' on the part of Pandit Deendayal Upadhyay is obviously rooted in the Vedantic principle: 'Ekam Sat, Vipra Bahudha Vadanti' (Truth is one, sages call it by different names.) Deendayalji naturally welcomes all the thought currents which articulate agonies over human sorrow, diagnose that sorrow and prescribe do's and don'ts for mitigating the sorrow. He, of course, expects the relevant thought currents to be positive or constructive, spiritual, integral, holistic, and so on. He, however, tries to find out pluses even in a thought current which is otherwise negative,

34. Quoted in Madhav Gadgil, "Development as a people's movement", in *The Hindu* (Chennai) 1.12.2014

35. *See* the Note no. 6, p. 74

materialist, fragmentary and partial. We have already referred to the fact that Pandit Deendayal Upadhyay is in agreement with Marx when he analyses phenomena of alienation and fetishism. How aptly has Shri Guruji Golwalkar stated that Pandit Deendayal Upadhyay resembled Yudhishthir who used to call Duryodhana as 'Suyodhana' !

Deendayalji's faith in 'as well asism' or his opposition to 'either or ism' deserves due attention, because it is woven around the core of the philosophy of Integral Humanism. Pandit Deendayal Upadhyay has referred to this core in the fourth lecture during his lecture- series in Mumbai in April 1965. His articulation is inimitable indeed:

> "Keeping in view the aim of human life we must endeavour to see how with the minimum of fuel, man proceeds to his goal with the maximum speed. Such a system alone can be called civilization. This system will not think of merely a single aspect of human life but of all aspects including the ultimate aim. This system will be constructive rather than destructive. This system will not thrive on the exploitation of nature but will sustain nature and will in turn itself be nourished. Milking rather than exploitation should be our aim..... If such human angle inspires the economic system then our thinking on the economic questions will undergo thorough transformation".[36]

Upadhyayji shakes hands comfortably with anybody who has faith in the just mentioned core of integral humanism. His philosophy accordingly becomes inclusive and accommodative, in the sense that seeds of alliance with several schools of thought are sown quite spontaneously.

It is the underlined portion of the just quoted extract which informs us of the emphasis on all aspects of the human life including its ultimate aim. And the fact that from the perspective of integral humanism the best human life is that which unfolds itself in the light of certain principles is simply obvious. Deendayalji offers salute to such human life! No wonder, he pays heartfelt tribute to Shri Hafij Mohammed Ibrahim, a former Muslim league M.L.A. who thought it indispensable to relinquish the post of M.L.A. in 1939 on his own before joining Congress, sought re-election on Congress ticket and got elected again as M.L.A.[37] He honours in the same vein those socialists like Acharya Narendra Deva, who followed the footsteps of Hafij Mohammed

---

36. *See* the Note no. 6, p. 73
37. *Ibid*, p. 10

Ibrahim and resigned as M.L.A.s with a view to fighting elections on socialist tickets.[38] It was the same accommodative spirit on the part of Pandit Deendayal Upadhyay which prompted him to be a bosom friend of principled personalities such as Acharya J.B. Kripalani, Jai Prakash Narayan, Dr.Ram Manohar Lohia, and so on.

Once we grasp such an accommodative spirit of integral humanism, we can conclude that the following extract from Asoka Mehta's write-up can very well be fitted into the framework of Upadhyayji's philosophy: "Wholeness of man is achieved only where he ceases to be at war with himself, at war with his fellowmen, at war with nature, where he recovers his traditional kinship and recaptures the feeling of continuity, the rhythm of harmony. Peace, poise, harmony, the blending of all notes, the stilling of tensions in a quickening equipoise, is the final achievement of man, the ultimate end of all quest".[39]

One and the same rationale goads to state that the philosophy of Integral Humanism accommodates the extract given below from the write-up penned by Jawaharlal Nehru on 25th May 1964:

> "The focus on the unity and quality of being behind the diversity and inequality of the functions is a must for being spiritual".[40]

Jawaharlalji here highlights very beautifully the crux of spiritualism, according to which the moment, the functions performed by anybody are ignored and concentrate our attention exclusively on the fact that the fellow concerned is a being, a divine being, it is realised that the diversity and inequality between the one and that fellow are replaced by unity and equality. It can be asserted quite confidently that the views of Pandit Deendayal Upadhyay as well as the just quoted views articulated by Pandit Jawaharlal Nehru deserve due welcome by everybody!

That Deendayalji's philosophy is accommodative in the sense that it embraces the whole humankind needs to be elaborated in the concluding section of this write-up. Such accommodativeness of this philosophy is clearly mirrored in the 'as well as 'ism' of this philosophy. A succinct comparison between integral humanism on the one hand and capitalism as well as Marxism on the other hand is a must in this connection. Capitalism considers individual as superior to society and prompts everybody to be greedy; to pursue his respective self-interest. Increase in the wealth at the cost of welfare, widening of

38. *Ibid*, p. 10
39. Asoka Mehta, Democratic Socialism, pp. 146-148
40. Quoted in 'Ekatma Manav Darshan-Governance,' in Raveendra Mahajan (ed.) Ekatma Manav Darshan-Vichar Samgraha (Ahmedabad, 2014), p. 93

the gap between the 'Haves' and the 'Have Nots' as well as the conversion of democracy into plutocracy are the inevitable consequences in capitalism. Emergence of the aristocratic government is the outcome in the capitalist polity.

Marxism occupies the opposite end, as it gives priority to society over individual. It prefers equality to liberty.

Initially it tortures wealthy tycoons and assures 'good days' for the destitute and downtrodden. It relies on the institution of the state for accomplishing this mission. Resultant statist grabbing of society causes incalculable harm; as the nourishment of bureaucracy with all its inherent evils like routine, rigidity and inertia generates a new class of cruel exploiters! Marxism, in short gives birth to totalitarian autocratic government. This is why, Pandit Deendayal Upadhyay rightly comments: "Both these systems, capitalist as well as communist have failed to take account of the integral Man, his true and complete personality and his aspirations..... Both result in dehumanisation of man".[41]

Pandit Deendayal Upadhyay articulates the aim of Integral Humanism in a very positive manner in the following extract: Man, the highest creation of God, is losing his own identity. We must re-establish him in his rightful position, bring him the realisation of his greatness, reawaken his abilities and encourage him to exert for attaining divine heights of his latent personality. This is possible through a decentralised economy.[42]

It is hardly necessary to point out that the implementation of such a positive or constructive approach relies obviously on 'as well as ism' in the place of either orism'. This is why, integral humanism is quite broad, accommodative and inclusive! It is in full consonance with the Indian ethos which informs us that if Shukacharya obtained Mukti (spiritual independence) in his dwelling in forest, Raja Janaka achieved very aim through his residence in the royal palace! We discard either orism,' in favour of 'as well asism'.

Integral Humanism has spelt out six objectives of Indian economy in the light of the salient features elaborated in the lines above. Thus the first two objectives emphasise holistic paradigm in the sense that they ask to pay attention to all entities from the individual to the entire universe. It can, for instance assure minimum living standard to each individual and be ever ready simultaneously for the defence of our

41. *See* the Note no. 6, pp. 83-84
42. *Ibid.* p. 44

nation. These very objectives ask in the same vein to go on raising the living standards with a view to enabling ourselves and the nation as well to contribute to the world peace on the basis of our 'Chiti', third and fourth objectives underscore integral approach, as they ask to be extremely cautious and sensitive while providing meaningful employment to each able citizen, as the unrestrained and unreasonable utilisation of resources will cause great harm to ecology. These objectives moreover imbibe the significance of the necessity to transform mind-sets for developing machines suitable for Bhartiya conditions. Fifth and sixth objectives inform the positive or constructive outlook of the Integral Humanism. They inculcate equally forcefully the pragmatic and the accommodative nature of Deendayalji's philosophy. They ask for instance to help the individual and to protect the cultural and other values of life. That the spiritual tune of integral humanism is mirrored in these objectives is crystal clear. Sixth objective, in particular is fully reflective of pragmatic, accommodative 'as well as ism' of Pandit Deendayal Upadhyay, as from its perspective the issue of the ownership, state, private or any other form of various industries is not akin to the holy cow !

Entire lecture series of Pandit Deendayal Upadhyay delivered for elaborating Integral Humanism is full of apt references to Indian ethos. Thus at one place Deendayalji informs how Bhartiya culture is integrated; at another place he reminds us that our national life continued uninterruptedly even after the state went in the hands of foreigners. He similarly conveys to us that the description of king Bharat after whom the nation has been named Bharat runs as follows: 'by maintaining and protecting his subjects (bharanat, rakshanat cha) he was called *Bharat*. Such a lecture series being in short the most apt Twentieth Century articulation of Indian ethos finds its culmination in the most memorable determination': "We shall create a Bharat which will enable every citizen in its fold... to become 'Narayan' from 'Nar'. This is the external divine form of our culture. This is our message to humanity at cross roads. May God give us strength to succeed in this task!"

Integral Humanism, which has been described above as the most apt Twentieth Century articulation of the Indian ethos continues to guide in the Twenty First Century and of its relevance for ever! It is in fact the uniqueness on the part of Indian ethos that it absorbs and retains eternal dimensions of every thought current and goes on strengthening the treasury of our civilization.

Implementation of Integral Humanism in Indian Economy

It is well known that Bhartiya Janata Party which has formed Central Government in the aftermath of its victory in the 2014 parliamentary election takes legitimate pride in carrying forward the legacy of Pandit Deendayal Upadhyay, as it was he who nurtured with utmost care Bhartiya Jansangh, the previous incarnation of B.J.P. This is why, the economic policies, sponsored and implemented by the present rulers reflect quite spontaneously the features of Integral Humanism. It is therefore quite legitimate to elaborate implementation of integral humanism by referring to schemes launched and the budgetary provisions made by the present rulers. Shri Narendra Modi and his colleagues are well aware of the fact that Pandit Deendayal Upadhyay was interested in changing the then existing economic and other institutions in the direction to be determined by the principles and goals set for human endeavour by the Indian ethos. They also know that Deendayal-sponsored Integral Humanism, a philosophy, least interested in status-quo paradigm expects them to be comprehensive and holistic while implementing policies and schemes.

Glimpses of the holistic approach are vividly observable in the linkage, or to be more precise, in the synergy between economic and foreign policies pursued by the Modi Government in the past two and half years. To anybody it is obvious that the distinct pillars or initiatives of the transformative agenda underpinning this government's budget proposals are closely linked with foreign policy initiatives of the present government.

The present government's foreign policy and its certain salient trends such as Narendra Modi's personal rapport with international leaders, thrust given to bilateral trade relations along with multilateral pacts like the WTO and GATT, leveraging India's powerful diaspora etc. have indicated that such an enhanced India's profile and this much self-confidence was never seen before. Narendra Modi has been successful in convincing the international community that India will realise its true potential as an economic power. As a result, India has now emerged as one of the world's top destinations for FDI flows. It has attracted investment of close to $ 200 billion from foreign investors.[43] Small wonder, present government's economic policy-initiatives like Make in India, Skill India, Stand up India, Clean India, Transform India through investment in infrastructure, etc. have obtained solid boost through innovative trends of the present foreign policy.

43. Gopal Krishna Agrawal , 'At ease with the world' in *The Indian Express* (Mumbai), 21 October. 2016, p. 15

This does not mean that the critique of the present government's economic policies should not be looked at as well because juxtaposition of the critical assessment side by side with the laudatory assessment will enable us to see both sides of the coin.

Here we refer to the write-up penned by one Pushparaj Deshpande, as it has launched an attack on the Smart Cities -initiative on the ground that as a result of this initiative rural areas will be damaged. This critique accordingly challenges the claim that the present government's approach is integral or holistic. According to this critique, the budget presented by the Modi-Government in 2014 has set aside Rs.7060/- crore for the development of 100 new smart cities and such a course of action is bound to affect most adversely indigenous and rural communities which have been displaced, deprived of their self-sufficient ways and ultimately marginalised.[44]

Pushparaj Deshpande has in fact asked the present Central Government to abandon the prevalent urban industrial version of development and opt for establishing more cooperative anti-hierarchical forms of socio-economic and political organisation, as envisaged by Mahatma Gandhi.[45]

Curiously enough even a cursory perusal of the 2014- budget presented by the Modi Government informs us of its faith in "the Rurban development model of urbanization of the rural areas through which people living in the rural areas can get efficient civic infrastructure and associate services". One and the same budget assures us that "Shyama Prasad Mukherji Rurban Mission would be launched to deliver integrated project based infrastructure in the rural areas which would include development of economic activities and skill development".

The latest budget presented by Arun Jaitley on 29 February 2016 highlights the Mukherjee Rurban Mission in a still more vigorous style: "300 Rurban Clusters which will be developed under this mission will incubate growth centres in rural areas by providing infrastructure amenities and market access for the farmers. They will also expand employment opportunities for the youth".

All the underscored portions of the extracts quoted above are adequately self-explanatory. They convey to us that the Modi-

44. Pushparaj Deshpande, 'Reconceptualising Indias Civilisational Basis' in *Economic & Political Weekly* (Mumbai), 24 September 2016.
45. *Ibid.* p. 19

Government is totally against 'the prevalent urban industrial version of development' causing trepidation to rural areas. They also inform us that this government believes in integrated Rurban Mission. And thirdly they convince that it has a faith in the A.P.J. Abdul Kalam-sponsored PURA system (Providing Urban amenities in Rural Areas) A.P.J. Abdul Kalam and Srijan Pal Singh have elucidated in the book : 'Target 3 Billion' the so called PURA Scheme, whereby sustainable development forces would be generated in villages through the provision of several attractive urban amenities.

The Rurban development model of urbanisation of the rural areas sponsored by the Modi-Government in fact assures us of quite cooperative and anti-hierarchical form of relationship between cities and villages. The 2016-2017 budget thus informs us of very vital government commitments such as achieving 100% village electrification by 1st May 2018, giving priority allocation from Centrally Sponsored Schemes to reward villages that have become free from open defecation, launching of Digital Saksharta Abhiyan (DISHA) for rural India to cover around 6 crore additional households within the next 3 years, launching of another campaign : 'Rashtriya Gram Swaraj Abhiyan' for strengthening Panchayat Raj Institutions with a view to developing governance capabilities etc. Pushparaj Deshpande's criticism of the initiative of Smart Cities is indeed quite wide of the mark! Such a Rurban mission actually mirrors Modi Government's resolve to implement Deendayalji's dream of supplying the flow of electricity to the remotest villages in India.[46]

The initiative of Smart Cities as well as all other initiatives mentioned above vividly actualise the following guidance of Pandit Deendayal Upadhyay: "The long term needs of development and the short term needs of satisfying the expectations of the people for a better standard of living have to be balanced".[47]

'Make in India' initiative is no doubt a right step in the direction of realising 'Swadeshi' principle enunciated by Pandit Deendayal Upadhyay. That it has acquired additional relevance at present due to the Chinese goods' intrusion in our economy is equally obvious. This year's budget rightly states that several startups (such as manufacturing of electronic equipments, hardwares, softwares, etc.) generate employment, bring innovation and become partners in Make in India

46. *See* Sharad Kulkarni, *Pandit Deendayal Upadhyay : Ideology and Perception : Part IV Integral Economic Policy* (New Delhi, 2014), pp. 54-55
47. Deendayal Upadhyay, 'The Third Plan x-Rayed,' in *Political Diary* (Bombay, 1968), p. 19.

programme.[48] It gives incentives through the offers of certain tax-exemptions. "Skill India mission is closely linked with Make in India programme as it creates comprehensive skilling eco-system and brings entrepreneurship to the doorstep of youth. Finance Minister has informed that 76 lakh youth have received due training under skill India mission. Stand up India Scheme deserves certain space here, as it aims at promoting entrepreneurship among SC/ST and women. Present budget has provided Rs.500 crore for this purpose. Actually it was in December 2015 that P.M. Shri Narendra Modi addressed the national conference of Dalit entrepreneurs organised by the Dalit Indian Chambers of Commerce and Industry in New Delhi. Shri. Modi said on this occasion that nearly 80 lakh people have been granted loans worth Rs.50,000 crore without any collateral under the Mudra Scheme. Mudra is an acronym for Micro Units Development and Refinance Agency. The extract given below from the address of Shri Modi informs of his faith in integral humanism as this philosophy gives priority to the upliftment of marginalised destitute".

"Banks are ready to go to the house of someone who creates 300 jobs but is setting up a hi-fi factory. But they don't see ten people running small shops in a village and creating 50 jobs. The government has now set up a venture capital fund for first generation entrepreneurs, which is fundamentally quite relevant for S.Cs and S.Ts. They don't inherit businesses or entrepreneurship, but only the hardships faced by their parents".[49] Noida city in U.P.witnessed on 5th April 2016 the unveiling of the 'Stand up India' Scheme at the hands of Narendra Modi who stated then that as a result of 'Stand up India' 2.5- lakh Dalits would come ahead as entrepreneurs, that job seekers would become job creators".[50]

Special attention paid in this year's budget to accomplishing Deendayal Antyodaya Mission as well as to Pradhan Mantri Krishi Sinchai Yojana is in line with Integral Humanism. Harish Damodaran has rightly invited our attention to the fact that the Modi-Government which initially allocated Rs.38,500/- crore towards Mahatma Gandhi National Rural Employment Guarantee Act in the present budget raised this amount to around Rs.60,000/- crore by October 2016 and accordingly set a record for this programme.[51] Shri Damodaran further

48. *See* Note no. 5, p.25.
49. *See The Hindu* (Chennai), 30 December 2015, p. 16.
50. *See The Hindu* (Chennai), 6 April 2016, p. 15.
51. Harish Damodaran, 'MGNREGA 2.0' in The *Indian Express* (Mumbai), 20 October 2016, p. 16.

informs us that this flagship rural jobs programme under the Modi Government has generated an all-time high person days of employment! No less important is the apparent improvement in the quality of MGNREGA (Mahatma Gandhi National Rurl Employment Guarantee Act) spending" and Shri Damodaran refers here to two impressive dimensions. Thus near about 94 per cent of around 11 crore active workers employed under MGNEREGA (Mahatma Gandhi National Rurl Employment Guarantee Act) would be the recipients of Direct Benefit Transfer (DBT) Initiative. (By March 2017 all such active workers would get their wages through Adhar Payment Bridge (APB) system.) Secondly, there is a direct linkage between MGNREGA and productive government programmes of water conservation and natural resource management. According to Amarjeet Sinha, Secretary, Department of Rural Development, work has already been taken up on 9.2 lakh ponds.[52] It was incidentally, the budget for 2004-2005 presented by the Manmohan Singh Government which chalked out a very impressive programme linked with millions of water tanks throughout India. Tragically, however, the whole programme was thrown into oblivion in subsequent years. The present Central Government has thus given a new life to this programme. Besides this, the Modi-Government has decided to strengthen the Pradhan Mantri Krishi Sinchai Yojana as well as the Accelerated Irrigation Benefit Programme (AIBP) and provided Rs.12,517/- crore in this connection. The whole approach is in full consonance with Deendayalji's thinking which has reminded us of our ancient, age old concept of 'Adeva Matrika Krishi' (Agriculture, least dependent on the ups and downs in the natural rainfall.) Pandit Deendayal Upadhyay asks us to keep in mind that ancient kings and queens in India used to dig and conserve wells, tanks, ponds and canals with a view to achieving the dream of Adeva Matrika Krishi!

It appears that the present Central Government is bent on making rural transformation more and more inclusive. Thus this year's budget intends to make our farmers well informed about nutrient level of the soil through putting into effect the soil health card scheme. Implementation of this scheme will prompt farmers to use fertilizers judiciously. Another scheme titled 'Paramparagat Krishi Vikas Yojana' will bring 5 lakh acres under organic farming within three years. Present budget similarly facilitates farmers' access to markets through the Unified Agricultural Marketing Scheme. I have already referred to

---

52. *Ibid.*

the Direct Benefit Transfer Initiative which makes it possible for the government to direct subsidies to the needy. Government has however realised that fertilizer and electricity subsidies are still likely to be diverted to non- agricultural uses. It has therefore provided a legal platform through the JAM trinity: Jan Dhan, Adhar and Mobile !

That our government is deeply committed to the upliftment of the weaker sections of our society is clearly evidenced in this year's budget proposal to ensure that the B.P.L. families are provided with a cooking gas connection, supported by a Government subsidy.[53] Our Finance Minister's statement in this connection that such a proposal will significantly improve the health of women and members of those B.P.L. families who suffer adversely from the ill-effects of chullha-cooking" reminds us of Deendayalji's concern for the Indian females.

Dr. Mahesh Chandra Sharma informs us of Deendayalji's views about the role of a female in society. He mentions that Upadhyayji has written a novel on Shankaracharya's life, wherein Mandan Misra's wife works as a mediator at the time of the debate between Shankaracharya and Mandan Misra. And Deendayalji articulates his thoughts about women through the mouth of Mandan Misra's wife. Mahesh Chandra Sharma's commentary deserves reproduction here:

"Neither a branch of R.S.S. accommodates females, nor does Vedic School recommend the stage of 'Samnyas' for females. Pandit Deendayal Upadhyay, nonetheless makes Mandan Misra's better half plead logically for the rights of females. The rhetorical questions raised and the appeals made by her during interactions with Shankaracharya are quite revealing: "Why should I feel ashamed of being a female? Does not a female think independently? Kindly note that a female does have a brain and a heart; she is also a part of the nation. And she has got every right to accomplish her duties towards the nation. Have not females engaged themselves in the past in the shastrartha ? (... in the debates over principles and practices?) Was Gargi a male? Was Sulabha a male? If great souls like Janaka and Yajnyavalkya did not hesitate while having dialogues with females, why do you refuse to do the same with me"?[54]

This budget proposal has elicited unalloyed kudos from everybody. Swaminathan S. Anklesaria Aiyar has thus showered praise in the following words: " I am not usually a votary of expanding subsidies. But I fully support subsidies for rural cooking gas to save rural lives. At

53. *See* Note no. 5, p. 3.
54. Mahesh Chandra Sharma, *Pandit Deendayal Upadhyaya* (A biography in Hindi), (New Delhi, 2002), p. 21.

last we have recognised a huge problem terribly neglected for decades".[55] As per the same well-known commentator the smoke from cooking chullahs made of clay or stones, fuelled by firewood or dung and used by 700 million Indians cause incalculable indoor pollution". Respiratory diseases caused by this smoke are the second biggest killers after unclean water".[56] The budget proposal pertaining to cooking gas subsidies has been rightly titled "Social Sector including health care".

I intend to conclude elaboration of the implementation of Integral Humanism through economic policies of the Modi Government by referring to the most significant paragraph of the speech delivered by Finance Minister Arun Jaitley while presenting this year's budget to Indian Parliament on 29 February 2016. The Finance Minister has informed our parliamentarians through this paragraph that 75 lakh middle class and lower middle class households have voluntarily given up their cooking gas subsidy, in response to the call given by the Hon'ble Prime Minister. Their gesture is a matter of great pride for the country.[57]

It is essential to point out here that the number of those households who have on their own said good bye to cooking gas subsidy has reached the figure 1 crore 6 lakh 30 thousand and 956 within eight months after the presentation of the current budget!

Why do I consider the just mentioned paragraph as most significant? There are two reasons. First, the content of the paragraph mirrors credibility of the present government, and secondly, it also reflects the faith of the present rulers in the transformation of the mind-sets of citizens. Shri Arun Jaitley has referred in the beginning as well as at the end of his budget speech to the aim of the present rulers to transform India for the benefit of the farmers, the poor and the vulnerable. He has thus given us to understand that he as well as all his colleagues in the present government are committed to fulfil the dream on the part of Pandit Deendayal Upadhyay to give utmost relief to the jobless youths, homeless destitute, shop less hawkers and landless farmers. And with a view to giving due relief to the unfortunate 'have nots' present leaders expect upper strata members of 'the haves' to come ahead willingly to sacrifice their benefits. I have highlighted in preceding lines seven salient features of the philosophy of integral humanism. The feature pertaining to the transformation of the mind-set

55. Swaminathan S Anklesaria Aiyar, 'The key Budget proposal that you probably' missed, in *Sunday Times of India* (Mumbai), 13 March, 2016, p. 16

56. *Ibid.*

57. *See* Note no. 5, p. 10.

is, no doubt quite crucial and if the present government seems determined to rely on this feature, any sane individual will welcome this policy of the present government!

One of the most thought provoking extracts from Pandit Deendayal Upadhyay's Mumbai lecture series on integral humanism appears to me quite befitting in the present context. It contains the aim as well as the means sponsored by Integral Humanism: "In a society even those who don't earn require food to eat. There are, for example children and the old, diseased and the invalids. Society is supposed to take care of such human beings. Parameter of man's social concern and his culture is his promptness to take care of the downtrodden".[58]

Man's social concern and culture no doubt, need to be consolidated on the war footing!

58. Deendayal Upadhyaya, Integral Humanism (Bombay 1967), p. 74. Also *see Ekatma Manav Darshan* (A book in Hindi) (New Delhi, 2012), pp. 65

12

Indian Nationalism from the Perspective of Integral Humanism

As Pandit Deendayal has elaborated his views on Indian nationalism during the course of his lecture series on Integral Humanism, it has been decided to pen the present paper for analyzing Indian nationalism from the angle of Integral Humanism.

Pandit Deendayal was extremely annoyed over the fact that during immediate post-freedom years, the then prevailing our leaders and thinkers were diffident about the potentialities of Indian ethos and that was why were enthusiastic in borrowing thoughts and ideas from Europe.

Pandit Deendayal must have felt it essential to inform us that the history of European nations is least inspiring. He has therefore, devoted first of his four lectures on Integral Humanism for bringing to our notice that these nations have emerged in reaction to the holy Roman Empire and that states have played crucial supportive roles in building and consolidating respective nations in their jurisdictions. He has also pointed out in the first lecture itself that the same European nations have caused a threat to the law and order in international arena.

Subsequent pages of the booklet based on the above-mentioned lecture-series on Integral Humanism convincingly prove how our nation is superior to European nations. Indian nation has thus arisen not in reaction to any idea or entity, but out of our conviction. It has not secondly, emerged due to the initiative on the part of the state but due to the vision and mission of saints and sages. Thirdly, Indian nation has never caused a threat to the global peace.

Unique Peculiarities of Indian Nation

Having mentioned above three peculiarities of our nation, it is logical now to highlight the uniqueness mirrored in such peculiarities.

i. That our nation has arisen in the hoary past not in reaction but out of conviction in certain principles is indeed a uniqueness which deserves due elaboration. Indians thus have deep faith in certain principles such as 'सत्यमेव जयते नाऽनृतम्' (It is the Truth and not a lie that prevails) 'एकं सत् विप्राबहुधावदन्ति' (Truth is one, sages call it through different names) 'सर्वं खल्विदंब्रह्म' (Whole cosmos is Brahma (Divine) 'शीलंपरम् भूषणम्' (Character is the supreme ornament), etc. The group comprising all such sublime principles has acquired the name (*Chiti*). And we observe throughout the land from Himalayas to Kanyakumari classes as well as masses believing in this '*Chiti*'. People, in fact try their level best to implement These-Principles' in their practices public as well as private. Dr. S. Radhakrishnan has beautifully stated about this phenomenon: "If you talk to a fairly intelligent Indian peasant about the Paramatma, Karma, Maya, Mukti and so forth, you will find that the terms are familiar to him, and that he has formed a rough working theory of their bearing on his own future".[1] There indeed prevails a unique inner cohesion among Indians. '*Chiti*', in short means the innate nature of the people residing in India. Indians generally honour righteous behavior — (धार्मिकव्यवहार) as according to them, such sort of behavior is an articulation of '*Chiti*'. They similarly condemn unrighteous transactions, because they are incompatible with '*Chili*'. So long as people have faith in 'Chid', they continue to live as a nation. '*Chiti*' is thus equivalent with the soul of the nation. Pandit Deendayal has therefore stated that the lack of '*Chiti*' demolishes nation, even when people continue to live together. Mere cohabitation of people on the particular piece of land does not shape a nation. Jews had to live for centuries with other peoples scattered far and wide, but because they have preserved '*Chiti*' they have emerged as nation in Israel. Sustainability of Indian nation as well as that of Jewish nationalism thus inform us of the role played crucially by '*Chiti*' in the life of a nation. Lokmanya Tilak has used in one of his write-ups a very interesting simile for high-lighting the role of '*Chiti*' in the nation building process. His argument runs as

1. Dr. S. Radhakrishnan, *The Hindu View of Life* (London, 1965) p. 40.

follows: "Take a glass full of water. Place a stick vertically in the glass and bring down the temperature of water upto zero Celsius. You will observe freezing; transformation of water into ice around the stick. In the nation building process also individuals assemble around certain common ideas, common pleasures and pains and stand unitedly".[2]

ii. A study of Indian nation informs us that in the pre-Islamic era, there existed in India a multi-state nation. The contrast between ancient Indian nation on the one hand and a European nation state as well as a multination state in the form of the Soviet Union on the other is quite revealing. One can thus aver that no state sowed the seeds of our nation, that several states put in their efforts to protect Indian nation. And when on 15th August 1947 Indian state obtained freedom from British subjugation, it began to protect Indian nation. In the case of Indian nation, one can accordingly state that nation precedes state and as has been mentioned above, our nation depends on '*Chiti*'. During our freedom struggle also, last decade of the 19th century strengthened Indian *Chiti*, thanks to activities of Lal, Bal, Pal who were inspired by Vivekananda's spiritual humanism and during the first decade of the 20th century we witnessed the most effective fight against political subjugation! Spiritual awakening in India thus shaped Indian polity. All stalwarts of modern India give credit to sages and saints for shaping the genesis and growth of India. Swami Vivekananda has thus pointed out that Indian nation has got a destiny to fulfil, a message to deliver, a mission to accomplish; and that mission is 'Mukti'- 'spiritual independence'. He has further stated in the same vein that sages and saints belonging to several schools (Vedic, Jain, Baudha etc.) have imparted to India, one and the same mission. As this mission has brought Indians together, there has arisen Indian nation.[3]

Hind-Swaraj, written by Mahatma Gandhi also contains a notable paragraph, in consonance with Vivekananda's views. The paragraph runs as follows:

"Our far-seeing ancestors established Setubandha Rameshwar in the South, Jagannath in the East and Hardwar in the North with a view to

2. Ram Shevalkar (ed.) *Essays of Lokamanya Tilak* (a book in Marathi) (New Delhi, 1997), p. 200.
3. Quoted in Eknath Ranade (ed). *Swami Vivekananda's Rousing Call to Hindu Nation* (Chennai, 2012), pp. 20-22.

informing us that India is one undivided land so made by nature".[4]

Gandhiji's comment immediately after this paragraph is equally quotable here:

> "Our ancestors therefore argued that it must be one nation. Arguing thus, they established holy places in various parts of India and fired the people with an idea of nationality in a manner unknown in other parts of the world".[5]

Dr. Ram Manohar Lohia, a genuine socialist leader of India also shares the viewpoint that Indian nation has been built and strengthened by sages and saints. His statement is as follows: "Great sages of India have woven the unity of India around the names of Ram and Krishna and Shiva, the three greatest myths of the country". [6-7]

It was the initiative of sages and saints and not that of kings and queens which caused the emergence of Indian nation. Pandit Deendayal therefore comments that state is not the sole representative of our nation. He points out that our national life continued uninterruptedly even after the state went in the hands of foreigners. Pandit Deendayal-sponsored Integral Humanism, of course, does accept the primacy, if not the supremacy of the state in the process of nation building. This paradigm, indeed reminds us of the fact that it was the lack of due alertness on our part regarding the primacy of state in the national life that enabled the Turks, the Mughals and the British to subjugate India. When however brave strategists like Chanakya-Chandragupta and Ramdas-Shivaji took into account the due role played by state in the life of a nation, India obtained vitality![8] Third peculiarity of our nation- 'no dogma about any creed, sect, religion and nation' under-scores India's distinctness from any European nation. Swami Vivekananda has highlighted very lucidly through his essay: 'The East and the West' that whereas European nations exterminated the aborigines and settled down in ease and comfort on their lands, Aryans, known for kindness and generosity never thought of extermination of the aborigines with a view to settling on their lands.[9]

---

4. *See* Jitendra Bajaj and M.D. Srinivas ed , *Mahatma Gandhi's Hind Swaraj* (Chennai, 2011), p. 52.
5. *Ibid.*
6. Rammanohar Lohia, "Ram and Krishna and Shiva", in *Think India*: Quarterly Vol. No.1, *January*- March 2010, p. 61.
7. Deendayal Upadhyay, Integral Humanism (Bombay, 1967), p. 50.
8. *See* the note no. 3, pp. 103-104.
9. S. Gurumurthy, *Eternal India and the Constitution* (New Delhi, 2005), pp. 15-16.

S. Gurumurthy, who opines that Indian nation is a sacred confluence of mass faith of the Indian people with Indian geography informs us of the unique significance of this faith through the following content: "this faith being basically tolerant, never had any conflict with any other faith. On the contrary it integrated all other faiths as part of its own ever accommodating creed. Since it is non-conflicting, it turned out to be non-aggressive and non-invasive".[10]

Geo-Cultural Nationalism of India

It is a fact that Indian nationalism is geo-cultural and not merely geographical or territorial. Mere cohabitation of people on the land does not generate national feeling among them. When, however, people feel from their heart-bottoms that they share common pleasures and pains, common memories of the past and common aspirations for the future, there emerges nation. Such a narration reminds us of the following extract from Ernest Renan's book on nation: "Two things, which in truth are but one constitute the soul or spiritual principle: One lies in the past, one in the present. One is the possession in common of a rich legacy of memories; the other is present day consent, the desire to live together, the will to perpetuate the value of the heritage that one has received in an undivided form".[11] This extract points out here that the concept of nationalism expounded originally by European thinkers happened to be geo cultural, though due to its association with nation states, it became (particularly during the years of 19th century) uncultured imperialist threatening global peace. Indian nationalism has however retained its cultural attributes, its affirmative, constructive, peaceloving and accommodative peculiarities.

Protagonists of cultural nationalism in India think that if a European thinker like Ernest Rennan feels confident that a nation can be built on spiritual principle on the basis of the rich legacy of memories, on that of the will to perpetuate the value of the heritage, Indians should be doubly confident in this regard. India's history is glorious; its nation has survived despite antagonistic state, despite huge challenges. It is important to say good-bye to Euro-centric thinking. It is essential here to explain how the political nationalists differ from cultural nationalists. The former thinkers rely on the institution of the state as well as on legal-rational lines for strengthening bonds of unity among people; the

10. Renan Ernest, *"What is a Nation?" Nation and Identities: Classic Readings* (Oxford, 2001), pp. 162-176.
11. *See* Selections from Swami Vivekananda (Calcutta, 1981), pp. 296-297.

advocates of cultural nationalism, on the other hand consider nations as organic beings, living personalities, natural solidarities like families. The latter therefore rely on history, culture and geographic profile for cementing nation and its distinctive civilization.

Political nationalism views state as a central and crucial pillar of the nation. Cultural nationalism views the state on the other hand as a peripheral and accidental pillar of the nation. Indian nationalism from the perspective of Integral Humanism, however plainly accepts that state's role in the building of our nation is quite significant. It informs in the similar vein that 'Dharma' is superior to the state in Indian nation.

What is Dharma?

Integral Humanism reminds us that 'Dharma' is not synonymous with religion, that Dharma is wider, broader and deeper than religion, a sect. Dharma sustains society, in fact it sustains the whole world. It comprises certain laws, certain principles which offer sustainability to the particular entity. In India, 'Dharma' plays a crucial, a fundamental role. Swami Vivekananda has explained the role played by 'Dharma' in the Indian nation by referring to the following shloka of Bhagavat-Gita:

"यदा यदाहि धर्मस्य ग्लानिर्भवतिभारत।
अभ्युत्थानमधर्मस्य तदात्मानंसृजाम्यहम्।।"

(Whenever, O descendant of Bharat, there is decline of Dharma, and rise of Adharma, then I body Myself forth.)

Each nation has its own peculiar method of work. Some work through politics some through social reforms, some through other lines. With us Dharma is the only ground along which we can move. The Englishman can understand Dharma through politics. The American can understand Dharma through social reforms. But the Hindu can understand even politics when it is given through Dharma, sociology must come through Dharma, everything must come through Dharma. For that is the theme, the rest are the variations in the national life-music.[12]"

Pandit Deendayal, relying on Vivekananda's message comments that Dharma is the repository of our nation's soul. Least wonder, he reminds us that Indian state is supposed to protect 'Dharma', it is expected to consider itself subordinate to Dharma. During the course of his lectures on Integral Humanism, Pandit Deendayal offers a very

12. *See* the note no. 7, p. 68.

convincing interpretation of Bhishma Maharshi's statement:

राजाकालस्य कारणम्

(King shapes the circumstances).

It runs as follows: "Some persons interpret this statement to mean that Bhishma considered the king above all. But this is not true. He did not suggest that the king was above Dharma. It is true that the king wielded a great deal of influence, and that he was the protector of Dharma in society, but the king could not decide what constitutes Dharma. In a way he was equivalent to the present-day executive".[13] In parliamentary democracy, cabinet under the captainship of Prime Minister plays the role of executive; it has to abide the decision taken by the parliament. In ancient Indian polity, rishis and munis formed the parliament; they accordingly drafted laws. Integral Humanism thus informs us that Dharma means innate or fundamental law of nature which offers the standard for deciding the appropriateness of behavior in various situations. When the state implements such innate or fundamental laws it mirrors Dharma-Rajya. As Dharma is sublime, sacred and holy, if compared to religion, Dharma-Rajya is also sublime and sacred, if compared to a theocratic state. It does not discriminate against any religion, nor does it cause any injustice to anybody on the ground of caste, creed and religion. It ensures genuine religious freedom! Indian nation-honours Dharma-Rajya and the latter honours Dharma! It is genuinely secular!.

Attributes of Indian Nationalism

Having deliberated over peculiarities of geo-cultural Indian nationalism, one can take into account notable attributes of Indian nationalism. I have ended the narration of the preceding section by referring to secular attribute of our nationalism. One may also add some other attributes such as receptivity, syncretism, eternality, etc. All these attributes however mirror the basic fundamental fact that Hinduism has been nourishing all these qualities and this is why, one must begin the elaboration of the present section by elucidating the role played by Hinduism in building and consolidating Indian nationalism.

Hinduism and Indian Nationalism

When a claim is made that Hinduism has laid the foundation of Indian nationalism, it informs us of two dimensions: Hindu society and

13. *See* the Note no. 11, p. 493.

Hindu philosophy. World knows it well that the followers of Hinduism have created myths around rivers, mountains, valleys and forests of India. The stories woven around all these entities continue to inspire contemporary Indians. The epics of Ramayana and Mahabharat and the scriptures and the songs like Bhagwat & Gita continue to provide insights to present generations as well. The imprints imbibed by rishis and munis on minds of Indians consolidate the spirit of unity among Indians. No wonder, an Indian takes pride in tracing his or her descent from this or that rishi. An Indian feels happy in moving on in the lines laid down by sages and saints. Hindu Gods like Rama, Krishna and Shiva have strengthened the unity of India and Hindu heros like Chandragupta and Yashodharma, Pratap, Shivaji and Guru Govind singh as well as Hindu kings like Janaka and Ashok still motivate us to pursue righteous paths. The invocation made by Swami Vivekananda, the great warrior monk to all of us is worth reproduction here, as it informs us of the thinking of all sages and saints of India. The following is the invocation: "O Indian, proudly proclaim at the top of your voice: The Indian is my mother, the Indian is my life. India's gods and goddesses are my God. India's society is the cradle of my infancy, the pleasure-garden of my youth, the sacred heaven, the Varanasi of my old age".[14] Hindu society has, in short imparted nationalism to India.

Hindu philosophy, the other dimension of Hinduism inculcates faith in spirituality, in inherent divinity. As each one in the world, each entity in cosmos is steeped in divinity, there emerges genuine equanimity (समत्वं) toward all, there arises selfhood, which is superior to brotherhood. Indian nation thus refuses to discriminate against any other nation, rather it assures global peace. Hindu philosophy secondly worships principles; it does not bind itself to a prophet or to a book. Rajiv Malhotra highlights this attribute in the following content.

"No authority pronounces someone a Hindu. There is no mandatory equivalent to baptism as a point of entry, nothing which is performed by a church-certified priest or minister and makes one a member of the Christian community.[14] Since Hinduism does not require membership in an organization, club or institution, and since it glorifies sadhus, who pursue their independent journey, the problem of excessive institutional control has never arisen. No authority has the power to excommunicate a person from Hinduism".[15]

14. Rajiv Malhotra, *Being Different* (Noida, U.P. India, 2013), p. 134.
15. *See* the note no. 11, pp. 184-185.

Hinduism thirdly, allows scope for new thoughts, as it respects rational, scientific basis. Its dexterity or ability to adapt ancient values to the modern times and modern, western values to indigenous conditions keeps it eternally evergreen. Philosophy of Hinduism fourthly asks us to pursue divine, sublime instincts such as compassion, empathy, devotion, sacrifice, and so on. This is why it cares for marginalized, vulnerable souls in society. Fifthly, it is least dogmatic, least sectarian. Here one can again refer to one of the speeches delivered by Swami Vivekananda for addressing Hindus: "If you are a lover of Shiva, you must see him in everything and in everyone. You must see that every worship is given unto him whatever be the name or the form; that all knees bending towards the Caaba, or kneeling in a Christian church, or in a Buddhist temple are kneeling to him whether they know it or nor; whether they are conscious of it or not".[16]

Hinduism, the fountainhead of Indian Nationalism has thus acquired the reputation of being receptive, syncretic, large hearted and tolerant. History of Hinduism, of course conveys to us that on occasions it does bless militant, assertive and selective transactions. It expects the followers of Islam as well as those of Christianity to reciprocate above mentioned lofty attributes. Actually, all the above-mentioned appreciable attributes of Hinduism, have converted Indian nationalism into a peculiar culture, akin to the unique solvent, which absorbs several sects, creeds and communities in such a way that they still retain their respective identities. Muslims and Christians, however do pose a challenge to this narration. Such a phenomenon must not, however prompt us or goad us to replace geo-cultural nationalism by geopolitical or territorial, political nationalism, because mere cohabitation of people under the common shelter of a state is not adequate enough to generate the feeling of oneness among people. We must remember that nonaggressive, non-conflicting and non-competitive Hinduism had succeeded in prompting aliens like Shakas and Hunas to become indivisible part of Indian nation. And if Muslims and Christians pose a challenge or a threat to Indian nationalism, we must boldly blame the organized and aggressive faiths pursued by Muslims and Christians. We must point out that Abrahamic religions which consider their texts, their precepts and their practices as inerrant and the texts, precepts and the practices of others as erroneous are responsible for their incompatibility with Indian nation. Followers of Abrahamic faiths are therefore expected to reciprocate receptive, liberal and syncretic Hinduism.

---

16. *Ibid.* p.356

Both Swami Vivekananda, the warrior monk as well as Lokamanya Tilak, the warrior householder have stated that Abrahamic religions are incompatible with Indian ethos. Swami Vivekananda's comment runs as follows: "I do not understand how people declare themselves to be believers in God, and at the same time think that God has handed over to a little body of men all truth, and that they are the guardians of the rest of humanity".[17] What is notable is the fact that the speech titled 'My Master' delivered by Swamiji highlights the contrast between receptive, accommodative Hinduism and the dogmatic and exclusive Abrahamic religions. Lokamanya Tilak has gone a step ahead as he has asked us to keep aside the principle of forgiveness while dealing with the followers of Abrahamic religions which ignore the doctrine of Self-identification. The doctrine of Self-identification (आत्मौपम्य द्रिष्टी) gives us the following advice: "Do not cause harm to others by doing such actions, as if done to oneself, would be harmful".[18]

Lokmanya Tilak, of course, informs us that Christianity does honour the doctrine of Self-identification. He however makes no mention of Islam in this connection, because 'Jihad', one of the pillars of Islam asks Muslims to launch a religious war against those who are unbelievers in the mission of Muhammad-the prophet.[19]

Luckily, present thinking among Muslims is appreciable, as it has endorsed sufi-interpretation of 'Jihad' according to which this pillar of Islam asks Muslims to wage a war against one's own lusts against one's own lower human tendencies or instincts such as desire, anger, greed, temptation, insolence and jealousy. (Incidentally, Gandhiji as well as Pandit Deendayal also expect us not to succumb to such lower instincts).

Though Christianity asks us 'To love your neighbour', and accordingly does establish a rapport with Indian nationalism, it must equally abstain itself from calling itself as the monopolist of the Truth.

Relevance of Indian Nationalism

In the present circumstances when 'nativism' seems to have taken roots in the Anglo-Saxon world, Indian nationalism has perhaps emerged as a light house! It is the growing number of migrants- Muslim migrants in the U.S.A. as well as in Europe that has caused a historical turmoil throughout the Anglo-Saxon world. According to Ashok Malik,

17. *See Sri Bhagwadgita-Rahasya* (English Translation) (Poona, 2012), p. 547.18
18. *See* B. B. Kumar, *Understanding Islam* (Delhi, 2016) p. 332.
19. Ashok Malik, "Implosion of the West", in *Times of India* (Mumbai), 5 March, 2015, p. 20.

a senior fellow in Observer Research Foundation, a resurgence in nativism and national identity in the U.S.A, France, Spain, Greece, Italy, Germany and east European countries is a backlash or a harsh reaction to Islamic terrorism.[20] What worries the world most is the clear discrimination made against Muslim migrants. In the U.S.A. for example, nativism has generated WASP-ism; in the sense that those who are neither Whites; nor Anglo Saxons, nor Protestants are marginalized! Such sort of backlash is no doubt anti-democratic.

The interview granted by Pierre Manent, a leading French philosopher to Wall Street Journal on 28 May 2017 shows a ray of bright hope against this setting. Mr. Manent first diagnoses the problem. He says that Euro-Americans are extremely worried due to the growing number of Muslim immigrants in the respective national boundaries because the spread of individualism in the Anglo-Saxon world has alienated a common man and a woman not only from the sacred communion of Judeo-Christianity, but also from political communion of modern states. Such common men and women are moreover constrained to face masses of Muslim immigrants who are proud of their affiliations to 'Ummah'- the faithful Muslim community spread all over the world. Common Euro-Americans thus face unequal and unjust scenario; they are isolated, alienated individuals whereas migrants coming from abroad are members of global Ummah. Muslim migrants consider themselves as members of the "house of submission"; they have moreover been trained to treat a non-Muslim nation as the "house of war". A common Frenchman or a common Dutchman develops fear complex in such a scenario. What is the way-out? French philosopher Pierre Manent suggests that cultural nationalism can resolve the crisis of Islam, provided, of course, Muslim migrants also reciprocate liberal, syncretic and accommodative life styles of Euro-Americans. Pierre Manent thus pleads for cultural nationalism, as it provides solid anchor to the ship of an individual. The French philosopher, of course asks native Christians to respect citizenship-rights of all non-Christians. He in other words opposes discrimination against non-natives. Mr. Manent's words are quotable here: "In the present circumstances relations between Europe and the Muslim world will be less fraught, if we accepted the Christian mark, while, of course, guaranteeing that every citizen, whatever his religion and lack of religion, has equal rights".[21]

20. *See* "How Nationalism Can Solve the Crisis of Islam", in the *Wall Street Journal*, 28 May 2017, p. All.
21. *See Times of India* (Mumbai), 29 January 2018, p. 14.

Mr. Manent further states: "We accept Muslims, but they must also accept us".

We all should be proud of the fact that the thinking of Mr. Manent; vividly mirrored in the geo-cultural nationalism of India is quite prevalent today in India. Choudhary Mahboob Ali Kaiser, Chairman of Haj Committee and an M. P. from Bihar has appreciated Indian nationalism through his opinion that India is the best place in the world of Muslims to live.[22] Ahmed Badreddin Hassoun, the Grand Mufti of Syria, who visited India as a speaker in the world Sufi Forum held in New Delhi in March 2016 has endorsed the just mentioned appreciation of Indian nationalism. He has stated that India's pluralist society is an inspiration for conflict prone countries of the West Asian region".

Recent invitation and honour extended by the Organization of Islamic Cooperation to Mrs Sushma Swaraj, India's external affairs minister to deliver a keynote address at its Abu-Dhabi conference has in fact approved India's nationalism. We are confident that Indian nationalism will continue to march ahead with flying colours.

---

22. *See Times of India* (Mumbai), 14 March 2016, p. 13.

13

Contemporary World

Challenges and Integral Humanism

The thought of writing a paper on Contemporary World Challenges and Integral Humanism occurred while going through the literature pertaining to the issue of Sustainable Development. The Human Development Report 2016 (HDR 2016) published by the United Nations Development Programme (UNDP) included the challenges faced by the contemporary world. It has also highlighted certain Indian initiatives for overcoming these challenges. The HDR 2016 contains a special chapter titled as 'Caring for those left out - National Policy Options'. As this Report, wishes to give a very significant message that in the human development journey no one should be left out, it is bound to analyse strategies which care for those left outs. It is, therefore, important to understand that if we aim at everyone's development, we must pay priority attention to the development of marginalized and vulnerable destitute citizens. HDR 2016 also underscores how Indian initiatives are the right programmes in this connection. It is a fact that initiatives and programmes are rooted in philosophy and ethos. Here Nineteenth Century born Indian philosophers in general and Swami Vivekananda in particular do deserve to be remembered gratefully, because their interpretations of our Dharma and Sanskriti have shaped Indian initiatives and programmes. Pandit Deendayal Upadhyay, the expounder of Integral Humanism, following the footsteps of Mahatma Gandhi has articulated Indian philosophy filtered through Vivekananda's and Gandhiji's thinking. This is why it is essential to study how Pandit Deendayal sponsored Integral Humanism has thought over world challenges and their solutions.

In the beginning, I attempt elaboration of the present world challenges as have been outlined by the HDR 2016. The innovative Indian initiatives as well as programmes mentioned admirably by several publications deserve to be analysed later on. Such an analysis will be followed by the elucidation of divine tendencies of the lives of Swami Vivekananda, Mahatma Gandhi and Pandit Deendayal Upadhyay, because one must highlight and underscore how the mindsets of these architects of modern India paid very spontaneous priority attention to the wellbeing of destitutes of society. The entire latter half of the present essay will be devoted to the line of thinking mirrored in the philosophy of Integral Humanism.

Present World Challenges

As has been stated above, the HDR 2016 does mention three types of challenges, 'lingering', 'deepening' and 'emerging' ! This report first invites our attention to the whole development - discourse unfolded itself since the emergence of the first definition of modern Economics in 1776. It was Adam Smith who thus expounded wealth oriented definition of Economics. Later it was Alfred Marshall, who advocated in 1890 the necessity of relying on welfare oriented definition of Economics. Still later, economists began to state that in the development-discourse, one must emphasise human acquisition of different kinds of abilities, physical, intellectual, psychological and so on with a view to measuring development in terms of the growth of such abilities. In subsequent years, the realization dawned on economists that ‘growth’ is inferior to ‘development’, that richness of economies is inferior to that of human lives. Present consensus among economists, in short avers that development processes which shape human lives must be influenced by the people at large. And this is why, people should enjoy full freedom. Logically therefore, HDR 2016 points out that ‘development means enlargement of freedoms’. It brings to our notice in this connection that ‘human freedom’ has got two dimensions freedom to enhance one’s own wellbeing and freedom to achieve one’s favourite goals or values. Present shift in the development discourse from the pursuit of material prosperity to that of enhancing human happiness is indeed quite visible in the HDR 2016. A discussion of challenges confronting human happiness is thus immensely relevant.

As far as 'lingering challenges' are concerned, one can refer to different sorts of deprivations caused due to hunger, malnutrition, air pollution etc. Besides these, one can also allude to certain basic deprivations such as gender discrimination, ethnic segregation, enforced separation of indigenous sons and daughters of the soil etc. One comes across discrimination against disabled persons and migrants as well. Such unfortunate souls remain deprived of ownership rights over land and other assets, in some other countries indigenous people are deprived of access to education in their own languages. Indigenous persons are also debarred in certain nation-states from access to water, forest and so on. Certain deprivations continue to linger even after people concerned move out of poverty. Poor people who can't afford to reside in posh localities, who are constrained to live near dirty factories, waste dumps and ecologically fragile lands suffer from environmental hazards. Such a poverty environment nexus causes, in fact adds to 'lingering challenges'. Veer Savarkar has attacked seven shackles such as prohibition to read Vedas, prohibition to enter certain professions, untouchability, ban on inter-dining, ban on inter-caste marriages etc., because these very shackles are 'lingering challenges' on the development-trajectory. One must also take into account prejudiced segregation based on colour and creed considerations. Despite laws banning colour discrimination, 'white' members continue to give inferior treatment to 'black' counterparts. Such lingering challenges do create hurdles on the path of sustainable development.

'Deepening and widening challenges' focus on increasing inequalities since 1970. Liberalisation, Privatisation, Globalisation (LPG) trends prevalent since 1991 have further accelerated inequalities. If liberalisation and privatisation have given a new boost to market forces, globalisation has enhanced the production of capital-intensive goods and facilitated the concentration of wealth in the topmost one percent section of the society. Joseph Stiglitz, the author of the famous book 'The Great Divide' has explained to us how and why the inequalities have got deepened during the era of LPG trends. He has thus mentioned causes triggering still deeper inequalities due to number of United States (US) Government policies such as replacement of Paul Volcker by Alan Greenspan as Chairman of the Federal Reserve Board, demolishing the wall between commercial banks and investment banks, offering tax cuts especially for individuals belonging to upper income groups, oblivious attitude towards perverse practices of rating agencies etc. It is essential here to elaborate how such U.S. Government policies deepened inequalities and challenged development-trajectory. Allan Greenspan, a villain-market fundamentalist indeed did play a crucial role in the capacity of Federal Reserve Chief in this connection as neither he regulated the flood of liquidity, nor he prohibited deceptive banking practices such as sanctioning of the no documentation loans, the interest free loans, etc; nor he restricted derivatives and gambles. Government demolition of the wall between commercial banks and investment banks prompted former to abandon typical conservative approach and to start investing recklessly. Declarations of tax cuts in favour of upper income citizens goaded such individuals to indulge in speculative activities. The ostrich like governmental oblivious attitude towards corrupt practices of rating agencies facilitated a quid-pro-quo relationship between the latter and investment banks. The U.S. Government practically bailed out banks, agencies and corporations at the cost of common masses whose interests were sold out. The comment made by Joseph Stiglitz over such a scenario is worth quotation. "The bail out package was like a massive transfusion to a patient suffering from internal bleeding". (*See*: The Great Divide, p.47)

Joseph Stiglitz shares with Thomas Piketty the view point that one percent people in U.S.A. have succeeded in amassing wealth at the cost of ninety nine percent causing 'deepening challenges' to the human development. Both these thinkers accordingly inform us that in capitalism there blossoms a caricature of democracy, in the sense that capitalism shapes the government of one percent which is run by one percent and which works for one percent only. Least wonder, Stiglitz endorses Piketty's worry mirrored in the following quotation: "The main question confronting me today is not really capitalism in the 21st century. It is about democracy in the 21st century. As Stiglitz rendered whole hearted support to Piketty's dissent with Simon Kuznets' assessment of the peculiar unfoldment of capitalism in the aftermath of the end of the Second World War, a succinct elaboration of this argumentation is 'a must' in this connection. Simon Kuznets had thus argued that in the post Second World War years, inequality which increased in the initial phase began to wither away later giving way to equality. Simon Kuznets, being a recipient of the Nobel Prize in 1971 succeeded in creating a consensus in favour of the viewpoint that as economies become richer they become more equal. Thomas Piketty however dared to question Kuznetsian viewpoint; he put forward through his book 'Capital in the Twenty-First Century' (welcomed in the world as a tour de force) a unique finding that "the trend of concentration of wealth with the richest few forms a 'U' shaped curve with the concentration being high in the beginning of the 20th century, then falling between the two world wars and remaining low till the 1970s, and thereafter increasing again rapidly". (Quoted by Mridul

Mehndiratta, “The Discourse on Inequality beyond Capital in the 21st Century”, in Economic and Political Weekly, December 15, 2018, p.28)

Kuznetsian viewpoint was thus countered quite convincingly by Thomas Piketty who proved that the rate of interest pocketed by the wealthy few overtook the rate of growth by the economy as a whole thus causing the rise in the ratio of capital to national income since 1971.

Besides Piketty and Stiglitz, more than twenty renowned economists came together in the aftermath of the publication of Capital in the Twenty First Century and endorsed the thesis of deepening inequality through publishing a compilation of works under the title: ‘After Piketty: The Agenda for Economics and Inequality (2017)’. These scholars have pointed out through such a compilation that the globalisation years have witnessed a rise not only in the incomes of few wealthy fortunates, but also a hike in the gains of super salary earners and super managers. Most of the ordinary wage earners thus continue to bear the brunt of inequality. Same globalisation years have also observed a unique expansion of trade, blessing more and more capital intensive production resulting in the exit of labour-intensive manufacturing products. During these very years, not only developed countries, but also the labour abundant developing countries as well experienced a rise in the capital intensive manufacturing units. Logically, therefore, there is a drastic fall in the employment of labourers and in the amounts of wages. The fact that the proliferation of Artificial Intelligence (AI) and the progress of labour replacing technologies have further fuelled socio-economic inequalities, has also been mentioned in the above referred compilation of Papers.

The HDR 2016 also refers to terrorist activities throughout the world as 'emerging challenges'. Astonishingly enough, the 2016 Report deals with these challenges very casually and perfunctorily. If it mentions on page number three violent extremism as an example of 'emerging challenges', it refers on page number 45 to the ruling of the International Criminal Court in the Hague whereby an Islamic militant from Mali who helped destroy the fabled shrines in Timbuktu was imprisoned for nine years. Actually such emerging challenges have acquired serious global dimensions. If the 'lingering' and 'deepening challenges' create hurdles on the path of human development, violent extremism and terrorism kill the human beings who belong to ‘other’ religious sects. What is note-worthy is the fact that the peaceful existence on the part of several sects and creeds in India does show a prescriptive path to end the above mentioned 'emerging challenges'.

Whoever reads development-pertaining literature, notes quite invariably that several innovative initiatives on the part of India for overcoming challenges, confronting human development have received due appreciation in the writings of scholars studying development issues.

(1) The HDR 2016 obviously deserves to be considered in the beginning only as each Human Development Report mirrors United Nation's views. The 2016 HDR has showered unadulterated appreciation on India's affirmative action programme launched in 1950 which aimed at benefitting Scheduled Castes comprising 16 percent of the population and Scheduled Tribes comprising eight percent of the population. Indian Government subsequently expanded this programme for providing reservation benefits to the Other Backward Castes (OBCs) as well. As the other backward castes also got benefitted, the HDR 2016 has expressed happiness over this Indian initiative for uplifting huge sections of Indian population out of the morass of poverty and ignorance. From the perspective of the 2016 HDR, India's affirmative or positive initiative of this sort has shown a worthy path to the world as it intends to end historical group disparities and group discrimination with a view to offering equal rights to every human being. India has indeed underscored the sublime principle that in an unequal society 'equity' is more relevant than 'equality'.

(2) Second Indian initiative, admired by the HDR 2016 is Mahatma Gandhi National Rural Employment Guarantee Programme which creates jobs for the poor people through launching special public works programmes. This programme serves several purposes, it facilitates the construction of infrastructure, improves agricultural productivity, besides offering employment opportunities to the needy people. India's success in these ventures is quite glaring against the background of the prevalent world trend favouring capital at the cost of labour.

(3) It is on the page no.142 of the HDR 2016 that one comes across a note titled "The WTO and India's national development policies", where India's National Food Security Act of 2013 has been welcomed as the biggest ever food safety net programme. It is a fact that India has been

distributing through the implementation of this Act 61 million tonnes of subsidized foodgrains to 67 percent of the population. As hunger is a major impediment on the path of human development causing deprivation to millions of poor people, India's programme of buying foodgrains from poor farmers for sale to poorer consumers rightly deserves to be admired. The HDR 2016 admires India not only for the concern shown in poverty-removal through the 2013 Act, but also for readiness to confront World Trade Organisation on the issue of agricultural subsidies. It appreciates India's decision to challenge WTO sanctions in this connection on the ground that the ceiling on its agricultural subsidies based on 1986-1988 prices is least justifiable. Here a very important footnote deserves to be added because the Narendra Modi Government succeeded in vetoing WTO sanctions in November 2014. Brahma Chellaney, a well-known geo-strategist has praised India's firm stand at the WTO on the food stockpiling issue in the Geneva-meeting in November 2014. When India faced the choice between feeding its citizens and creating jobs for wealthy economies, it opted for the former and shielded poor destitutes from external world pressures. (See Brahma Chellaney, "Deconstructing the Modi Foreign Policy" by 'The Hindu', December 4, 2014, p.10)

(4) India's success in the field of road construction has also received accolade from the HDR 2016. The following extract on the page number 39 mirrors HDR-appreciation - "In 2005 India aimed to connect every community with more than 1000 people (and every community with more than 500 people in hilly, tribal and desert areas) to an all-weather road. Four years later, 70 percent of the target communities were connected". As the human development depends to a large extent on the linkage between backward and hilly areas on the one hand and the all weather roads on the other, India's achievement in this field, no doubt happens to be quite praiseworthy.

(5) We have elaborated so far how has the HDR 2016 admired certain Indian initiatives. Now let me refer to the admiration on the part of Ban Ki Moon, the then Secretary General of the U.N. in favour of India's ratification of Paris Climate Deal of 2015. It was on 2nd October 2016 (the birthday of Mahatma Gandhi) that India declared its intention to take essential

climate action, provided,it got financial and technological support to move towards a low carbon growth path. (See Times of India, 3/10/2016, p.12)

India's declaration in this regard is simply unique, it mentions not only its resolve to eradicate poverty but also its commitment to follow the low carbon path of progress. It underscores in the similar vein its expectation that developed countries must provide cleaner sources of energy, technologies and financial resources as well. The Indian declaration moreover states that it would review its promises if other countries don't fulfill their promises on the transfer of finance and technology. India has thus endorsed U.N. sponsored Sustainable Development Goals pertaining to growth, social inclusion and environmental protection, provided other countries also share the burden. It seems that not only Ban Ki Moon but also Barak Obama, the then U.S. President felt happy over the fact that India became a member of the Club of early ratifiers of the Paris Climate Deal.

(6) We must also give a thought to India's participation in the Kigali-Convention held in October 2016, as this Convention involving representatives of developed as well as developing countries held in Kigali, in Rwanda aimed at chalking out a due plan to concretise the phase down of Hydrofluro carbons (HFCs), a very powerful greenhouse gas used in refrigerants and air conditioning. India showed its readiness to jointly work with advanced countries in the field of research and development for manufacturing climate-friendly refrigerants. India's collaborative initiative plus its success in using renewable sources like solar and wind were acclaimed by Ajay Mathur, Director of The Energy and Resources Institute (TERI) through the following commentary: "Now India has decided to leapfrog to climate friendly technologies while achieving its development goals". (See Times of India, Mumbai, October 6, 2016, p.14)

(7) HDR 2016, which is devoted to the theme of human development for everyone, finds it indispensable to pay priority attention to eighteen million people living with HIV because most of them are young and adolescent and each one of them faces endangered survival. This report moreover, expresses its worry over the unavailability of badly required antiretroviral

treatment. Joseph Stiglitz refers in this connection to India's success in the production of antiretroviral drugs. His narration, glorifying India's initiative is quotable here: "Production of antiretroviral drugs by Indian generic manufacturers such as Cipla has reduced the cost of life-saving AIDS treatment in sub Saharan Africa to just 1 percent of the cost a decade ago". (See Stiglitz, *The Great Divide*, p.281)

(8) Reforms in stressed sectors like agriculture, infrastructure, banking, etc. prescribed by thirteen senior economists, including former RBI Governor Raghuram Rajan, IMF Chief Economist Gita Gopinath and many more have been implemented by the present Narendra Modi Government; thus underscoring the significance of innovative initiatives. One can begin the listing of such programmes by alluding first to 'Ease of Doing Business'. The World Bank Chief Mr. Jim Yong Kim has acclaimed the fact that within four years (from 2014 to 2018) India's rank improved from 142 to 100. The above mentioned thirteen Indian economists have admired 'Pradhan Mantri Fasal Bima Yojana'. Dr. Vinayak Govilkar has rightly stated that Indian farmers face yield risk as well as price risk. The uncertainty regarding the quantity and quality of agricultural product harvested at the end of an agricultural cycle, triggers yield risk. And the price risk is caused due to uncertainty about prices of foodgrains. If the previous governments announced relief packages to farmers and tried to help distressed farmers, the Modi Government launched a comprehensive insurance scheme for insulating farmers from multiple risks. Dr. Govilkar has mentioned that 'Pradhan Mantri Krishi Sinchai Yojana' aims at ridding farmers from the exclusive reliance on rainy season and the 'Soil Health Card System' intends to provide a printed report to every farmer for each of his holdings containing the status of his soil with respect to 12 parameters. (See Govilkar, Modinomics, Chapter 3)

That Modi Government has achieved remarkable success in implementing integrated infrastructure programme involving construction of roads, railways, waterways and airports, is quite visible to everybody. The suggestion made by well-known thirteen Indian economists that Indian banks need to be recapitalized has also been endorsed by the recently formed Governing Council of the RBI.

Every sane man and woman in India, of course, appeals to Indian Government that in no case interests of common masses be sacrificed for facilitating the growth of sustainable enterprises. "Ease of Doing Business should never be converted into the Ease of Closing Business". (See Saji Narayanan C.K., Saga of India's Labour Law Reforms, p.27)

(9) I have elaborated so far several initiatives of the Government of India for giving due relief to the common man. The objective of India through all the seven post-independence decades has been to uplift vulnerable masses from poverty and ignorance. Peculiarity of the Indian march lies in the fact that each government during seven decades stick to the path of democracy. Barring the Emergency era of 1975, all post-independence years have demonstrated to the world, India's conviction in democracy. Pursuit of human development for everyone through the march on democratic path is itself an impressive initative on the part of India. This uniqueness of India is impressive against the background that in China, Turkey and Russia, chief captains of the respective governments are fascinated by autocratic style of governance. It is also remarkable as democracy in capitalism generally morphs itself into plutocracy. In India, however, all rulers have put in conscious efforts to end deprivations of common masses within the boundaries of democratic framework.

(10) What is most impressing in the post globalization India is the scenario that several philanthropists have come ahead to shoulder social responsibilities. Such a scenario shows the 'third way' to the world, different from Capitalism and Marxism as well. Jaco Cilliers, the country director for the United Nations Development Programme informs us that during post globalization years, there have emerged partnerships inter se government, philanthropists and business houses for offering financial assistance as well as technical skills and energy for development programmes. (See Jaco Cilliers, "Lending a hand, filling a gap" in *The Indian Express*, Mumbai, February 22, 2017, p.13)

Mr. Cilliers further conveys to us that according to India Philanthropy Report 2015, India has added since 2009 more than 100 million private donors who have contributed a lot to a wide array of social causes. India has thus shown that society also takes essential initiative for strengthening priority areas. As for the government initiative in this regard, one may refer to the Corporate Social Responsibility Act passed in 2013. The Act obliges companies and corporations to go beyond the pursuit of profit with a view to serving the interest of people and planet. Vikram Mehta, Chairman of Brookings India has made a memorable commentary in the context of philanthropy and the 2013-CSR Act: "Helping hand of collaborative partnerships between the social enterprises and the community is, no doubt superior to the invisible hand of the market". (See Vikram Mehta, "Corporates should reach out", in *The Indian Express*, Mumbai, August 4, 2015, p.13)

(11) A discussion of Indian initiatives for overcoming 'emerging challenges' like terrorism is a 'must' in the present paper because human survival has become problematical, but India has succeeded in overcoming these emerging challenges. India is a land of spirituality, tranquillity and harmony. It believes in the ancient maxim: Ekam sat, Viprabahudhavadanti ("Truth is one; wise people call it by different names".) This is why, it welcomes all religions. It never discriminates against any religion. It respects all places of worship and picks up sublime values from all corners of the world. No wonder, a grand Mufti of Syria acclaimed Indian scenario during his visit to India on the occasion of Sufi Conference held in 2015. The Citizenship Amendment Bill is also in tune with Indian ethos, as it provides that "persons belonging to minority communities, namely Hindus, Sikhs, Buddhists, Jains, Parsis and Christians from Afghanistan, Bangladesh and Pakistan shall not be considered illegal migrants". This Bill, in vogue at present thus does away with injustice caused to minorities in neighbouring Muslim countries, the minorities which have sought shelter in India. It informs the world at large that no government can afford to ignore culture, history and politics. As the present Indian Government refuses to discriminate or segregate vis-à-vis any religion and concentrates its attention exclusively on minorities persecuted in the neighbouring Muslim countries, it enriches Indian ethos. This type of initiative, uniquely innovative, no doubt deserves to be admired as it provides appropriate antidotes to the world facing 'emerging challenges' of violent extremism.

Divine Tendencies of the Architects of Modern India

It has been stated in the beginning of the present Paper that several world-acclaimed initiatives and programmes launched in India for putting an end to human deprivations have been shaped by Indian philosophy and Indian ethos. And the roles played by Swami Vivekananda and Mahatma Gandhi in offering proper interpretations of our philosophy and ethos have also been mentioned in the beginning of this Paper. Pandit Deendayal Upadhyay picked up very interpretations and built the paradigm of Integral Humanism. His reliance on divine human tendencies for uplifting common masses is rooted in his conviction that the temple of civilization is built on the basis of very divine human tendencies, like love, sacrifice, compassion, empathy etc. His diagnosis is that, whereas capitalism based its paradigm on desire, greed and temptation, Marxism built its framework on the basis of anger, insolence and jealousy. Pandit Deendayal Upadhyay reminds us of the fact that all such lower tendencies have been condemned by the Indian philosophy as six enemies of human beings. No wonder, Swami Vivekananda and Mahatma Gandhi happened to be concrete epitomes of divine tendencies! Neither they believed in reaction, nor they opted for compartmental or fragmentary thinking, nor did they endorse materialistic or mechanistic outlook. Both of them emphasized social dimensions of spiritual ethos of India. The quotations given below from the writings and speeches of Swami Vivekananda, mirror social dimensions of Indian ethos. Swamiji has asked us to implement in our individual and social transactions, these very dimensions as they demonstrate our pursuit of divine tendencies.

(A) We want a religion..... which will give us faith in ourselves, a national self-respect and the power to feed and educate the poor and relieve the misery around us. If you want to find God, serve man.

(B) Do you love your fellow-man? Where else should you go to seek for God? Are not all the poor, the miserable, the weak-Gods? Why not worship them first?

(C) Service to man should be the future religion of the world!

(D) Educate the masses for their upliftment. This only will bring redemption to them from their present day down-trodden condition, as it will put life into this dead mass, dead to almost all moral aspiration, dead to all future possibilities!

It was a solid faith in divine tendencies and in social dimensions of spiritualism that spurred Vivekananda to ask his elite audiences in the

United States of America (U.S.A.) and United Kingdom (U.K.) to pay priority attention to the other world of the deprived and disprivileged citizens.

Mahatma Gandhi carried forward Vivekananda's legacy. It was he who launched a crusade against inhuman colour– conscious 'Whites' of South Africa. It was he who attacked the status-conscious and insensitive Indian elites assembled at Varanasi at the time of the inauguration of the Banaras Hindu University (B.H.U.). It was he who rushed to Champaranya with a view to giving relief to the poor indigo-farmers.

Pandit Deendayal Upadhyay taking inspiration from Swamiji and Mahatmaji underscores the eternal relevance of imbibing divine tendencies in every being and concludes his 1965-Mumbai lecture series on Integral Humanism through the memorable content which deserves quotation here:

"With the support of universal knowledge and our heritage we shall create a Bharat (India) which will excel all its past glories and will enable every citizen in its fold to fully progress in the development of his manifold latent abilities and achieve through a sense of unity with the entire creation, a state even higher than that of a complete human being, to become 'Narayan' from 'Nar'".

Upadhyayji beautifully reminds us during the course of his lecture series that the transformation of 'Nar' into 'Narayan' depends on the pledge on the part of the former to shoulder the responsibility of caring for the old, the diseased, and the invalids. The philosophy of Integral Humanism has, no doubt, enriched the legacy of Swamiji and Mahatmaji. What is badly needed for facilitating sustainable development of the world is to imbibe on everybody's mind the imprints of divine tendencies. These very imprints have led rulers of post-independence India to launch world-acclaimed innovative initiatives to overcome lingering, deepening and emerging challenges!

USPs (Unique Selling Points) of Integral Humanism

That the paradigm of Integral Humanism, mirroring Indian philosophy and ethos can help the world in facing contemporary challenges needs to be elucidated now in the latter half of this Paper. This issue has been elucidated through highlighting eight USPs of Integral Humanism.

(i) Humanism sponsored by the paradigm is quite distinct from West-sponsored Humanism. In the West, when the nation states in alliance with respective state religions began to crush common human beings, there emerged humanism with a view to shielding a human being from the autocracy and theocracy. West-sponsored humanism thus emerged in reaction. Logically therefore, the pendulum of individualism did swing to another extreme. A Human being accordingly occupied monopolistic centrality at the cost of everything else. Indian philosophy however worships Humanism not in reaction but out of conviction. Secondly, unlike the West sponsored homocentric or anthropocentric humanism, Integral Humanism is cosmocentric. A human being, from the perspective of Integral Humanism, in consonance with Bhagavad Gita is expected to be सर्वभूतहितरत: the western humanism however teaches a human being to be स्वहितरत:. Indian Philosophy believes that divinity permeates entire universe, this is why, you and me are expected to worship समष्टी, सृष्टी and परमेष्टी! In this sense, Humanism, rooted in India is cosmocentric, whereas Western humanism is homo-centric or anthropocentric. Thirdly, understanding of a human being from the angle of Integral Humanism comprises body, mind, intellect and soul, whereas the Western understanding of a human being is confined to the biological needs only.

(ii) Secondly, Integral Humanism is affirmative and constructive. Pandit Deendayal Upadhyay, no doubt criticized capitalism and Marxism. He however stated categorically that the paradigm of Integral Huamnism emerged not in reaction to any 'ism' but out of spontaneous faith in the divinity of each human being.

(iii) Integral Humanism reflects 'Swaraj in Ideas', reminding us of the historical speech delivered by Krishnachandra Bhattacharya at Chandranagar in 1931, wherein this great thinker asked Indians to worship distinct indigenous Indian culture. Krishnachandra Bhattacharya was in favour of assimilation, though he fought against subjugation. Integral Humanism similarly accepts, in fact welcomes, all the sublime divine values from other cultures though it insists that such values must be adapted and adjusted with the Indian ethos.

(iv) Integral, or holistic thinking is the Fourth feature of Pandit Deendayal-sponsored paradigm. It accepts that each human being has his own specific characteristics, though it points out in the similar vein that every being expects society to provide congenial climate. Man cannot live as an isolated being. He needs family, village, state and several social institutes. He, whose vision is broad, embracing wider canvass can live happily. Integral Humanism, therefore emphasizes that there is a symbiotic relationship between an individual and society. Compartmentalized or fragmentary thinking sponsored by Rene Descartes is least acceptable in India. As per Descartian thinking, universe is a machine and if anybody wants to know how it works, he dismantles the machine into tiny parts and reassembles it subsequently. One can similarly dismantle the universe, one can reduce it into parts and reassemble it later. Descartian approach which is fragmentary, reductionist and mechanical is generally presented through concentric circles around an individual. Hence individual occupies the central position, which is surrounded first by family circle, later by village circle, still later by the district circle and subsequent several outer circles. All these circles are parallel to each other, separate from each other.

Integral Humanism being rooted in Indian philosophy believing in symbiotic relations between an individual and society begs to differ with Descartes-sponsored concentric circles. Integral Humanism here sponsors spiral circles around individual. It is obvious that all such circles emerge out of individual, quite akin to a spider's web. We all know that Indian ethos teaches everybody of us to be broad hearted through the following subhashit:

त्यजेदेकं कुलस्यार्थे ग्रामस्यार्थे कुलं त्यजेत्।
ग्रामं जनपदस्यार्थे ह्याऽत्मार्थे पृथिवीं त्यजेत्।।

(One must sacrifice one's interests for the family, the family should sacrifice its interests for the village.... And ultimately one should renounce the world and its pleasures for one's own emancipation.)

Surprisingly enough, the HDR 2016, which does mention concentric circles around individual, underscores the relevance of spiral circles and gives India-centric message through the following content:

"People should consider themselves part of a cohesive global whole rather than a fragmented terrain of rival groups and interests". (See the HDR 2016, p.6)

(v) Faith in the 'survival of the weakest' is the Fifth feature of Integral Humanism. Mahatma Gandhiji as well as Pandit

Deendayalji totally oppose Darwinian principle: 'survival of the fittest'. They call it the law of the jungle. They rightly point out that human beings believe in a civilized life. The Human Development Reports published so far by the United Nations Development Programme seem to have endorsed that the weakest human beings must be protected by the rich counter parts because nobody should remain vulnerable. The HDR 2016 rightly recommends that the marginalized and deprived persons must be identified through the use of disaggregated measures for monitoring progress in human development. Thus people need to be disaggregated by age, gender, ethnicity, sub-national units and other parameters. The analyses through such measures will help us in locating marginalized and deprived people. The 2016 HDR goes a step ahead and asks us to pressurise policy-makers to draft policies for mitigating worries of marginalized people. It also calls 'Haves' to volunteer for social cause. The world think-tank has indeed given some acceptance to the spiral circles and symbiotic relations between an individual and society as it has realized that the weakest members can be uplifted through the operation of spiral circles only. It has, as if, backed the memorable statement uttered by Pandit Deendayal Upadhyay, the statement which runs as follows: "Parameter of man's social concern and his culture is his promptness to take care of the downtrodden".

Incidentally, Alwin Tauffler has also rejected Descartes-sponsored reductionist approach, as in his opinion holistic technology is reliable for the 'third wave-manufacture'. (*See* Capra Fritjof, *The Turning Point*, pp.194-195)

(vi) Integral Humanism's conviction that 'cooperation, and not conflict' is the sign of civilization can be called the Sixth U.S.P. of this paradigm. If the world has survived so far, credit must be given to the human spirit of completion. This spirit asks you and me to help each other with a view to doing away with any inadequacy. To complete-is the Mantra-well accepted at present. We are not supposed to compete with each other. Alfred Wallace thus seems to have overtaken Charles Darwin. One must however, note that if any 'Shylock' throws the spirit of cooperation to the winds, if he sticks to the path of exploitation, Integral Humanism does expect the State to bring him to the track.

(vii) It is in the Seventh U.S.P. that Integral Humanism spells out its idea regarding the institute of the 'State'. State is thus called one of the social institutions carved out for defending nation from attacks external as well as internal. It is the responsibility of the State to chalk out a strategy for defending nation. It is not supposed to succumb to the enemy; nor it is expected to surrender in front of exploitative elements within society. It should however confine itself to certain boundaries. Pandit Deendayal Upadhyay interprets the Mantra: राजाकालस्य कारणम् in a very unique way. He argues that the King undoubtedly plays a very crucial, influential role in the sense that he protects Dharma, though he cannot decide what constitutes Dharma. The King resembles the executive in the present state. He executes the laws properly, but does not enact these laws as the legislative assembly is supposed to enact laws. Integral Humanism, in short, argues that 'State' should never overpower 'Nation'.

(viii) Deendayalji's viewpoint regarding 'Nation', the Eighth U.S.P. of Integral Humanism has also received acceptability at present. The genesis and growth of fifteen nations in the aftermath of the disintegration of Soviet Union have endorsed Deendayalji's viewpoint that a nation is shaped by its intrinsic nature-the Chiti. No wonder, Vladimir Putin, the Present Chief of post-Soviet Russia has scrapped 7th November public holiday and replaced it with 4th November holiday. The day of 7th November used to be celebrated as public holiday during Soviet era for honouring the Bolshevik uprising of 1917. The present Russia however wants to commemorate 4th November because it was on this day in the year 1612 that Russian nation succeeded in driving out Polish invaders. Withering away of the artificial Soviet nationality and the birth of intrinsic Russian Nationality, no doubt sanction the concept of Chiti. Integral Humanism, of course rejects Trump sponsored nativism because the latter respects White Anglo-Saxon Protestants and offers secondary citizenship to those who are neither Whites, nor Anglo Saxons, nor Protestants.

Integral Humanism is thus all inclusive, all accommodative, it does not discriminate against non-Hindus. It honours each and everyone who leads his life in the light of Dharma, who is righteous, who worships sublime principles. Pandit Deendayal Upadhyay has remembered during his lecture series on Integral Humanism how Mr. Hafiz Mohammed Ibrahim, a Muslim League MLA in Uttar Pradesh said good bye to the assembly seat before joining Indian National Congress. Mr. Hafiz Mohammed Ibrahim thus implemented healthy principles of public conduct, he accordingly pursued 'Dharma'. That is why, Pandit Deendayal Upadhyay found it necessary to remember him gratefully.

'Sustainable Development' opposes discrimination on the ground of colour, creed and caste. And, Integral Humanism fully shares the viewpoint.

World Acclaim of Integral Humanism

It has been elaborated in the lines above how have Human Development Reports and development related write ups appreciated Indian initiatives launched for mitigating inequalities and disparities. It has also been mentioned that as initiatives are shaped by philosophy and ethos, development pertaining literature has admired such sources of Indian initiatives as well.

Now, an effort needs to be made to elucidate commonalities between HDR-sponsored recommendations for overcoming world challenges and the prescriptions made in this connection by Integral Humanism. It is quite logical because the paradigm of Integral Humanism mirrors the crux of age old Indian philosophy and ethos: the source of above analysed Indian initiatives.

It is important to bring to the notice of reader how has Pandit Deendayal Upadhyay claimed that Integral Humanism would succeed in reconstructing Indian economy through the pursuit of Indian initiatives in the light of Indian philosophy and ethos. Later, it will be highlighted as to how HDR-sponsored development strategy relying on integrated public functions and societal transitions for facilitating development would march towards sustainable development goals. Finally, an explicit and detailed elaboration of commonalities between the development path sponsored by Integral Humanism and the development-strategy put forth by Human Development Reports will be presented. Unintentional global support to Integral Humanism will thus be underscored. As for the development-path hinted broadly in Integral Humanism, one can refer to the concluding part of lecture-series. Pandit Deendayal Upadhyay has stated while concluding his lecture series on Integral Humanism that, if capitalism relies on encouraging selfishness of a human being, Marxism believes in converting a human being into a feeble lifelong cog in the scheme of rigid rules. He has also stated that if capitalism honours market fundamentalism and leaves a human being at the mercy of the law of the jungle and the resultant fierce competition, Marxism asks a human being to blindly follow dialectical materialism and to throw away inherent dynamism. "Both 'isms' avers Upadhyay, "thus result in dehumanization of man". Pandit Deendayal sponsored Integral Humanism therefore pledges to restore dignity to the human being. The extract, most relevant in this context runs as follows:

> "Man, the highest creation of God, is losing his own identity. We must re-establish him in his rightful position, bring him the realization of his greatness, reawaken his abilities and encourage him to exert for attaining divine heights of his latent personality. This is only possible through a decentralized economy".

It is indeed the paradigm of Integral Humanism alone which considers a human being as the highest creation of God and aims at enabling him as well as her to reach highest divine peak of his/her personality. It is again the paradigm of Integral Humanism which places before us the concept of a 'complete human being', an integrated human being as a goal as well as a path. This paradigm thus asks everybody of us to try to be an integral man through the pursuit of integrated development path.

Incidentally, the strategy of development chalked out by the HDR 2015 asks us to reach Sustainable Development Goals "through inclusive and transparent intergovernmental process which takes into account interests of all stakeholders". (*See Human Development Report 2015*, p.132) What is most significant and relevant is the fact that the five areas of critical importance for humanity and the planet, mentioned by the HDR 2015 also happen to be the goals placed before us !

The indivisibility of goals and path is in short a commonality between Integral Humanism and the U.N. sponsored Human Development Reports. The objectives of Indian economy from the angle of Integral Humanism are, no doubt worth comparison with HDR sponsored sustainable development goals. Just as the objectives placed by Integral Humanism before Indian economy are interlinked with each other, the HDR sponsored five areas of critical importance for humanity and the planet are also indivisible from each other. Both paradigms are thus least fragmentary or compartmental and most holistic or integral.

Let us, first elucidate, six objectives which Integral Humanism expects our economy to achieve. They are as follows:

(1) Our economy must first provide minimum living standard to

every individual, it must provide simultaneously full defence preparedness to our nation.

(2) It must, secondly, pay constant attention to the further increase in the above mentioned living standard whereby our individuals as well as our nation would acquire ability to contribute to the world progress on the basis of the Chiti (spirit) of our nation.

(3) Thirdly, it must offer every able bodied person meaningful employment, whereby he or she would be able to achieve just mentioned two objectives and to prompt him or her to use natural resources parsimoniously.

(4) It must, fourthly, develop suitable Indian technology compatible with India's resource-endowments.

(5) Fifthly, it must not disregard any person; it must, in fact facilitate full development of every person. It must protect the cultural and other values of life, because no economy can afford to disregard cultural as well as other values.

(6) It must, sixthly, opt for pragmatism while deciding about the ownership, state, private or any other form of various industries.

Even a quick glance at these objectives prompts one to comment that they are interlinked with each other. It also informs us that if an individual is linked with the society, with the entire broad cosmos, the present generation is also connected with its future counterparts. This is why, the third objective asks our economic system to use natural resources parsimoniously. It also conveys to us that it is the cosmo-centric human being, rather than the homo-centric person who deserves to be worshipped. Such type of Integral Humanism is, no doubt quite superior to the homo-centric humanism.

If the first three objectives take into account symbiotic, spiral relations between an individual and all circles around him, the fourth objective is India-centric, it refuses to apply single panacea to all diseases. It's message that "One size fits all policy does not work" is really golden. Fifth objective is immensely crucial, because not only it places cosmocentric human being in the center of the paradigm, it also underscores the relevance of cultural and other values in the march towards sustainable development goals. Sixth, that is, final objective points out that we all should be pragmatic, zero dogmatic while considering the issue of ownership of a firm.

It has been explained so far how the objectives placed by Integral Humanism before Indian economy are closely interlinked with each other, how they are integral and holistic ! It is against this setting that I intend to elaborate now how the HDR 2015-sponsored sustainable development goals are closely interrelated with five areas of critical importance for humanity and the planet. The HDR 2015 expects people to achieve development goals through dealing with five significant areas which are inseparable from the former. First, they must end their poverty, hunger, indignity and inequality in a healthy environment. Secondly, they must ensure their socio-economic and technological progress without causing any harm to natural system. They must thirdly, protect the planet from degradation, because it is the planet which supports the needs of the present and future generations. Fourthly, they must build inclusive, peaceful societies, because peace and sustainable development are mutually supportive. Fifthly, they must revitalize participation of all countries, all stakeholders and all people for achieving sustainable development goals. The HDR 2015 informs us through this narration that the five 'P's (People, Prosperity, Planet, Peace and Partnership) are interwoven and linked closely with sustainable development goals. The development paradigm built by the 2015-Report thus endorses, inadvertently, of course, the objectives prescribed by Integral Humanism for Indian economy.

Unintentional Global Support to Integral Humanism

In this section of the Paper, a number of statements, akin to golden nuggets from Human Development Reports are quoted as they resemble positions and views articulated in Integral Humanism. Human Development Reports, published by the United Nations Development Programme give expression to the views of scholars and leaders representing different corners of the world. One can therefore, aver that these reports articulate world-opinion and as these articulations are quite similar to those one comes across in the paradigm of Integral Humanism, one can claim that Integral Humanism has obtained unintentional global support.

It has been stated above that Western philosophers, taking cue from Rene Descartes draw concentric circles around individual with a view to informing us that a person is cut off from the society. The HDR 2016 however amends the concept of concentric, social circles by calling them as extensions of the individual. (See the p.128 of HDR 2016) This type of amendment is, of course immensely crucial, because it expects an individual to treat surrounding social circles as his or her extensions and the relations with these circles as symbiotic and spiral.

The HDR-2016-appeals to people at large to consider themselves part of a cohesive global whole rather than a fragmented terrain of rival groups and interests. The contemporary global thinking thus says a good-bye to the fragmentary Descartian thinking and extends welcome to the holistic outlook. Same thinking logically asks us "To put empathy, tolerance and moral commitments to global justice and sustainability at the centre of individual and collective choices". (*See* the HDR 2016, p. 6) The HDR 2016, in fact asks people to have a concern in the wellbeing of people who belong to future generations as well, as it remarks that "Sustainable development relates to intergenerational equity-the freedoms of future generations and those of today". (*See* p. 9) The HDR 2016 thus seems to be a replica of the approach on the part of the World Commission on Environment and Development (1987), as this approach comprises the following content- "Sustainable development means that development which meets the needs of the present without compromising the ability of future generations to meet their own needs". (Quoted in HDR 2015, p. 131) Present global thinking indeed encompasses a very wide range of integral worldview.

A reader comes across one of the most quotable quotes on the page no. 9 of the HDR 2016. It runs as follows: "Human development requires recognizing that every life is equally valuable and that human development must start with those farthest behind". This quote reminds us of the speech delivered by Pandit Deendayal Upadhyay while inaugurating the Zopadpatti Janata Parishad in Mumbai in 1965. Deendayalji's remark in the course of his speech is worth reproduction here: "As even a single weak thread causes a threat to the strength of a rope, one must pay serious attention to the strengthening of each thread. The weakest thread obviously deserves priority attention". Pandit Deendayal Upadhyay reminded his audience through this remark that as no locality in a city affords deprivation and inequality, one must pay priority attention to the development of slum areas.

What is most relevant here is the similar comment made by the HDR 2016 on page number 32. This comment informs that "lingering deprivations and inequalities present serious challenges to human development because first they slow down the capabilities of people, secondly they strengthen the process of exclusion whereby poor, vulnerable people are kept out of the decision-making process on the development path, and thirdly they create unjust and inhuman society".

Present global thinking thus shares with Integral Humanism not only holistic or integral outlook, but also the perspective that the issue of the development of the most vulnerable people deserves our priority attention. Contemporary world thinking logically expects us to reinforce the spirit of cooperation and coordination in the place of clashes and conflicts. (*See* p. 29)

It seems that the scholars and leaders representing different nation states involved in the UN sponsored deliberations over human development have formed their opinions and observations on the empirical basis. The remark given below mirrors the just mentioned empirical basis: "cooperation and commitments to eliminating deprivations and promoting sustainable human development have improved the lives of billions of people over the past 25 years". (*See* the HDR 2016, p. 29)

Present human development approach naturally relies on cooperation between 'Haves' and 'Have-Nots'. It expects members belonging to the category of 'Haves' to take initiative for uplifting vulnerable people out of the morass of poverty. The following extract is quite relevant here: "People may thus volunteer for causes that do not advance their own wellbeing. They may thus protect the rights or improve the conditions of vulnerable groups or conserve ecosystems, etc. People may put themselves in gruelling situations, working to promote causes they believe in at the cost of their own health or security". (*See* the HDR 2016, p. 87)

Contemporary human development approach, in short believes in integral or holistic outlook, cares utmost for the most vulnerable people, appeals to 'Haves' to volunteer for mitigating the deprivations of downtrodden destitutes and relies on the spirit of cooperation.

Finally, it can be legitimately concluded that the paradigm of Integral Humanism is acclaimed by the world at present!

14

Integral Humanism

A Timely Treatise

Introduction

Certain recent events have prompted me to pen this essay as they have brought to my notice how the tenets of Integral Humanism are immensely relevant at the present juncture. These events are as follows : a) The decision on the part of the Travancore Dewaswam Board to appoint five Dalit youths as Temple Priests in Kerala, b) The approval given by the so called secularists in India to the necessity to take pride in the Indian ethos, c) The healthy shifts in the development discourse mirrored in the human development reports during post-cold war years, and d) The incisive expert assessment of the genesis, growth and demise of the Soviet Union on the occasion of the centenary of the Bolshevik Revolution. It is essential to elaborate just mentioned events, because such an elaboration will enable us to set the tone required for highlighting how Pandit Deendayal's line of thinking is quite timely at present!

Elaboration of Events Pertaining to Integral Humanism

The news of the appointment of five Dalit youth as temple priests in Kerala reminds us of Pandit Deendayal's deep interest in shaping homogeneous India. Pandit Deendayal enriched the legacy of social reformers since the days of the Vedic sages and of the Upanishads who have asked us to retain essentials and to abandon non essentials of the customs and traditions of our motherland. He therefore, launched an attack on outdated customs such as untouchability. He has asked us through his lectures on Integral Humanism to discard status quo mentality and to abandon such institutions and traditions which have outlived their utility.[1] He has also drawn a line of demarcation between Jan Sangh (the party nursed by him) and the Rama Rajya Parishad by calling the former "reformist" and projecting the latter as "orthodox".[2]

Pandit Deendayal, being the leading mentor of Jan Sangh was eager to see the end of untouchability and lifting of ban on the Dalit-entry in the temples. No wonder, the recent appointment of Dalit-Priests in Temples of Kerala must have gladdened the advocate of Integral Humanism. Such an appointment has put an end to the ban on the Dalit entry not only in the sanctum — sanctorum of a temple, but also in a profession of a priest. Another recent event, endearing to Pandit Deendayal is the realization dawned on the secularists like Sharad Yadav, the founder president of Swaraj India' that political formations in India need to respect Indian Culture.[3] The present enthusiasm shown by Indian Marxists in the participation in religious festivals is equally noteworthy. We cannot, of course forget that whereas Pandit Deendayal's affection and respect for Indian ethos are natural and spontaneous, the apparent respect shown by pseudo secularists for Indian Culture is occasional and opportunistic. That day is not far away, when Indian Marxists will be competing with theists in visiting temples, if Indian polity lends credence to the stances and viewpoints of the protagonists of cultural nationalism.

The development discourse, one comes across in the UNDP-sponsored Human Development Reports during post-cold war years is also quite relevant in the present context, as it endorses a comprehensive people-centric approach to development.[4] Such a discourse is no doubt in tune with Integral Humanism which aims at the progress and happiness of 'Man', the Integral Man. The very discourse informs us that if material opulence occupied the centre in the previous development—approach, enlargement of human freedoms has got primacy in the present development debate.

It was the centenary of the Bolshevik Revolution on 7th November 2017 that gave an opportunity to several thinkers to articulate their views regarding the birth and decay of the USSR. As the USSR tried to implement Marxism in practice in the aftermath of the Bolshevik Revolution, its tragic demise in 1991 triggered incisive assessment of

1. *Ekatma Manav Darsan*, New Delhi, (2012), p.76.
2. *Political Diary*, Bombay, (1968). p.131.
3. *Times of India* (Mumbai), 14 March 2017, p. 12.
4. *Human Development Report 2016*, New York, (2016), p. 12.

the Bolshevik Revolution, Yogendra Yadav has thus stated that he would oppose tooth and nail the centenary celebration of the Bolshevik Revolution, because it had generated the bubble of the USSR. The conclusions drawn by him in connection with the Bolshevik Revolution are reflective of Pandit Deendayal's views about Marxism. They are as follows:

1. One should never delineate the time table of revolution.
2. Revolution in the sphere of human consciousness is a 'must' in the socio-economic and political transformation of the nation.
3. Level of the power of the state fails in uplifting economy and polity. It is interesting to find that all these comments remind us of similar observations made by Pandit Deendayal more than five decades back. These observations are as follows:
   i. Clash and conflict can never be made the bases of history,
   ii. Followers of Marx remained deprived of bread as well as of voting rights.
   iii. Nations whose lives are centered in the institutions of states cannot survive in the aftermath of the demise of the state.

I have highlighted so far how the recent events have lent imprimatur to Pandit Deendayal's line of thinking. I would like to substantiate the central theme of this essay through elucidation of Pandit Deendayal's mission and vision in the next sections.

Even a cursory glance at Pandit Deendayal's lectures on Integral Humanism enables one to notice unique peculiarities of the mission and vision of the mentor of Jana Sangh. Let us first try to study the mission of Pandit Deendayal. It is the last paragraph of the final lecture in Integral Humanism which summarised Pandit Deendayal's mission in the following words: "With the support of universal knowledge and our heritage, we shall create a Bharat which will excel all its past glories, and will enable every citizen in its fold to develop his manifold latent potentialities and to achieve, through a sense of unity with the entire creation a state even higher than that of a complete human being. It is a state in which '*Nar*' (Man) becomes '*Narayan*' (God). This is the eternal and continuous divine form of our culture. This is our message to humanity at the crossroads. May God give us the strength to succeed in this task"!

Pandit Deendayal wanted India to achieve unprecedented glories because India is the lone survivor who keeps the integral vision and the embodying culture alive.[5] Arnold Toynbee, a great historian has

5. P. Parameswaran, 'Introduction', in K R Rao, *Integral Humanism*, Hydrabad, (1995) p. LJI

showered praise on India through the inimitable content: "Today we are still living in the transitional chapter- of the world history, but it is already becoming clear that a chapter which had a western beginning will have to have an Indian ending if it is not to end in the self-destruction of the human race. At this supremely dangerous moment in human history, the only way of salvation for mankind is the Indian way".[6] Swami Vivekananda, the great warrior monk took pride in awakening India, because according to him, this sacred land which has preserved spirituality for centuries together deserves our unalloyed worship. No wonder, Pandit Deendayal's mission gives first priority to rebuild India with a view to making it unprecedentedly glorious.

Pandit Deendayal's aim to make each Indian aware of individual's symbiotic links with entire creation is not only congruent with our ethos but also conducive to sustainable development goals placed before the world at present by the United Nations Development Programme. The *Human Development Report 2015*, addresses five areas of critical importance for humanity and the planet. A succinct elucidation of these areas will highlight how Pandit Deendayal's mission is quite relevant for accomplishing the United Nation's mission.

1. *People*: The UN is determined to end all forms of dimensions of poverty and hunger. It is equally committed to keep every human being in dignified, equal status.
2. *Prosperity*: The UN intends to ensure that all human beings enjoy prosperity without causing any damage to nature.
3. *Planet*: The UN is determined to save planet from degradation, because it is concerned with the fulfilment of the needs of the present and future generation.
4. *Peace*: The UN is interested in preserving and amassing social capital through fostering peaceful, just and inclusive societies because peace and sustainable development walk hand in hand.
5. *Partnership*: The UN desires to revitalize Global Partnership for Sustainable Development, of course, for accomplishing on a priority basis, the needs of the poorest and the most vulnerable sections of the world.

The UN think-tank has informed through its concern for five crucially significant areas that it favours holistic approach vis-a-vis Cartesian view point relying on fragmentation. It has also conveyed to us its faith in cooperation and harmonization and its disbelief in Marx

6. Quoted by P. Parameswaran, Op.Cit.

sponsored dialectical materialism. The fact that the United Nations think tank shows concern in the upliftment of vulnerable and destitute citizens mirrors its rejection of the Darwinian principles of the survival of the fittest. As Deendayal-sponsored 'Integral Humanism' has articulated views in April 1965, one can legitimately comment that the present global think-tank has merely echoed Pandit Deendayal's vision of development.

World has observed the end of the Soviet Union and the demise of the experiment deduced from the determinist view of history that development of productive forces helps in facilitating social, intellectual and cultural progress of human beings. If the last decade of the previous century has witnessed the end of Communism, first decade of the present century has seen the end of Capitalism through the unfoldment of the Lehman crisis. We have realised the futility of the exclusive reliance on industrial civilization, the civilization which enables us to fly in the air and to move freely under the surface of the ocean but forgets to teach us how to have brotherly relations with our neighbours. We have indeed comprehended that it is culture which is an attribute of the soul that gives the promissory note of eternal happiness. Obviously, it is Indian culture filtered through Integral Humanism that shows the third way. Integral Humanism reconciles contemplative East with active West; it discards futile metaphysical discussions, attacks outdated customs like untouchability as well as superstitious practices and recommends replacement of fatalism by industriousness. Integral Humanism, moreover exhorts us to share a certain community feeling, a sense of belonging together because this sort of sense enables us to realize the human potentialities.

Pandit Deendayal's Vision: India-Centric Approach

It is through his lectures on Integral Humanism as well as through his speeches and writings on various topics that Pandit Deendayal informed of his vision as well. India-centric dimension is the first salient feature of this vision. Pandit Deendayal felt that during pre-independence years, Indians showed great interest in asking foreign government to quit India. In post-independence years, however Indians took pride in importing foreign ideologies to India. He shared the view the anguish and the agony of Chandrashekharendra Saraswati articulated through the following rhetorical question: “We have become free, when shall we be genuinely independent?” That the answer to this question lies in the adoption of India- centric approach is more than obvious.

Pandit Deendayal, being confident in Indian ethos challenged Rene Descartes and Karl Marx. He thus projected India sponsored holism as an effective antidote to Cartersian, fragmentary approach. His advocacy of the organic view of production, vis-a-vis reductionism and his prescription of cooperation and harmonization vis-à-vis Marxist dialectism are also rooted in his faith in the India-centric approach.

Pandit Deendayal's rationale behind his urge to pursue India-centric approach while thinking about strategy for development process is quite convincing. He thus argues that socio-economic and historical situation differs from one country to another and this is why when the problems confronting a specific country need to be resolved, the solutions prescribed are required to be in sync with above mentioned peculiarities of the country concerned. One and the same rationale prompted Professor Radhakamal Mukherjee, hundred years ago to refer to the inapplicability of Western economic theories to Indian economic and social conditions and to urge that India should develop its own strategy for its development[7].

Spiritual Tune

Pandit Deendayal's Integral Humanism articulates spiritual tune and one may call this tune as the second feature of Pandit Deendayal's vision. Swami Vivekananda's definition of India informs us that India is the union of those hearts which beat to the same spiritual tune. The fact that Swamiji was the advocate of spiritual humanism deserves to be underscored. Integral Humanism shares with spiritual humanism, in all five convictions. First, it points out that every human being is a spark of divinity. Secondly, it considers principles as more important than prophets and books. Third conviction, is logically deduced from the second one. It proclaims that the humanism advocated by Indian sages is fully compatible with science in the sense that it is quite objective. Fourthly, it honours compensatory discrimination in favour of Scheduled Castes and Scheduled Tribes in India. Integral Humanism is thus committed to uplift our downtrodden and destitute brethren through the level of reservation policies. Fifthly and lastly, it rejects sectarian dogmatic approach and fosters global partnership in resolving problems.

It is the spiritual tune of Pandit Deendayal's vision which asks everyone of us to go beyond a materialistic view of the world and to strengthen one's bonds with the planet as a whole. I have already

7. "From the Hindu Archives", in *The Hindu* (Mumbai) 7 November 2017, p. 9

mentioned that the United Nations Development Programme addresses five areas such as people, prosperity, planet, peace and partnership. Once we are convinced that everybody has a spark of divinity, we can overcome hierarchy and heterogeneity and worship justice and humanity. Pandit Deendayal, of course expects us to practice spirituality, in our individual as well as public transactions.

Reliance on *Dharma*

Third feature of Pandit Deendayal's vision lends credence to '*Dharma*', to the righteous thoughts and practices. Dharma' sustains society, teaches values to us and rehabilitates our mindset. If each and every one in society engages himself or herself in unattached, unselfish and unegoistic activities, society will be benefitted at large. As '*Dharma*' teaches me to be compassionate and kind, it enables me to strengthen silken bonds with other members of society. *Dharma* thus facilitates vertical as well as horizontal progress of a human being. It is the institution of *Dharma* which asks everyone to overcome animal instincts like anger, greed, jealousy, etc and to worship divine tendencies such as love, altruism, sacrifice and so on. *Dharma* is different from religion and that is why it does not confine itself with a specific sector creed. According to Pandit Deendayal, *Dharma* provides basis to economic and political transactions as well. No wonder, whoever pursues sublime principles deserves respect. Pandit Deendayal appreciated Hafij Mohammad Ibrahim, a Muslim political leader who tendered his resignation letter to the UP Assembly in 1939, said good-bye to the seat of MLA when he defected from Muslim League to Indian National Congress. Pandit Deendayal's interpretation of the concept of `Raja- *Dharma*' is quite revealing. According to Pandit Deendayal, raja or king is expected to protect '*Dharma*', but no king can decide what constitutes `*Dharma*'. It is the responsibility of the rishis to lay down the tenets of *Dharma* and the king is supposed to follow these tenets, the king is supposed to see that the people at large lead their lives according to *Dharma*. A king is under compulsion to respect the supremacy of *Dharma* as a principle. Pandit Deendayal, in short informs us that in the Indian ethos, a king plays the role of executive, whereas rishis and munis form the legislative assembly.

Constructive or Positive Perspective

Pandit Deendayal always refused to be negative or reactionary. He rejected "Western' version of nationalism, democracy and socialism, because of their reactionary origin. While nationalism emerged in the west in reaction to the so called 'Holy Empire', democracy originated itself against greedy, ambitious and corrupt autocracy. However, it was the alliance between democracy and capitalism and resultant genesis and growth of plutocracy that triggered the rise of socialism. Pandit Deendayal's conviction that it is the positive or constructive perspective that keeps one on the right track and prompts him to be altruistic which shaped his vision. He narrated in one of his speeches a very interesting story entitled 'Two Swimmers'. As per this story, in a swimming competition only two swimmers remain energetic and kicking in the final phase. The second swimmer, lagging behind the first one makes a strange appeal to the Almighty. The second swimmer appeals to God: "Oh Bhagavan, kindly generate a high tide in front of my rival, as a result of which he will be drowned, and I will emerge as winner in flying colours". Pandit Deendayal's commentary over this appeal has got eternal value. The commentary is a quotable quote. "The desperate second swimmer forgot that the high tide which will drown the first competitor will cause equally existential danger to his follower as well". Pandit Deendayal's advice to Jan Sangh workers in this context is similarly quotable here: "Some of my party workers strangely think that evil minuses such as dishonesty, corruption, indiscipline, Mafiosi, etc will drown 'Indian National Congress and in the aftermath only Bharatiya Jan Sangh will succeed in occupying seats of power. I request these friends to keep aside such negative thinking, because if the evil minuses take roots in India, they will cause disaster to all political parties including Jan Sangh. Let us therefore think positively". What Pandit Deendayal's Integral Humanism teaches has, no doubt, shaped Jan Sangh and its present avatar the BJP as well.

Cosmo–Centric Viewpoint

Integral Humanism, being a legitimate repository of the crux of Indian culture, has proclaimed proudly its faith in cosmo-centric viewpoints. If Adam Smith and David Ricardo have asked people to accomplish individual self-interests and to undertake transactions in the light of homocentric or anthropocentric viewpoints, Bhagvad Gita has asked readers to be "*Sarva Bhoota Hite Ratha*" that is cosmo-centric in human lives. That cosmo-centric viewpoint asks every human being to broaden and widen his or her mind is crystal clear. As per Indian ethos individual and society are interlinked to each other. The Indian culture, actually underscores that during childhood one may play the role of an individual, but during adulthood, each one is expected to play the role of society. Only a walk on such trajectory will shape a welfare society.

And if everyone believes in divinity, if each one treats all creations as divine articulations, our planet will reap the benefits. Pandit Deendayal advocated Integral Humanism, but refused to be utopian. Since the world is bound to confront exploitative, egoistic tycoons, corrupt corporate and dogmatic violent terrorists, such anti socials need to be tackled through appropriate, befitting actions by the governments concerned.

Pandit Deendayal thus expects the institution of the state to be sufficiently harsh while dealing with such people. Integral Humanism prescribes the use of "*Ugra Danda*", the reliance on harsh measures in such scenarios. If however, the government opts for alliance with antisocials, Integral Humanism condemns such a regime as the epitome of "*Ksheena Danda*", the incarnation of a vulnerable government. Post-Soviet Russia, in the last decade of the previous century suffered a lot due to Yeltsin-regime signing alliance with corrupt mafias. From the perspective of Integral Humanism, if the Soviet citizens underwent inhuman tortures during *Ugra Danda*-era in particular, their Russian successors in post-Soviet Russia suffered from alienation during "*Ksheena Danda*" Yeltsin regime. Integral Humanism, of course favours society with cosmo-centric viewpoint, but it does not ignore the role of "*Mridu Danda*" State, the normal state, acquiring apt role or stance in response to the circumstances.

Distinct Outlook about 'State'

Pandit Deendayal's outlook about state and nation deserves a special space in this essay, because it has acquired special relevance at present juncture. It was during 1960s when 'statism' used to win friends and influence people specifically in the then developing countries. Pandit Deendayal challenged the pursuit of statism. It was Pandit Deendayal's firm faith in the Bharatiya way of life which led him to point out that in a healthy society people at large carryout several activities and that is why the state plays a limited role. Pandit Deendayal's write up titled 'Growing dependence on the State' must be considered as noteworthy, because it informs that Pandit Deendayal was well aware of the impact of the then prevailing world trend towards centralization on Indian elites. The very write up, however contains a clear articulation of Pandit Deendayal's faith in the Indian way of life. Pandit Deendayal argues that "The impact of the world is not as forceful and as unavoidable as we imagine it to be. We can still hold to our own and pave the way for others to follow. But this calls for a total reorientation of our outlook towards life towards policies and towards planning. We should admit their limitations. It is therefore necessary that Government should be persuaded ..., to give up their socialist fads and stop their inroads into what is, in principle, and in practice, legitimately and conventionally the people's sphere.[8]

The latter part of this quotation is immensely revealing, as it clearly depicts Pandit Deendayal's faith in the Indian way of life, in the abilities of the people vis-a-vis limitations of the state. One may refer as a wonderful specimen to the write up titled, "Success and Slowdown" penned by C.P. Chandrasekhar, wherein a reader comes across a penetrating post-mortem of the slowdown in the Soviet Union since 1950s. As per this post-mortem, Soviet Union failed in sustaining the advances made earlier because the area of control of the state was limited even in a society with extensive social ownership of the means of production".[9] What impresses most is the vivid contrast between present admission of the limitations of the state in the aftermath of the demise of the Soviet Union and Pandit Deendayal's bold initiative in hinting at the same phenomenon in the 1950s when Indian elites were pleading for the spread of public sector in Indian economy. Pandit Deendayal then argued that state is not supreme, although it also happens to be an important social institution, serving certain needs of the nation like a limb of the body.

The line of demarcation drawn by Pandit Deendayal between state and society is simply marvellous and highly relevant forever. As Dr. M. Mohandas has pointed out, Pandit Deendayal expected society to evolve and develop as self-actuating and self-regulatory system, enhancing public welfare. Pandit Deendayal exhorted that the state should play the facilitating role through simplified laws and regulations.[10]

The state, from Pandit Deendayal's perspective, is a caretaker or a guardian of society. It must enhance public welfare by playing a catalytic role through encouraging individuals and autonomous social institutions to undertake socially conducive activities. Joseph Stiglitz, an American economist has coined a phrase — 'managed markets' for pleading that the state should manage markets with a view to putting an end to market distortions causing disasters to the vulnerable, destitute citizens. He has thus prescribed a pursuit of a golden mean between market and Marx in tune with Pandit Deendayal's Integral Humanism.

8. "Growing dependence on the state" — August 4, 1959- in *Political Diary*, Bombay (1968) p. 157.
9. *Frontline*, Chennai, December 22, 2017. p. 65.
10. M. Mohandas, "Ekatma Manav Darsan and Economic Development" in K.C. Sudhir Babu (ed) *Integral Humanism: Vision for Tomorrow*, Thiruvananthapuram, (2017), pp. 115-121.

Integral Humanism and 'Nation'

The emergence of fifteen nations simultaneously with the demise of the Soviet Union in Central Eurasia and the subsequent rise and growth of 'nativism' in the Euro American world have lent credence to the elucidation of 'nation' in Pandit Deendayal's lectures on Integral Humanism. Post-Soviet Russia has thus scrapped 7th November public holiday marking the Bolshevik uprising in 1917 and replaced it with the new 4th November holiday commemorating the 393rd Anniversary of the End of Polish intervention.[11] Present Russia has accordingly conveyed to the world that from its perspective, it is nationalism, and not Marxism that deserves due honour. The so called Soviet Nation, an artificial creation was bound to wither away on the lines predicted by Pandit Deendayal. The story of five Central Asian Muslim nations unfolded itself during post-soviet years is equally significant because it reminds us of Pandit Deendayal's viewpoint regarding 'nation'. A search has been going on in the post-Soviet Central Asian Nations to find out the roots not only in pre Soviet years, but also in pre Islamic years. One hears at present in these nations the following lines from the Uzbek poet's ballad, 'Dear Soul'.

> "Every Nation has its own desire, its own song, its
> own epic. It has its own place.
> Its own garden, so far preserved
> Thousands of years".[12]

Do we not remember here Pandit Deendayal's elucidation of 'Chiti'?

As for the strengthening of 'Nativism' in the Euro American world, one may comment that this sort of 'ism' is rooted in the desperate urge to survive on the part of the sons and daughters of this world, in reaction to the entry of Islamic immigrants there. Such sort of urge in the USA has transformed 'Nativism' into WASPism. White Anglo Saxon Protestants of the USA have thus come together and pronounced the superiority of their colour, race and creed. It is essential to point out the notable dissimilarities between these types of 'Nativism' on the one hand and 'Nationalism' on the other hand favoured and advocated by Integral Humanism. It is obvious that the rise and spread of 'Nativism' in the Euro-American world is a recent phenomenon, whereas Indian

11. Bal Ananda, "Cultural Diplomacy : From Old to New Connectivity" in Pramjit Sahai (ed), *India- Urasia: The Way Ahead*, Chandigarh (2008), p. 248
12. Quoted in Ashok Modak, *Uniquness of Integral Humanism*, Nashik (2016), p. 6.

Nationalism favoured by Deendayal Upadhyay has emerged in the hoary past. If the Nativism has emerged in reaction to the Islamic immigrants there, Indian Nationalism has come into existence out of conviction that genuine spiritualism needs to be spread everywhere. If Nativism is propagated by the government agencies, Indian Nationalism has been shaped by sages and saints. If Nativism distinguishes between natives and non-natives and offers secondary citizenship to each non-native, Indian Nationalism believing in spirituality opts for faith neutral polity and worships equity and justice.

The interview granted by the French philosopher Pierre Manent to the issue of Wall Street Journal in connection with 'Nativism' acquires certain significance in this context. Mr. Pierre Manent justifies the emergence of Nativism in the Euro- American world though he adds a significant proviso to this 'ism'. He calls it nationalism and argues that a common Euro American feels lonely in front of Islamic immigrants because while the former has dispensed with Judio-Christianity, the sacred communion as well as with the modem nation state, the political communion, the latter, an Islamic immigrant proudly displays his faith and his relationship with Ummah', the world wide empire without an emperor. Mr. Manent therefore pleads that French or a German or an American badly needs an anchor in the form of nationalism. He, however, wants to guarantee that every citizen whatever is his religion and lack of religion, has equal rights. This French philosopher thus discards faith driven polity implicit in the 'Nativism' and prescribes the acceptance of faith neutral polity. He asserts that the rise of nationalism in the form of Nativism in the Euro-American world, of course with the provision of faith neutral polity deserves to be pursued. However his assertion that, "however weakened the idea of the nation, nations do not want to die"[13] reminds us of Pandit Deendayal's s view point regarding nationalism.

Integral Humanism put forth by Pandit Deendayal through Mumbai lectures in April 1965 is, no doubt, a timely treatise at present.

---

13. "How Nationalism Can Solve the Crisis of Islam", in *The Wall Street Journal*, May 27-28, 2017, p. A11.